CW01370905

KING'S COLLEGE LONDON
MEDIEVAL STUDIES

XXVI

King's College London
Centre for Late Antique & Medieval Studies

Co-Directors: Dr Sarah Salih and Dr Lawrence Warner

King's College London Medieval Studies

General Editor:
Professor Julian Weiss
Executive Editor:
Ms WM Pank

Editorial & Advisory Board:
Dr Sarah Bowden, Professor Julia Crick, Professor Emma Dillon,
Dr Serena Ferente, Professor Simon Gaunt, Professor Clare Lees,
Dr Sarah Salih, Dr Dionysios Stathakopoulos, Dr Lawrence Warner

Distinguished Members:
Professor David Carpenter, Professor Judith Herrin,
Mr Martin Jones, Professor Dame Jinty Nelson, Professor Charlotte Roueché

Since 1987, the Centre for Late Antique & Medieval Studies (CLAMS) has published 'King's College London Medieval Studies', a series devoted to high quality monographs, critical editions, and collected essays on a rich variety of topics of interest to scholars and students of Late Antiquity and the Middle Ages. Our publications reflect the broad range of research sponsored by the Centre, whose members are specialists in both eastern and western Europe from the earliest centuries of the Christian era to the start of early modernity.

We welcome publication proposals in any area of Late Antique and Medieval Studies. For further details, contact the General Editor of the series, Professor Julian Weiss (julian.weiss@kcl.ac.uk).

KCLMS is distributed by Boydell & Brewer. For our list of books and details of how to order, visit our website www.kcl.ac.uk/artshums/ahri/centres/clams/publications/kclms.aspx

Punishment & Penitential Practices in Medieval German Writing

Punishment & Penitential Practices in Medieval German Writing

edited by
Sarah Bowden & Annette Volfing

King's College London
Centre for Late Antique & Medieval Studies
2018

© 2018 named authors
All images are printed with permission.

All rights reserved. No part of this publication may be reproduced, stored in a retrieval system, or transmitted in any form or by any means, electronic, mechanical, photocopied, recorded, or otherwise without the prior permission of the publisher.

ISBN: 978-1-897747-34-6

Typeset by WM Pank, Faculty of Arts & Humanities, King's College London

Printed in England

2018

Contents

Acknowledgement	ix
Notes on Contributors	x

1. Punishment and Penitential Practices: An Introduction
   Sarah Bowden — 1

2. *râche* zwischen ‚Vergeltung eines Unrechts durch den Geschädigten' und ‚Strafe': Semantische Spielräume im *Alexander* Rudolfs von Ems
   Henrike Manuwald — 19

3. 'und wolt iuch hân gebezzert mite': Keie, Cunneware and the Dynamics of Punishment
   Annette Volfing — 43

4. Sünder, Prediger, Dichter: Rollenspiele im *Beichtlied* Oswalds von Wolkenstein
   Andreas Kraß — 65

5. Legal Process and Fantasies of Torture: Reality and Imagination in Oswald von Wolkenstein
   Almut Suerbaum — 79

6. *Offenlich und unter ogen*: Honour and Punishment in Late Medieval Urban Life
   Jamie Page — 95

7. 'schneident mir beid oren ab': The Comic Potential of Corporal Punishment in Sixteenth-century *Schwankbücher*
   Sebastian Coxon — 115

8. Penitential Punishment and Purgatory: A Drama of Purification through Pain
   Racha Kirakosian — 129

9. Körpergebrauch, Kontrolle und Kontrollverlust in den
 Askeseschilderungen der Vita Elsbeths von Oye
 Björn Klaus Buschbeck 155
10. Strafen und Leiden im Martyrium: Überlegungen zu
 Konrads von Würzburg *Pantaleon*
 Katharina Mertens-Fleury 175
Abstracts of German-language articles 195
Index 207

Acknowledgements

This book started life as a conference of the same name, which took place at King's College London in September 2014. The aim of the conference was to bring together scholars working on various aspects of punishment and penance in the medieval German context to share and develop ideas. We are very grateful to all participants at the event for their lively and open-minded discussion. The majority of the papers presented have made their way in revised form into this book and we are also pleased to be able to include an essay by Racha Kirakosian, who was unable to attend the original event.

The conference was generously supported by the Faculty of Arts and Humanities and the Department of German at King's College London, and Oriel College Oxford; we are extremely grateful to all of these bodies for making the event possible. We would also like to thank Julian Weiss, series editor for KCLMS, for accepting our volume and for all his invaluable help and advice during the editing process. Thank you, too, to Wendy Pank for the typesetting, to all contributors for being so accommodating and efficient, and to Susen Vural from Susen Vural Design for invaluable help with the final stages of production.

Sarah Bowden & Annette Volfing
London/Oxford, September 2017

Notes on Contributors

Sarah Bowden is Lecturer in German at King's College London. Her research has focused on medieval bridal-quest epic and on 11th- and 12th-century German literary culture, and she is the author of *Bridal-quest Epics in Medieval Germany: A Revisionary Approach* (London: MHRA, 2012).

Björn Klaus Buschbeck is a PhD student in German Studies at Stanford University, having previously studied at Albert-Ludwigs-Universität Freiburg and the University of Oxford. His research focuses on the transmission and poetics of later medieval and early modern religious cultures and on German mysticism.

Sebastian Coxon is Reader in German at University College London. He has published widely on later medieval comic narrative and on laughter, jest and ridicule, including the monograph *Laughter and Narrative in the Later Middle Ages. German Comic Tales 1350-1525* (London: MHRA, 2008).

Racha Kirakosian is Assistant Professor of German and the Study of Religion at Harvard University. Her publications include studies on medieval German mysticism, female sanctity, and religious law, and her book *Die Vita der Christina von Hane: Untersuchung und Edition* (Berlin: de Gruyter) appeared in 2017.

Andreas Kraß is Professor of Medieval German Literature at the Humboldt-Universität zu Berlin. He has published widely on medieval German literature, including monographs on the Stabat mater tradition and on clothing in courtly texts. His book *Ein Herz und eine Seele. Geschichte der Männerfreundschaft* (Frankfurt a. M.: Fischer) appeared in 2016.

Henrike Manuwald is Professor of Medieval German Studies at Georg-August-Universität, Göttingen. She has published widely on German literature of the high and late Middle Ages, on mediality (text-image relations) and on fictionality, and is the author of *Medialer Dialog. Die "Große Bilderhandschrift" des Willehalm Wolframs von Eschenbach und ihre Kontexte* (Tübingen: Basel 2008).

Katharina Mertens-Fleury is Privatdozentin and Oberassistentin in Medieval German Literature at the Universität Zürich. She has published widely on courtly epic and is the author of monographs on *compassio* in Wolfram's *Parzival* and on medieval allegorical narrative.

Jamie Page is Leverhulme Early Career Fellow in Late Medieval and Early Modern European History at the University of Durham. He is a historian of late medieval Germany and Switzerland, working primarily on gender, sexuality and crime.

Almut Suerbaum is Associate Professor in German at Somerville College, Oxford. Her research focuses on the dialogue between Latin and vernacular culture, between manuscript and voice and between lay and institution, and she has published widely in all these areas.

Annette Volfing is Professor of Medieval German Studies at Oriel College, Oxford. She has a particular interest in later medieval religious, mystical, philosophical and allegorical writing, and her most recent book, *The Daugher Zion Allegory in Medieval German Writing* (Abingdon: Routledge), appeared in 2017.

1

Punishment & Penitential Practices: An Introduction

Sarah Bowden
King's College London

In *Discipline and Punish* – first published in 1975 as *Surveiller et punir* and translated into English two years later – Michel Foucault analyzes the historical changes in the penal systems of the West, highlighting the disappearance of physical torture in modern penal systems and the move from corporal punishment to discipline and the birth of the prison. This difference between the the modern and pre-modern penal ages is made immediately apparent in his startling opening descriptions of the spectacular execution of the regicide Damiens in 1757 – whose flesh is torn from his limbs with pincers in a botched fashion, whose body is quartered by horses (again, gruesomely and not very efficiently) and who is finally burnt – and, in contrast, the set of rules drawn up for the 'House of young prisoners in Paris' just eighty years later (Foucault 1977: 3-7). As such, Foucault stresses the move from a focus on the punishment of the body to the punishment of the mind and, correspondingly, from punishment as a public event or spectacle to punishment as discipline behind closed doors (even if it is paradoxically made just as 'visible' for being shut away). His analysis of these differences is also a means to investigate forms of power and the interrelation between power and knowledge. For Foucault, punishment is a complex social function, which plays a central role in the exercise of political power; it is a political tactic, not simply a consequence of legislation or an indicator of social structures. Different forms of punishment also expose the way in which the human body is invested with power relations: the body's symbolic currency, the body's political history, the body's relationship with the soul.

Foucault's primary interest is in modern cultures of discipline and surveillance – for him, punishment is to a certain extent a lens through which he can explore the modern bourgeois 'disciplined society' – and he does not concern himself to any serious degree with the medieval period. Yet his writing looms large in much contemporary scholarship on medieval penal systems and cultures, and it has become almost impossible to discuss the theory and practice of punishment in any period without reference to his work. Much as I am doing now, it is common for authors writing about aspects of medieval punishment to start with a discussion of Foucault and then to establish some form of revisionary standpoint (or indeed an extension) to his relatively brief comments about the medieval period. Depending on the particular focus of the study in question, there are inevitably different points of emphasis to such revisions. First, and most fundamentally: to what extent does Foucault represent accurately the historical reality of medieval penal culture? What was actually going on? Then, to what extent do Foucault's observations on role of power relations and the body in acts of punishment still apply to a perhaps more nuanced recalibration of the historical situation? More broadly, what opportunity do acts of punishment offer us as medievalists to comment on the mechanics of power in various social siutations, as well as on the symbolic capital of the body?

Foucault's ideas and what I understand as these areas of critical response to them form a point of crystallization for the two main aims of this introduction: to introduce and discuss some current critical trends on medieval punishment, and to establish in this context the specific questions that shape this book. For this purpose, I divide the introduction into two main sections: first, I examine the historical situation and outline various critical trends; second, I explore the various ways in which we interpret acts of punishment, working outwards from the Foucauldian emphasis on power structures and the body, but also highlighting further interpretative problems that this collection aims to bring to light.

Before I turn to this, however, it seems sensible to set out the basic parameters of the present volume. Thus far I have written only of 'punishment', yet the title of the book points to a concurrent emphasis on 'penitential practices', which suggests a broader focus on actions (or restrictions) performed voluntarily or imposed upon the person in response to a perceived sin or crime. Given the clear overlap between punishment and penitential practice in both theory and practice, it seems surprising that the two are not considered in conjunction more frequently. Punishment can be penitential; a penitential practice can punish. An exploration of both areas demands that one interrogate the difference between them – and this in turn clarifies the difficulty of defining and delineating each term. Taken strictly, punishment is conventionally understood as a penalty or sanction imposed as a kind of retribution for a crime according to a secular legal framework, and a penitential practice as the performance (habitual or otherwise) of some sort of action to atone for a sin, either imposed by a priest or confessor or undertaken voluntarily.[1] Broadly, then, punishment occurs in a secular legal context and penance in a religious one, with punishment imposed by a superior authority of some kind and penance relying at

---

[1] I follow the definitions found in the Oxford English Dictionary (http://www.oed.com; accessed 26/2/16). Here, punishment is defined as: 'The infliction of a penalty or sanction in retribution for

least to some extent on the motivation of the penitent, but such a distinction is rarely easy (or sensible) to uphold.[2]

It is however, not the aim of this book to define with any finality what we might mean by punishment or a penitential practice in a medieval context. Unlike many studies of punishment in the Middle Ages, this book does not have at its centre the historical realities of judicial punishment. It is not our intention to make a clear statement about the penal or penitential system of the German lands in a particular period. Inevitably many of the essays do analyze historically attestable practices and events, but it is our primary aim to consider how such events and practices – 'real' or otherwise – were written about in the German vernacular, and how they find currency in a variety of different text types. As such, many of the essays do not discuss solely officially sanctioned acts of punishment or penance, but rather instances or actions that have a punishing or penitential character. The authors of the individual essays this volume contains are, primarily, literary scholars, and therefore one of the main aims of the collection is to investigate the way in which literary texts can function as a means to consider the conceptualization and problematization of punishment and penance, and – correspondingly – the challenges posed for writing about them in different contexts and in different genres. The areas of investigation extracted from Foucault above therefore resonate with us in a particular way, as I set out in more detail below: we consider the representation of lived experience in literary texts, and how literary depictions intersect with such lived experience; we interpret acts of punishment and penance both within literary texts and with respect to their extra-textual communicative function; we explore the complex power structures inherent in these acts; and we consider the symbolic and communicative capital of the body that results from them.

---

an offence or transgression; (also) that which is inflicted as a penalty; a sanction imposed to ensure the application and enforcement of a law.' Penance is: 'The performance of some act of self-mortification or the undergoing of some penalty as an expression of sorrow for sin or wrongdoing; religious discipline, either imposed by ecclesiastical authority or voluntarily undertaken, as a token of repentance and as a means of satisfaction for sin; (also) such discipline or observance imposed by a priest upon a penitent after confession, as an integral part of the sacrament of penance.' Penitence is the 'state of being penitent', so penitential practices are actions undertaken as penance, whether self-imposed or imposed by another, typically a confessor or priest.

[2] See for instance Merback (1999: 17): 'the interrelationship of criminal justice and religion was a fact of life beyond dispute. [...] We find learned jurists enthralled by the rationalism of the neo-Roman law then being studied in the universities, yet beholden to theological precepts and para-religious practices rooted in popular culture and enshrined by custom. And we find, on the other side of the scaffold as it were, a popular audience for executions that experienced the performance of justice as an opportunity for cultic devotions, prayers and transactions with the community of the dead.' The interrelationship between punishment and penance is further explored in this volume by BUSCHBECK.

Punishment and Penitential Practices in the Middle Ages: Historical Approaches

Foucault first provides a springboard for a discussion of the historical reality of medieval punishment. It is an old adage now that there are weaknesses in the accuracy of Foucault's historical analysis and that his use of archival material is rather slim (Spierenburg 1984: vii; Merquior 1991: 101-04). Although the basic premise of the move from corporal punishment in the pre-modern world to discipline in the modern is held to be largely sound, it has been argued in various different ways that the change occurred in a more gradual and complex fashion than Foucault might lead us to believe. Spierenburg (1984), for example, argues that Foucault's picture is too simplistic and his model of change too sudden, and aims to qualify it by inquiring into the reasons for and the nature of the transition between penal systems, stressing in particular the role of urbanization in the development of criminal justice; Dean (2001), on the other hand, argues that we should not understate the role of incarceration as punishment in the Middle Ages or overstate the role of public execution or corporal punishment, when most offenders were punished with monetary fines.[3]

More broadly, there has been an attempt to rehabilitate the Middle Ages through engagement with the modern perception of the 'medieval'. When it comes to 'medieval punishment', the public perception has not moved far from Huizinga's classic description of 1921 (here cited in the 1996 English translation), in which he writes of 'the perverse sickness, [...] the dull, animal-like enjoyment, the country fair-like amusement' of judicial cruelty (1996: 20). There persists the cliché of a bloody and violent Middle Ages, in which punishment consists in sadistic blood-letting, perhaps even with some sort of erotic charge – and this is a perception that extends to penitential practices as well. In the words of Mills, '[C]apital punishment functions as a metonym for the brutality of the past, establishing an uninhabitable space fantasized by the speaker as threatening to his or her integrity and consequently disavowed.' (Mills 2005: 7). It comes as no surprise, therefore, that much effort has been expended in scholarship to rationalize violent judicial practice or qualify it by emphasizing non-violent practices as well (Cohen 1990; Althoff 1999). Starting from the presumption that punishment was not simply an expression of an untamed lust for blood, and that practices were conventionally much less extreme and more mundane than we might think, various scholars have begun to investigate not only why modern perception has been shaped as it has but also why medieval representations of punishments, in both art and literature,

---

[3] On the role of prisons in the pre-modern world, see Peters (1995).

often paint a more gruesome and extreme picture than historical reality (Braun and Herberichs 2005; Mills 2005; Tracy 2012; Caviness 2013).

What, then, was the historical reality of medieval punishment? It is first important to clarify that there is no one 'historical reality', that any notion we might have of 'medieval punishment' (whether an 'imaginary' perception of constant brutality or otherwise) needs specification and clarification. Practices of both punishment and penance were constantly in flux and varied widely in different regions and at different times. Nonetheless a brief overview of the complex history of the development of both punishment and penance in the German lands in the Middle Ages may be useful.

The Middle High German word *strafe* is not used to mean 'Strafe' or punishment in the modern sense until relatively late; *strafe* 'findet sich erst ab 1200 für ein Phänomen, das zuvor noch als "rächen" oder "körperl. züchtigen" oder "beaufsichtigen" bezeichnet worden war' [is first used from 1200 for a phenomenon previously marked out as 'vengeance', 'bodily chastisement' or 'bodily control'] (Schild 1997: 198) and was only used as a judicial or legal term from around 1400 (Achter 1951: 10). This semantic development corresponds to the gradual development of secular law in the period; it is possible to trace, from about 1200, a move towards what nowadays is thought of as a system of criminal justice. This shift occurred throughout the whole of Western Europe and is often attributed to the increase in intellectual study in the twelfth century, and particularly that of learned Roman law (Kuttner 1982). This increased reception of Roman law led to a gradual move from a personal, accusatorial way of dealing with crime to an inquisitorial approach, with the institution of written evidence and the use of specialized personnel. We can thus trace a gradual shift in the German lands from the personal, accusatorial settling of conflicts, in which criminal deeds were responded to with vengeance (*râche*) or were paid off with a set sum of money known as 'Buße' (or *wergeld*) and in which methods of proof were based around judicial battle, ordeals or oath-taking, to the inquisitorial system, with the institution of written evidence, torture and the use of specialized personnel. The culmination of this move was the *Carolina* of Emperor Charles V in 1532, Germany's first fully-fledged criminal code.[4] Yet the situation in German-speaking lands was somewhat different from others parts of Europe, primarily it seems because of the absence of one unified ruling body; the influence of Roman law was not as great and changes to the accusatorial system arguably not as wide-reaching. Changes that did occur were brought about primarily by the so-called 'Friedensbewegung' [movement of

---

[4] Good overviews of the development of judicial punishment in Germany are offered by Langbein (1974: 140-66); Schild (1997).

peace], especially the expansion of various 'Landfrieden' agreements [declarations of 'territorial peace'] from the eleventh century (Langbein 1974: 141-52; Wadle 1999).[5] Nonetheless, despite the general shift throughout the Middle Ages from *rache* [vengeance] to a more codified judicial punishment, it is extremely difficult to trace any kind of linear development and it seems clear that various forms of punishment existed concurrently (Kéry 2006; in this volume see MANUWALD).

Current research on medieval penance also has a strong focus on breaking down preconceptions; in this case the focus is not potentially erroneous contemporary understandings of the 'medieval', but rather the conventional narrative of the development of penitential theology and practice throughout the Middle Ages, which is now widely considered to be misleading. As with the legal developments outlined above, this penitential change is often attributed to the understanding of the twelfth century as an age of reform (Constable 1998). According to historiographical tradition, the twelfth century witnessed a move towards a greater emphasis on individual responsibility in the act of sin and on contrition in absolving oneself of it, which can be summarized as follows (the classic accounts are Jungmann 1932 and Poschmann 1951). The early medieval period inherited the notion of canonical penance from late antiquity, a kind of penance that was centred around public shame and could be undertaken only once in a lifetime: it was common, therefore, for it to be put off until the deathbed. The idea of the possibility of repeatable penance seems to have originated in Ireland, where the monastic way of life was understood as a perpetual state of penance; this spread to continental monastic life and thence to the laity. Thus in the Carolingian period there appear to have been two forms of penance, which we can refer to as 'public' and 'private'. 'Public' penance, the heir of early medieval penance, was undertaken for more serious sins, such as murder or incest, and was also, it seems, a useful political tool; 'secret' or 'private' penance was administered for lesser crimes. The next step, which is thought to have occurred in the twelfth and thirteenth centuries, is the move from penance – public or secret – performed externally according to a penitential tariff to a greater emphasis on the contrition of the individual. The culmination of this was the *omnis utriusque sexus* decree of the Fourth Lateran Council in 1215, which declared that everyone, male or female, must confess to a priest at least once a year.[6] In sum, then, the changing emphases with respect to the performance of penance seem to point to

---
[5] Langbein (1974: 152-55) also stresses the influence of the inquisitorial process of canon law on the development of secular law. In canon law, which is more clearly regulated and less regionally diffuse than secular law, we see the firm establishment of the inquisitorial procedure in the twelfth century under Innocent III and excommunication as the main punishment for offending clergy.

[6] More recent and critical summaries of the conventional history of penitential development are offered by Hamilton (2001: 1-15) and Bruchhold (2010: 19-28).

an interiorization of sin: a move from an understanding of sins as external forces to an understanding of sins as products of human intention. This is connected more broadly to the idea that the twelfth century saw the rise of the 'individual', that is, a new understanding of human nature as independent and self-governing and a greater sense of one's own personal identity (Morris 1972; Benton 1982).

The possibility of 'individuality' in the contemporary sense of an awareness of personal human uniqueness has, however, been fundamentally questioned (Bynum 1980) and the theory that the *omnis utriusque sexus* decree of 1215 was a manifestation of a particularly new and growing importance of interiority in religious experience has equally been thrown into doubt. Various scholars have emphasized the role of interiority in the penitential process in the earlier medieval period (Meens 1998; Hamilton 2001; Firey 2009) and it has also been shown that rituals of public penance and humiliation did not fall out of use after 1215 (Mansfield 1995). In this volume, the complexities of the role of interiority are tackled by KIRAKOSIAN, who explores interior and exterior forms of penance with respect to the emergence of the notion of purgatory.

Yet even if the historical reality of penitential practice is often difficult to pin down, we can nonetheless consider the Middle Ages as a deeply penitential period, a time in which people were acutely aware of their own sinfulness, their potential for salvation and also the work that they have to undergo in order to achieve this salvation. Art and literature are saturated with penitential imagery; penance is the subject of numerous theological discourses. It is inevitable that we come across actions that are not officially bestowed by a confessor as penance that nonetheless acquire a penitential nature; equally, that punishments of all sorts can be in some way penitential. Actions with some sort of penitential or punishing character extend beyond the official situations set out above. The punishments and penitential actions discussed in this volume are rarely located explicitly within the framework of a clearly regulated social practice. One of the aims of this volume is, therefore, to explore the way in which literary texts alter, and interact with, lived experience.

Interpreting acts of punishment and penance: power and the body

The intersection between literary writing and historical reality is not, however, the only point of interest of this volume. More broadly, we seek to interpret acts of punishment and penance in different forms of vernacular writing in ways appropriate to the texts and contexts in question. As such, the contributions to this volume aim to expose and discuss the communicative functions inherent in the actions we investigate: we consider what individual acts of punishment and penance communicate, how they communicate it, and to whom.[7] Our investigations inevitably take a number of different directions, but coalesce around two main areas that can be isolated for further discussion, both of which connect back to Foucault: power and the body.

As discussed above, Foucault asserts that punishment is a key practice in the exercising of social control and can also function as a political tool. The socially controlling aspect of punishment can, however, be overstated – and not just when it comes to punishment but also to penance, which was long thought of in scholarship as bringing out what was worst in medieval religious culture: the oppression of society, the mechanization of human life (Frantzen 1983: 1-8).[8] It is all too easy to generalize about the role of social control in acts of punishment and penance; here, we aim to contextualize and pay attention to time and place, and to particular social groups and behaviours that may be targeted by such acts (see for instance PAGE on late medieval Zurich). Moreover, power relations are not always clear-cut – instead of understanding power being imposed by one person (the punisher) onto another (the punished – or indeed a wider community who are affected by the punishment or threat of it), we can find evidence of situations where power structures are reinterpreted, and where roles oscillate. VOLFING, for instance, explores the ways in which an act of punishment can lead to further actions and reactions, which can bring about a reinterpretation of roles and recalibration of structures of power. Equally, it is not always the person who punishes or prescribes penance with whom the power lies. The punishments of saints and would-be martyrs, for example, may bestow them with a new sacred, even miraculous power (MERTENS-FLEURY); extreme penitential practices may also be interpreted as a sign of power over one's body and can have an effect on power relations within the community in which the penitent lives (BUSCHBECK; KIRAKOSIAN).

The potential role of God lies behind many actions of both punishment and penance. Worldly authority in the Middle Ages is, ideally, performed on behalf of spiritual authority; leaders, both secular and spiritual, should perform God's work on Earth and – when taken fundamentally – God is surely the only real judge of sin and crime. The extent to which punishments are presented, implicitly or explicitly, as

---

[7] A similar stance is taken by Braun and Herberichs (2005) in their volume on the depiction of violence in medieval German writing.

[8] See also Murray (1993: 52-53), who discusses the difference between Protestant and Catholic readings of the history of confession. He argues that Catholic scholars were more likely to suggest that confession was an older practice than perhaps it might be, whereas Protestants were prone to attribute it to papal authority, specifically that of Innocent III in the 1215 decree *Omnis utriusque sexus*. For Protestants (from the very beginning), Murray argues, confession was a 'bad thing', giving priests too much 'social control' and either leading to 'moral laxity' or 'scrupulosity'.

divine punishment is often of great importance (how can the agency of God be made apparent?), as is the depiction of the relationship of punishing authorities to God. In the case of depictions of Christian martyrdom, these sorts of power structures can become perversely complicated: on the one hand, the heathen 'punisher' is exerting and upholding his worldly power, but on the other, the otherworldly triumph of the Christian martyr (as well as the resulting power bestowed upon her through the punishments she has undergone) asserts the supremacy of the power of God and the punished (Mertens-Fleury).

The agency of God leads to a consideration of the way in which this-worldly forms of punishment and atonement relate to afterlife experiences, that is, the potential correlation between earthly and otherworldly punishments. Extreme penitential practices may be perceived as merging in some way with (or even pre-empting) post-death purgatorial experience (Kirakosian); on the other hand, the this-worldly 'punishment' of martyrs does not correlate at all with their fate after death. Capital punishment may pose different questions: is the fate of the criminal cast as a representation of his otherworldly fate (presumably pretty bleak), or does his eternal damnation remain largely irrelevant, that is, is the desired effect really an improvement of the spectating (or reading) audience? Is it the eternal fate of the audience or even the punisher here that is in question, rather than the punished?

Not all acts of punishment and penance are prescribed by one person to another, however. Penitential practices in particular are often performed by the self upon the self at the behest of the self. The power dynamics inherent in such actions can be particularly intriguing: on the one hand, these practices suggest the power of the self, which can direct and control; on the other hand, they manifest simultaneously a power over the self, resulting in (or aiming for) a total annihilation of selfhood. Extreme penitential or ascetic practices thus oscillate between both control and a loss of control: control in directing one's own actions and not succumbing to the easy way out or to bodily desires, but a lack of control in a complete resignation of the self to a particular penitential state of being (Buschbeck). Such paradoxes pose vital questions concerning the composition of texts themselves. Focusing in particular on the changes in the penitential system in the twelfth century, Kramer and Bynum (2002) explore the problems of negotiating between outer behaviour in demonstrating repentance for sin and inner feelings of contrition and sorrow. Both, they argue, are vital, but how can they be expressed?[9] The challenge is one of correlation – is the outer merely a visible manifestation of something hidden? How

---

[9] Kramer and Bynum (2002: 65): 'According to much early twelfth-century ethical theory, the moral quality of an act lay not in the deed itself but in the intention of affect of the actor. The disjunction between inner and outer in defining sin was, moreover, accentuated by an understanding that a person's

is the inner made manifest to an external audience, and expressed in words? True contrition is of course knowable only to God, and a state of extreme repentance which has led to a kind of penitential life that is so deep as to have absolved itself from intention is accordingly very difficult to put into words.

Considering this problem rather more broadly, and taking power rather more metaphorically, we explore the power of the act of writing about acts of punishment and penance, as well as of texts themselves. Power may be exerted not only within a text but by a text: the representation of a punishing or penitential action may itself be a way of exerting social control. Mills (2005), for instance, argues that spectacular *representations* of punishment and pain can be a way of maintaining institutional authority and social control, but that power can also lie with the punished in terms of fantasies of empowerment and resistance, as well as transgressive eroticism.[10] Given the emphasis of this volume on written texts, many of which are self-consciously literary, several contributions focus at least partly on the poetics of individual texts as well as how the particular challenges of the subject-matter of punishment and penance are tackled and perhaps overcome. Coxon, for instance, shows how the brutality of certain acts of punishment can be glossed over entirely or tempered with humour; in their essays on Oswald von Wolkenstein, Krass and Suerbaum explore the ways in which punishment and penance can provide an opportunity for authorial display and an examination of the self not only as penitential subject but also as author; Buschbeck shows how for Elsbeth von Oye, a fourteenth-century nun, (divinely inspired) writing can be a powerful tool for asserting and legitimizing a religious identity that her gender would not normally allow.

In the background of much of this discussion of power we can trace the presence of the body. The somatic aspect has as yet been only implicit, however, in order that its fundamental importance be given the dedicated space it deserves. Actions of punishment and penance are not necessarily bodily; as mentioned above, it is easy to overestimate the role of medieval corporal punishment, and penitential practices need also not always be expressed physically. Yet there is no ignoring the fact that most actions do involve the body in some way and the somatic aspect accordingly

---

true intention could be known only by God. Outer behavior was not a direct gateway to inner attitude. The bifurcation was troublesome. If only God can know intention, a theory which interiorizes sin means that only God can determine the moral quality of an act. Such a theoretical position could hardly offer a practical scenario to a church passionately concerned with the reform of its members. If sin is to turn on intention alone, then intention must somehow be externalized so that sin can be measured, punished and remitted.'

[10] See also Cohen (1990), who shows the ways in which the inconsistency of capital punishment in late medieval Paris was connected fundamentally to its potential effect on the general public.

features heavily in this volume; examples discussed include torture, execution, mutilation and ascetic self-chastisement.

In order to engage with the body in more detail we can return to Foucault one last time. According to his interpretation, one of the primary changes in the move from pre-modern to modern punishment is a shift from an emphasis on bodily chastisement or 'an art of unbearable sensations' to 'an economy of suspended rights' in discipline (Foucault 1977: 11). The body of the pre-modern criminal has a particular symbolic capital and stands in inversion to that of the King. The royal body, following the famous analysis of Kantorowicz (1957), is doubled: as well as the natural body, there exists the more mythical, eternal body, representative of the eternal dignity of kingship. Foucault argues, here in the words of Merquior, that just as the sovereign has a 'sacral body, symbol of the body politic, so the scaffold had in its victim a body which was the very antithesis of the right and might of royal power' (Merquior 1991: 88–89). Such an argument offers a good starting point, as does Foucault's broader observation that the punished body is a 'body politic', understood 'as a set of material elements and techniques that serve as weapons, relays, communication routes and supports for the power and knowledge relations that invest human bodies and subjugate them by turning them into objects of knowledge' (Foucault 1977: 28).

It is certainly true that both punishment and penitential practices can be read as a means of reasserting positive normativity or an ideal state of being. In this sense, both have a purifying function: the punishment of criminals by driving out or dehumanizing the criminal body purifies the society (who may well be watching);[11] penitential practices purify the soul, driving out the sins of the body by 'punishing' it with physical suffering. Yet this is by no means the whole picture. Foucault can lead us into traps – an overemphasis on subjugation, on political submission and on the use of punishment to assert normative power structures; an overemphasis on the tortured, dismembered body and on capital punishment – resulting in an 'othering' of the medieval body and the medieval period in general as a distant and barbaric place of critical condemnation (Mills 2005: 13; Geltner 2014: 62-68).

Bodies function differently in all of the texts explored in the essays of this volume. They are complex – their function and symbolic value is often hard to grasp with any finality – and encoded in different ways dependent on different sorts of contexts. Although some of the texts explored are presented as depictions of historical reality (or even as (auto)biography), all are self-consciously shaped written objects that bestow the body with a kind of representative function (one

---

[11] On the ways in which the body of the criminal is dehumanized through punishment and marked out through torture, dismemberment, and so on as an undesirable 'Unmensch', see Schild (1997: 200-01).

might even speak of 'literary' bodies). As a result, the symbolic capital of the body is vital; the complex forms of meaning we can read into individual bodies help to illuminate or reinterpret historical realities or ideas about punishment and penance, or indeed the texts themselves. Broadly, then, we consider the body as a carrier of signs. The punished body, for instance, may bear a sign of the particular crime or sin it has committed – a permanent trace with, perhaps, a memorial function, which can then exert an effect on others as well. The condemned body, the punished body, and the penitent body are all inscribed with different kinds of meaning – meaning bestowed by missing limbs, stigmata, traces of whipping, signs of starvation, perhaps, or by specific gestures, or by non-bodily markings such as ropes, chains or other ephemera, particular clothing or even a lack of clothing.

Penitent bodies in particular lead us to consider the relationship between body and soul. The body, with its connection to worldly temptation, is of course the locus of sin, so punishing the body may, in various ways, be an effective means of driving out that sin. Bodily suffering can thus enable the salvation of the soul. The relationship between body and soul is not, however, always a simple one; KIRAKOSIAN, for example, shows how penitential practices can allow us to explore the tension between the simultaneous identity and difference between body and soul. Moreover, suffering and pain need not always function directly as a form of 'punishment' for a specific sin; that is, a simple correlation between sin committed and physical pain to atone does not necessarily exist. Bodily sensation (and the way it is written about) is just as complex as the depiction of the body itself.

First, suffering bodies as depicted in texts are not always particularly sinful ones; in this volume we consider the 'punishment' of saints, and even of Christ, and the extreme penitential practices of female mystics. Penitential actions need not, therefore, be a response to one's own sin, but may offer a way of responding to the universal sinfulness of mankind through bodily suffering (BUSCHBECK); alternatively, they can take on a kind of proxy role (KIRAKOSIAN), atoning for the sins of others or assuming a didactic function. The relationship of suffering bodies to Christ, and the ways in which they are shown to engage with a kind of *imitatio Christi*, is therefore key; the (capital) punishment of Christ, and Christ's punished body are implicitly – or explicitly – present in so many medieval penitential or punishing actions. Physical suffering can recreate the suffering of Christ in order to replay (in a differently coded way) his acts of sacrifice, and thus restate an action which functions to establish and secure the Christian community; equally, it can provide a way to demonstrate *compassio* and to participate in his suffering. Bodily suffering and physical pain can, therefore, fulfil a devotional function, and punishing oneself may offer an articulation of some form of desire. The correlation between pain and desire can be a problematic, ambiguous one, however, explored here in particular with respect to the question as to whether extreme ascetic, penitential practices can go 'too far' (BUSCHBECK; KIRAKOSIAN).

* * *

The nine essays that follow address the issues raised in this introduction from a variety of different angles. Many deal with the productive 'grey areas' I hope to have set out above (the grey areas between punishment and penance, literature and history, vengeance and judicial punishment, pain and desire, to name just a few). In a volume with an emphasis on literary texts – on *writing* – it seems sensible to begin with an analysis of the specific terminology used to describe acts that we might think of as 'punishing'. Henrike MANUWALD investigates the complexities of the Middle High German term *râche*, which we might conventionally translate as 'vengeance', but which she demonstrates has a much wider field of reference. Through a case study of the twelfth-century *Alexander* of Rudolf von Ems as well as through a wider contextual approach, she shows that there is no linear development from a system of retribution based on personal vengeance [*Fehdewesen*] and that *rache* can denote (simultaneously) both vengeance of a misdeed by the aggrieved party *and* punishment. Annette VOLFING also discusses the complex intersection between revenge and punishment in the medieval context. Through a close reading of one series of events in Wolfram's *Parzival* – the beating of Cunneware by Keie and actions that result from it – she exposes the range of changing inter-personal dynamics caused by punishment and how they relate to gender roles and social normativity.

The contributions by Andreas KRASS and Almut SUERBAUM both concern the poet Oswald von Wolkenstein. Through a close reading of Oswald's *Beichtlied* [*Song of Confession*], KRASS investigates the opportunities that the subject matter of confession and penitence offers to writing poetry, in particular with respect to self-exploration and self-presentation. In this song, he argues, Oswald interweaves different roles, simultaneously presenting himself as sinner, poet and preacher. SUERBAUM also explores Oswald's self-presentation. Using both historical records of his life as well as his poetry, she employs the themes of torture, punishment and the penal system as a way in to investigate the complex intersections between poetry, autobiography and the penal system in his writing; she argues that we should not aim to distinguish between historical truth and fiction in Oswald's texts, but rather understand that his work is a unique and literary amalgamation of the two, shaped by different, contextually-determined first-person voices.

Jamie PAGE continues the focus on the intersection between historical sources and literary texts, investigating punishment in later medieval urban legal and fictional narratives. He argues that punishment was embedded in the 'everyday' actions of urban life, and through its informal practice was connected to the management of honour (*Ehre* or *fama*), which facilitated social cohesion. As such, punishment (whether real or imaginery) is largely shown to be part of a masculine discourse, aimed at maintaining not only masculine honour, but also patriarchal social order. Sebastian COXON also explores late medieval narratives, investigating the comic potential of corporal punishment in sixteenth-century collections of short comic and serious anecdotes. He shows that the stories in these so-called *Schwankbücher* [books of jest] play down pain and suffering in their depiction of punishment – in fact, the subject of law and order is treated with more restraint that other themes in this genre of writing – and focus instead on the witty or foolish speech of the criminal or others.

Racha KIRAKOSIAN'S contribution shifts the focus of the volume into a more profoundly religious sphere. Through a close reading of *Life* of the little-known thirteenth-century Premonstratensian mystic Christina of Hane, she explores the interrrelationships (both practical and theological) between penitence, penance, punishment and purgatory. The thirteenth century was a period in which developing ideas about the interiority of the penitential experience were being concretized, yet – as she shows – private internal penitence does not mean that penitential actions are less externalized or corporeal. This is demonstrated, for instance, through her analysis of the pain caused by Christina's extreme penitential practices: it is at once a materialization of a more abstract (internal) pain, and a 'proxy' pain which reflects the experience of others (here primarily souls in purgatory). Björn BUSCHBECK also investigates the penitential practices of a female mystic. In his exploration of the *Vita* of the fourteenth-century Dominican Elsbeth von Oye, he works from the starting point that her penitential practices are not a response to a specific sin, but rather to the intrinsic sinfulness of human nature. This leads to a consideration of the way in which her extreme bodily chastisement leads paradoxically both to a loss and gain of control of her religious experience. On the one hand, power over her body is a ways of establishing legitimacy and identity, giving her a form of religious control she would not normally have as a woman; on the other hand, her bodily practices become so extreme that they get 'out of control', leading to a potential annihilation of the self.

In the final essay of the volume, Katharina MERTENS-FLEURY considers the martyrdom of St Pantaleon, in particular the fourteenth-century narrative about the saint by Konrad von Würzburg. Through her close reading of this text, she uncovers the paradoxical power structures inherent in martyrdom narratives. Sanctions imposed on Christian martyrs do not function as punishments (even if they are intended to be punishments within the context of the punisher); instead, they are encoded as acts of triumph on the part of the 'punished' Christian. In this sense, Christians who are *not* powerful in this world are paradoxically enabled to become more powerful through their triumphant 'punishments'.

Works Cited

Achter, Viktor. 1951. *Die Geburt der Strafe* (Frankfurt a. M.: Klostermann)

Althoff, Gerd. 1999. 'Schranken der Gewalt: Wie gewalttätig war das 'finstere Mittelalter'?', in *Der Krieg im Mittelalters und in der Frühen Neuzeit: Gründe, Begründungen, Bilder, Bräuche, Recht*, ed. Horst Brunner, Imagines Medii Aevi, 3 (Wiesbaden: Reichert), pp. 1-23

Benton, John F. 1982. 'Consciousness of Self and Perceptions of Individuality', in *Renaissance and Renewal in the Twelfth Century*, ed. Robert L. Benson and Giles Constable (Oxford: Clarendon), pp. 263-95

Braun, Manuel and Cornelia Herberichs (eds). 2005. *Gewalt im Mittelalter. Realitäten – Imaginationen* (Munich: Fink, 2005)

Bruchhold, Ullrich. 2010. *Deutschsprachige Beichten im 13. und 14. Jahrhundert: Editionen und Typologien zur Überlieferungs-, Text- und Gebrauchsgeschichte vor dem Hintergrund der älteren Tradition*, Münchener Texte und Untersuchungen zur deutschen Literatur des Mittelalters, 138 (Berlin/New York: de Gruyter)

Caviness, Madeline H. 2013. 'Giving "the Middle Ages" a Bad Name', *Studies in Iconography*, 34: 175-235

Cohen, Esther. 1990. '"To Die a Criminal for the Public Good": The Execution Ritual in Late Medieval Paris', in *Law, Custom, and the Social Fabric in Medieval Europe. Essays in Honor of Bruce Lyon*, ed. Bernard S. Bachrach and David Nicholas, Studies in Medieval Culture, 28 (Kalamazoo: Medieval Institute Publications), pp. 285-304

Constable, Giles. 1998. *The Reformation of the Twelfth Century* (Cambridge: Cambridge University Press)

Dean, Trevor. 2001. *Crime in Medieval Europe, 1200-1550* (Harlow: Longman)

Firey, Abigail. 2009. *A Contrite Heart: Prosecution and Redemption in the Carolingian Empire*, Studies in Medieval and Reformation Traditions, 145 (Leiden: Brill)

Foucault, Michel. 1975. *Surveiller et punir: Naissance de la prison* (Paris: Gallimard)

—. 1977. *Discipline and Punish. The Birth of the Prison*, trans. Alan Sheridan (London: Penguin)

Frantzen, Allen. 1983. *The Literature of Penance in Anglo-Saxon England* (New Brunswick: Rutgers University Press)

Geltner, G. 2014. *Flogging Others: Corporal Punishment and Cultural Identity from Antiquity to the Present* (Amsterdam: Amsterdam University Press)

Hamilton, Sarah. 2001. *The Practice of Penance, 900-1050*, Royal Historical Society Studies in History (London: The Royal Historical Society)

Huizinga, Johan. 1996. *The Autumn of the Middle Ages*, trans. Rodney J. Payton and Ulrich Mammitzsch (Chicago: University of Chicago Press)

Jungmann, Josef Andreas. 1932. *Die lateinischen Bußriten in ihrer geschichtlichen Entwicklung* (Innsbruch: Rauch)

Kantorowicz, Ernst. 1957. *The King's Two Bodies: A Study in Mediaeval Political Theology* (Princeton: Princeton University Press)

Kéry, Lotte. 2006. *Gottesfurcht und irdische Strafe: Der Beitrag des mittelalterliche Kirchenrechts zur Entstehung des öffentlichen Strafrechts*, Symposien und Synthesen, 10 (Cologne: Bohlau)

Kramer, Susan R. and Caroline Walker Bynum. 2002. 'Revisting the Twelfth-Century Individual: The Inner Self and the Christian Community', in *Das Eigene und das Ganze: Zum Individuellen im mittelalterlichen Religiosentum*, ed. Gert Melville and Markus Schürer, Vita regularis, 16 (Münster: LIT), pp. 57-85

Kuttner, Stephan. 1982. 'The Revival of Jurisprudence', in *Renaissance and Renewal in the Twelfth Century*, ed. Robert L. Benson and Giles Constable (Oxford: Clarendon), pp. 299-323

Langbein, John H. 1974. *Prosecuting Crime in the Renaissance: England, Germany, France*, Studies in Legal History (Cambridge, MA: Harvard University Press)

Mansfield, Mary C. 1995. *The Humiliation of Sinners: Public Penance in Thirteenth-Century France*. (Ithaca: Cornell University Press)

Meens, Rob. 1998. 'The Frequency and Nature of Early Medieval Penance', in *Handling Sin: Confession in the Middle Ages*, York Studies in Medieval Theology, 2, ed. Peter Biller and A. J. Minnis (Woodbridge: York Medieval Press), pp. 35-61

Merback, Mitchell. 1998. *The Thief, the Cross and the Wheel: Pain and the Spectacle of Punishment in Medieval and Renaissance Europe* (London: Reaktion)

Merquior, José Guilherme. 1991. *Foucault*, 2nd ed., Fontana Modern Masters (London: Fontana)

Mills, Robert. 2005. *Suspended Animation: Pain, Pleasure and Punishment in Medieval Culture* (London: Reaktion)

Morris, Colin. 1972. *The Discovery of the Individual, 1050-1200*, Church History Outlines, 5 (London: SPCK)

Murray, Alexander. 1993. 'Confession before 1215', *Transactions of the Royal Historical Society*, 6th ser. 3: 51-81

Peters, Edward M. 1995. 'Prison Before the Prison: The Ancient and Medieval Worlds', in *The Oxford History of the Prison. The Practice of Punishment in Western*

Society, ed. Norval Morris and David J. Rothman (Oxford: Oxford University Press), pp. 3-47

Poschmann, Bernhard. 1951. *Busse und letzte Ölung* (Freiburg: Herder)

Schild, W. 1997. 'Strafe, Strafrecht C.I.', in *Lexikon des Mittelalters*, VIII (Munich: Lexma), cols 198-201

Spierenburg, Pieter. 1984. *The Spectacle of Suffering: Executions and the Evolution of Repression. From a Preindustrial Metropolis to the European Experience* (Cambridge: Cambridge University Press)

Tracy, Larissa. 2012. *Torture and Brutality in Medieval Literature: Negotiations of National Identity* (Cambridge: Brewer)

Wadle, Elmar. 1999. 'Zur Delegitimierung der Fehde durch die mittelalterliche Friedensbewegung', in *Der Krieg im Mittelalters und in der Frühen Neuzeit: Gründe, Begründungen, Bilder, Bräuche, Recht*, ed. Horst Brunner, Imagines Medii Aevi, 3 (Wiesbaden: Reichert), pp. 73-91

2

râche zwischen ‚Vergeltung eines Unrechts durch den Geschädigten' und ‚Strafe': Semantische Spielräume im *Alexander* Rudolfs von Ems

Henrike Manuwald
Georg-August-Universität Göttingen

Die Art, wie auf Gewalttaten reagiert wird, ist prägend für die Organisation einer Gesellschaft: Werden sie von den Betroffenen – also den Opfern oder deren Sozialverband – mit Gegengewalt beantwortet, oder wird ihre Ahndung an eine dafür zuständige Instanz übertragen? Bei Beschreibungen der verschiedenen Umgangsformen mit Gewalttaten wird nicht selten ein Fortschrittsmodell entworfen, indem die von Parteien ausgeübte Blutrache, die eine Kettenreaktion auslöst, primitiven Gesellschaften zugewiesen und von der späteren Übertragung der Gerichtsgewalt an Institutionen abgesetzt wird. Dieses zweipolige Fortschrittskonzept, das prominent von René Girard (1972) in seinen kulturtheoretischen Überlegungen formuliert wurde, ist unter anderem aus der Perspektive der Ethnologie und der Rechtsanthropologie kritisiert worden.[1] So bezweifeln Bertram Turner und Günther Schlee (2008) nicht nur die Linearität einer solchen Entwicklung, sondern heben weiterhin hervor, dass auch in Gesellschaften ohne politische Zentralinstanz meist nicht ein entfesselter Blutrachevollzug vorherrsche, vielmehr seien vergeltungsbasierte Konfliktregulierungsverfahren oft stark reglementiert.

Richtet man den Blick auf das deutsche Mittelalter, dann findet man dort im Fehdewesen als Interaktionsmodell zwischen Geschädigtem und Schädiger solche – jedenfalls in Grundzügen – geregelten Verfahren.[2] Insbesondere die ältere rechtshistorische Forschung hat aber das Fehdewesen seinerseits wieder in ein lineares Entwicklungskonzept eingeordnet: Die Landfriedensbewegung (ab dem elften Jahrhundert) zeige, dass sich nach und nach ein staatliches Gewaltmonopol herausgebildet habe, mit dem die Etablierung eines öffentlichen Strafrechts

---
[1] Vgl. dazu auch Nowakowski (2014: 77-78), die ebenfalls den Einfluss Girards hervorhebt. Zur Einordnung Girards vgl. Thomas (2011).
[2] Zum Verhältnis von Fehde und Recht vgl. Hyams (2010a); Renz (2012: 181-95); Reinle (2013); Isenmann (2013: 347-400).

einhergegangen sei. Parallel dazu sei im Rechtswesen der Gedanke eines Täter-Opfer-Ausgleichs zugunsten einer täterorientierten Bestrafung zurückgetreten. Rechtshistorische Arbeiten aus den vergangenen Jahren haben dagegen ein differenzierteres Bild entworfen. Danach lässt sich weder die Chronologie aufrechterhalten noch die Vorstellung, dass ein Modell das andere abgelöst habe. Vielmehr sei bis zum Spätmittelalter mit dem Nebeneinander verschiedener Konfliktlösungsmodelle und damit auch mit der Konkurrenz von Täter-Opfer-Ausgleich und Strafe zu rechnen.[3]

Wenn ein lineares Entwicklungskonzept nicht ohne Weiteres vorausgesetzt werden kann, ist anzunehmen, dass der Weg der Konfliktlösung in hochmittelalterlichen Gesellschaften immer wieder neu bestimmt werden musste. Im Folgenden soll die Frage erörtert werden, ob sich solche Prozesse auch in mittelhochdeutschen Erzähltexten beobachten lassen. Dabei dienen nicht *Motive* wie Rache oder Fehde, die aus heutiger Perspektive als solche erkannt worden sind, als Ausgangspunkt, sondern die Bezeichnungspraktiken in den Texten, weil sie für die Diskursivierung des Problemfeldes besonders aufschlussreich sind.

Zunächst einmal fällt auf, dass das Mittelhochdeutsche keine direkte Entsprechung für neuhochdeutsch ‚Strafe' im Sinne einer täterorientierten Sanktionierung kennt: Das Substantiv *strâfe* kommt erst im 13. Jahrhundert auf, und zwar in der Bedeutung ‚Tadel mit Worten' (Weitzel 2007: 23-25).[4] Bei mittelhochdeutsch *zuht*, das mit ‚Strafe' übersetzt werden kann, liegt der Akzent auf der Bildung und Besserung (Buck 1968), bei *pîn* (im Sinne von ‚Leibesstrafe') auf dem zugefügten Schmerz, bei *buoze* auf dem Ausgleich für Unrecht durch eine Kompensationsleistung (Schumann 2003).[5] Das Wort *râche* – die Nominalbildung zu *rechen*, wofür ein germanischer Verbalstamm mit der Bedeutung ‚verfolgen' zu rekonstruieren ist – lässt sich weder der Konfliktregelung zwischen Parteien noch der Bestrafung durch eine übergeordnete Instanz klar zuordnen:[6] Das *Deutsche Rechtswörterbuch* umschreibt ‚Rache' mit ‚gewaltsame Rechtsverfolgung als Form der Selbsthilfe einer Person, der vermeintliches oder wirkliches Unrecht angetan wurde [...]; eine Bedeutungsverschiebung zu Strafe ergibt sich aus der Ausübung der Rechtsverfolgung durch eine andere Instanz als den Geschädigten (Obrigkeit,

---

[3] Vgl. den Forschungsüberblick von Kéry (2006: 1-8); vgl. außerdem Weitzel (2007) (zum Strafgedanken im frühen Mittelalter) und Willoweit (2007) (zu den verschiedenen Formen des Ausgleichs von Unrecht im Spätmittelalter).
[4] Das Verb *strâfen*, von dem die Nominalbildung abgeleitet ist, trat leicht früher auf (vgl. Kluge (2011), s.v. ‚Strafe').
[5] Vgl. jeweils BMZ, Lexer, für *pîn* und *buoze* auch DRW, für *buoze* außerdem MWB.
[6] Zur Etymologie vgl. Möbius (1993: 13–15); Holzhauer (1997: 12-15); Kluge (2011), s.v. ‚Rache' und ‚rächen'; Beck (2003: 45).

Gott); die rechtliche Bewertung der Rache wandelt sich mit der Inanspruchnahme des Monopols legitimer Gewaltausübung durch den werdenden Staat' (DRW s.v. ‚Rache').

In diesem Eintrag wird also die Reaktion des Geschädigten selbst von der einer übergeordneten Instanz unterschieden. Die Ausführungen sind offenkundig von dem oben skizzierten Modell geprägt, dass das Konzept von ‚Strafe' mit der Herausbildung staatlicher Strukturen verknüpft sei. Wie sich die Verfolgung von Unrecht durch Gott in den zeitlichen Prozess einordnet, der mit dem Terminus ‚Bedeutungsverschiebung' aufgerufen ist, bleibt in dem Eintrag des *Deutschen Rechtswörterbuches* unklar. Eindeutig ist, dass Gottes Aktivitäten dort dem ‚Strafen' zugerechnet werden, da es als maßgeblich dafür angesehen wird, ‚Rache' von ‚Strafe' zu differenzieren, dass nicht der Geschädigte selbst das Unrecht ahndet. Vor dem Hintergrund der neueren rechtshistorischen Erkenntnisse würde ich für das Wort *râche* eher von einem *Nebeneinander* der Bedeutungen ‚Vergeltung eines Unrechts durch den Geschädigten' und ‚Strafe' ausgehen, was auch durch den in den mittelhochdeutschen Wörterbüchern dokumentierten Befund gestützt wird.[7]

Wegen des breiten Bedeutungsspektrums von *râche*, das sich entsprechend für das Verb *rechen* nachweisen lässt, ist die Wortfamilie besonders geeignet dafür zu beobachten, wie Bedeutungen kontextuell festgelegt werden bzw. werden mussten.[8] Wenn im Folgenden Bedeutungsnuancen der Wörter *râche* und *rechen* in Verwendungszusammenhängen nachgespürt wird, so soll der seinerseits aus Texten gewonnene Befund in den Wörterbüchern nicht einfach zurückprojiziert, sondern der Prozess der jeweiligen Bedeutungsaushandlung nachvollzogen werden. Der hier verfolgte Ansatz ist der semasiologischen historischen Pragmatik zuzuordnen (Weidenbusch 2005: 102-03), wobei sowohl die (konstruierten) sprachlichen Interaktionen zwischen Figuren im Text als auch die kontextuellen Bedeutungseingrenzungen in den Blick genommen werden, die in der direkt an die impliziten Rezipienten adressierten Erzählerrede zu beobachten sind.[9] Als

---

[7] Vgl. BMZ, Lexer, WMU. Vgl. auch den Abschnitt ‚Rache in der Bedeutung 'Strafe'' bei Holzhauer 1997: 160-62, deren Beispiele allerdings nicht primär ‚obrigkeitliches' Strafen betreffen.

[8] Vgl. die im BMZ angegebenen Grundbedeutungen ‚verfolgen, strafen, genugthuung verschaffen, rächen'. Schwächer ausgeprägt als im Althochdeutschen, wo auch die Bedeutungen ‚heilen, erretten, befreien' nachzuweisen sind (Schützeichel, s.v. *rehhan*), ist der Bedeutungsaspekt der Wiedergutmachung, der aber vor allem dann spürbar ist, wenn *rechen* mit dem Akkusativ der Sache konstruiert wird. Zum Bedeutungsspektrum von *rechen* vgl. auch die Wortfelduntersuchungen, die Möbius (1993) für einzelne Texte durchgeführt hat. Danach begegnet neben *rechen* zum Ausdruck der Wiedergutmachung entstandenen Schadens im *Nibelungenlied* büezen und *vergelten* (Möbius 1993: 46), zum Ausdruck der ‚Zurückzahlung einer Verletzung oder eines Totschlags im *Eneasroman* auch *geanden* (Möbius 1993: 152), das den Aspekt der Rüge mit umfasst.

[9] Zu Fragen der Bedeutungskonstitution (im Gespräch) vgl. den Überlick bei Deppermann (2007:

Beispieltext dient der im zweiten Viertel des 13. Jahrhunderts (in zwei Phasen) entstandene *Alexander* Rudolfs von Ems:[10] Der Text weist eine hohe Zahl von *râche*-Belegstellen auf; außerdem sind gute Herrschaft und die Übertragung göttlicher Gewalt auf Menschen darin thematisch wichtig, so dass Problemkomplexe wie der Charakter göttlicher *râche* oder das Verhältnis obrigkeitlicher *râche* zum Täter-Opfer-Ausgleich verhandelt werden. Obwohl der Alexanderroman Rudolfs von Ems mit dem Leben Alexanders des Großen einen antiken Stoff behandelt, kann er Aufschluss über die Einschätzung bestimmter Konfliktregelungsmechanismen zu seiner Entstehungszeit geben, denn der Stoff wurde gerade in Bezug auf die gesellschaftliche Ordnung mediävalisiert.[11]

Legitime und illegitime *râche*

Der Alexanderroman Rudolfs von Ems beginnt gattungstypisch mit der Kindheit und Jugend Alexanders (der Text folgt hier der *Alexandreis* Walters von Châtillon). In einer umfangreichen Rede, die Aristoteles als Erzieher an den jungen Alexander richtet (vv. 1401-830), formuliert Aristoteles Grundprinzipien für ein auf das Richtige ausgerichtetes Leben, zu dem die Achtung vor den Vorfahren, dem Recht und Gott gehört (vv. 1789-806), und äußert sich in diesem Rahmen auch grundlegend zur *râche*:[12]

rich der schuldigen getât	Ahnde die Taten der Schuldigen
als altez reht geboten hât!	gemäß dem alten Recht!
dû solt mit schœnen listen	Du sollst mit geziemender Klugheit
dîn **leitrechen** vristen,	die Rache für dir zugefügtes Leid aufschieben,

---

211-22). Anders gelagert ist die Arbeit von Möbius (1993: 41), der analysieren will, ‚[i]nwieweit [...] der Gedanke der Vergeltung eines Totschlags, einer Verletzung oder einer Beleidigung in Selbsthilfe Einzug in die zu untersuchende Dichtung gehalten' hat. Holzhauer (1997: 9) hat das Ziel ‚anhand der Begriffe "Rache" und "Fehde" Gemeinsamkeiten und Unterschiede ihrer Verwendung in der höfischen Literatur des 12./13. Jahrhunderts festzustellen und ihren Gebrauch mit der historischen Wirklichkeit zu vergleichen'; sie beschäftigt sich also ebenfalls nicht primär mit der Bedeutungsaushandlung. Auch Renz (2012: 176-339) ist bei seiner Untersuchung von Kriemhilds Rache im *Nibelungenlied* am inhaltlichen Verhältnis von Rache und Recht interessiert. Für die Rekonstruktion von Wertekonzepten in Rudolfs von Ems *Alexander* verfolgt Cölln (2002) bezogen auf das Wort *werdekeit* einen wort- und begriffsgeschichtlichen Ansatz.

[10] Zu den Entstehungsphasen des Texts vgl. Walliczek (1992: 323; 332-33); Lienert (2001: 49-58).

[11] Vgl. Lienert (2001: 56-57); Cölln (2002). Ob der Text sogar als Fürstenspiegel für staufische Adressaten (Konrad IV.) anzusehen ist, was in der Forschung kontrovers diskutiert wird (Schmitt 2002: 316-22; Weber 2012: 188-92), kann hier nicht erörtert werden.

[12] Vorher war vom *rechen* bereits im Abschnitt zur Trunkenheit (vv. 1765-88) die Rede gewesen, in dem auch vor unrechtem Zorn (v. 1773) gewarnt wird. Trunkenheit könne dazu führen, dass Leid in einer Weise ‚gerächt' werde, die das Ansehen nicht steigere: ‚urliugen, übersprechen, / leit ân êre **rechen**, / lêret allez trunkenheit' (vv. 1777-79). Die Hervorhebungen in Fettdruck in den mittelhochdeutschen Zitate stammen alle von H. M.

biz daz dîn zorn verende sich.	bis dein Zorn ein Ende hat.
ræchestû in zorne dich,	Wenn du dich im Zorn rächtest,
sô müeste der und dirre jehn,	dann könnte dieser und jener sagen,
ez wære in zorne geschehn.	es sei im Zorn passiert.
zorn ist ein hagel rehter zuht	Zorn verdirbt die angemessene Beherrschung
und von bescheidenheit ein vluht,	und führt von der Verständigkeit weg.
durch daz soltû dîu **rechen** sparn	Deshalb sollst du die Rache unterlassen,
biz daz der zorn sî vervarn.	bis der Zorn verraucht ist.
dû solt ouch dar nâch niemer mêr	Du sollst auch danach niemals mehr
gerechen dînes leides sêr,	den durch das Leid verursachten Schmerz rächen,
sô dir dîn leit benomen sî.	wenn du vom Leid befreit bist.[13]

(vv. 1807-21)

Die (einem zukünftigen Herrscher angemessene) rechtskonforme Vergeltung eines Normverstoßes wird hier abgesetzt vom vorschnellen Rächen selbst empfundenen Leides, das nicht in einer Situation emotionaler Aufgeladenheit erfolgen soll, zumal das Leid unter Umständen – mit Abstand betrachtet – gar nicht mehr einer Vergeltung bedarf. Dass auch eigenes Leid durch eine schuldhafte Tat ausgelöst werden kann, wird an dieser Stelle nicht thematisiert, so dass ein Gegensatz zwischen *râche* für ein objektiv bestehendes Unrecht und subjektiv empfundenem Leid suggeriert wird.[14]

Die Bewertung verschiedener *râche*-Motivationen ist für Rudolfs gesamten Alexanderroman relevant, wie exemplarisch an der Erzählung von einer geplanten Verschwörung gegen Alexander und deren Aufdeckung gezeigt sei. Die Handlungsführung in dieser knapp 1800 Verse umfassenden Episode (vv. 18765-20544) ist – wie bereits in der verwendeten Quelle, den *Historiae Alexandri Magni* des Quintus Curtius Rufus (IV,VII[25]-VII,II[10]) – äußerst komplex und kann hier nur in groben Zügen nachvollzogen werden. Anders als bei Curtius Rufus ist bei Rudolf von Ems *râche* der Auslöser für die Verschwörung: Wie er einem Vertrauten erklärt, fühlt sich Dimnus, ein Gefolgsmann Alexanders, von Alexander

---

[13] Junk (1928) hat nach *sêr* in v. 1820 einen Punkt gesetzt und ordnet den Nebensatz in v. 1821 den folgenden Versen zu: ‚sô dir dîn leit benomen sî, / wont dir solhiu vuore bî / sô wirt an lobe ein iemerleben / dînem namen und dir gegeben'. (vv. 1821–24). Die Bedingung für das hohe Ansehen wird aber in v. 1822 formuliert, während sich v. 1821 meines Erachtens nicht sinnvoll in die in die Wenn-dann-Aussage integrieren lässt.

[14] In der *Alexandreis* (vv. 180-84) wird – ebenfalls im Kontext des Dienstes am Recht (zu dessen religiösem Aspekt vgl. Schnell 1969: 156) – dagegen nur gesagt, dass die Ahndung von Unrecht aufgeschoben werden soll, bis der Zorn vorbei ist (‚Vindictam differ donec pertranseat ira', v. 181), und dass nach der Bestrafung (‚post ueberam', v. 182) der Hass vergessen sein soll. Für eine systematische Gegenüberstellung der Aristotelesreden bei Walter von Châtillon und Rudolf von Ems vgl. Wisbey (1969: 102-03).

nicht ehrenvoll genug behandelt. Dieser habe kein Zutrauen zu ihm (vv. 18859-64). Daraus sei ihm Leid erwachsen, das er ohne Beschädigung seiner *triuwe* an Alexander rächen könne. Er habe Mitstreiter gewonnen, die ebenfalls einen Ausgleich für Leid anstrebten, das sie von Alexander erlitten hätten:

‚[...]	‚[...]
swaz ich im leides tæte,	Was auch immer ich ihm an Leid zufügte,
mîn triuwe belibe stæte,	meine Loyalität bliebe bestehen,
diu wær ungebrochen	die wäre ungebrochen,
würd ez von mir **gerochen**.	wenn das [sc. die erlittene Missachtung] von mir geahndet würde.
des hân ich guote helfe erkorn,	Dafür habe ich mir gute Unterstützung gewählt:
mir hânt ze helfenne gesworn	Mir gegen ihn zu helfen
aht edele herren über in,	haben acht vornehme Herren geschworen
daz ich selpniunde bin,	(so dass wir insgesamt zu neunt sind),
den er ouch leide hât getân.	denen er [Alexander] ebenfalls Schmerz zugefügt hat.
die weln alle mir gestân	Die wollen mir alle darin beistehen,
daz wir über drîe tage	dass wir in drei Tagen
an im **rechen** unser klage.‘	an ihm Vergeltung für unser Leid üben.‘

(vv. 18865-76)

Die von Dimnus postulierte Legitimität dieser *râche* für eine subjektiv empfundene Ehrverletzung erscheint allerdings von vornherein als problematisch, weil der Erzähler das Verhalten Alexanders damit rechtfertigt, dass dieser vom schlechten Charakter des Dimnus überzeugt gewesen sei (vv. 18820-27).

Nach der Aufdeckung der Verschwörung wird sie in Verhandlungen vor Alexander aufgearbeitet, bei dem die Rollen des Gerichtsherren und des Geschädigten (als Objekt der Verschwörung) zusammenfallen. Alexander lässt Dimnus (der schon Selbstmord begehen wollte) vorführen; als der bei der Befragung nichts zu sagen weiß, kommentiert der Erzähler, dass es Schuldigen immer so ergehe. Auch handlungsimmanent wird das Schweigen als Schuldeingeständnis gewertet: Alexander lässt Dimnus das Haupt abschlagen (vv. 19085-89). Die Todesstrafe wird vom Erzähler als Vergeltung für die geplante Ermordung Alexanders bezeichnet: Alexander hieß ‚daz mort rechen über in‘ (v. 19086). Indem die Tat und nicht Alexanders persönliche Betroffenheit in den Mittelpunkt gerückt wird – er erscheint daher mehr als Gerichtsherr denn als Geschädigter –, gewinnt die Vergeltung hier den Charakter einer Strafe (für den begangenen Verrat).

Bei der weiteren juristischen Aufarbeitung der Verschwörung kommt Alexander aufgrund einer Aussage, die unter Folter von Philotas, einem Sohn des bewährten Feldherren Parmenion, erpresst wird (vv. 19947-20018), zu dem Schluss, dass

Parmenion des Hochverrats schuldig sei.[15] Die Aussage wird von Alexander nicht weiter geprüft, sondern er hält, wie er seinem Gefolgsmann Polîdâmant mitteilt, die Schuld Parmenions damit für erwiesen:[16]

‚[...]	‚[...]
mir ist an disen stunden	mir ist jetzt
des lîbes schuldec vunden	die todeswürdige Schuld Parmenions bekannt geworden,
Parmênîôn des valscher rât	dessen hinterlistiger Rat
mir den lîp verrâten hât.	mein Leben aufs Spiel gesetzt hat.
an dem wil ich **rechen** mich	An ihm will ich mich ‚rächen'
[...]'	[...]'

(vv. 20277-81)

Ob Parmenion tatsächlich Mordpläne gehegt hat, bleibt offen, doch schreibt ihm der Erzähler später in seinem sonst lobenden Nachruf (vv. 20459-523) zu, dass er Gegner Alexanders zu Gast gehabt habe und sich Alexander habe gleich machen wollen (vv. 20490-96).[17] Insofern erscheint die *râche* Alexanders nicht grundlos. Über Polîdâmant, dem er einen Brief mitgibt, erteilt Alexander seinen Leuten in Medien den Auftrag, den ebenfalls dort weilenden Parmenion zu töten (vv. 20282-318).[18] Die Tatsache, dass Alexander (anders als in der vorangegangenen Verhandlung) den Beschuldigten gar nicht erst befragt, und die personale Formulierung der angestrebten Vergeltung (‚an dem wil ich **rechen** mich', v. 20281) könnten darauf hindeuten, dass er hier nicht primär als Gerichtsherr, sondern als Betroffener agiert. Jedoch verleihen die Akteure der Tötung Parmenions den Charakter einer kontrollierten Strafaktion.

Trotzdem ruft die Tötung Parmenions bei dessen Sozialverband den Wunsch nach Vergeltung hervor (‚und wolden dô **gerochen** hân | swaz im ze leide was getân'; vv. 20403-04). Das ist kein Wunder, hatte doch Cleander, einer der Empfänger von Alexanders Brief, Parmenion erschlagen, als dieser unbewaffnet und wehrlos durch den Wald ritt (vv. 20343-95). Für das ihm zugefügte Leid wollen die Leute aus Parmenions Heer in Selbsthilfe mit Waffengewalt Vergeltung erwirken und reiten zum Ort der Tat, wohin sich auch Cleander begibt (vv. 20396-410). Cleander

---

[15] Zum zweifelhaften Verhalten Alexanders im Prozess gegen Philotas vgl. Wisbey (1969: 71-73). Zur Gestaltung der Alexanderfigur in der Philotas und der Parmenion-Episode vgl. demnächst auch Lienert (2018). Ich danke Elisabeth Lienert dafür, dass sie mir Einblick in ihr Manuskript gewährt hat.

[16] Zur Gestaltung der Rolle Parmenions bei Rudolf von Ems im Vergleich mit den Alexanderdichtungen des Pfaffen Lambrecht und Ulrichs von Etzenbach vgl. Krämer-Seifert / Kern (2003).

[17] Zur *unmâze* Parmenions als Grund für seinen Sturz vgl. Weber (2012: 171-72).

[18] Alexander sichert die Ausführung seines Auftrags dadurch ab, dass er Polîdâmant seine Brüder und dessen zwei Begleiter ihre Familien als Geiseln stellen lässt (vv. 20286-90; 20295-301; 20308-10; 20317-18).

führt dort mithilfe von Alexanders Brief den Beweis, dass er im Auftrag Alexanders gehandelt habe (vv. 20411-17):

den brief er sie dô schouwen liez,	Den Brief ließ er sie da anschauen,
dâ was vil gar geschriben an	da stand in allen Einzelheiten,
wie der künec sîne man	wie der König seine Leute [zum Vorgehen]
hæt ûf den vürsten gemant	gegen den Fürsten [sc. Parmenion] aufgefordert hatte
und wie gewærlîch er bevant	und wie er sicher herausgefunden hatte,
daz er hæt im sîn lebn	dass dieser sein Leben
verrâtèn und hin gegbn	verraten und preisgegeben hatte,
und wie er sie daz **rechen** bat.	und wie er sie [sc. seine Leute] um Vergeltung dafür bat.
der vürste sprach ‚an der stat	Der Fürst [sc. Cleander] sagte: ‚Auf der Stelle
hân ich den mein **errochen**,	habe ich den Verrat geahndet,
daz grôze mort zerbrochen.	den ungeheuerlichen Mordplan zunichte gemacht.
swer sich des wil nemen an	Wer sich dieser Sache annehmen will,
der muoz mit dem selben man	der macht sich zwangsläufig mit demselben Mann [sc. Parmenion]
des grôzen mordes schuldec wesn	schuldig an dem ungeheuerlichen Mordplan,
und mac ich doch vil wol genesn.'	während ich doch sehr gut ungestraft bleiben kann.'
	(vv. 20418-32)

Cleander deutet also die von den Leuten Parmenions beabsichtige Vergeltung, die aus ihrer Sicht legitim ist, zu einem justiziablen Verbrechen um.[19] Den Ausgleich, den er für den nach seiner Auffassung nachweislich begangenen Verrat des Parmenion geschaffen hat, klassifiziert er als *rechen*. Die Leute Parmenions akzeptieren daraufhin Parmenions Schuld und stellen die Legitimität seiner Bestrafung über ihr eigenes Ansinnen, Vergeltung für das ihnen dadurch zugefügte Leid zu üben:

Dô dise rede vernâmen	Als sie diese Worte hörten,
die dar ûf dar kâmen	die dort hinauf gekommen waren,
daz sie den vürsten **ræchen** dô,	um da den Fürsten zu rächen,
die sprâchen al gelîche alsô	sagten sie übereinstimmend Folgendes:
‚swie leid uns nû sî geschehn,	‚Auch wenn uns jetzt Schmerz zugefügt wurde,
sît wir rehte hân gesehn	da wir wahrheitsgemäß erkannt haben,

---

[19] Vgl. Jendorff (2013) mit einer Parallele für die Ausdeutungsmöglichkeiten von Fehdehandlungen als Verbrechen und umgekehrt. Auch in der Genelun-Handlung des *Rolandsliedes* sind entsprechende Verfahren der Uminterpretation zu beobachten (s. dazu u. Anm. 34).

daz er dem künge hât getân,	was er [sc. Parmenion] dem König getan hat,
sô müezen wir ez scheiden lân.	müssen wir es auf sich beruhen lassen.
swie ez anders wære,	Wenn es anders wäre,
daz wære uns iemer swære.'	würde es uns für immer belasten.'
	(vv. 20433-42)[20]

Zwar wird bereits bei Curtius Rufus (VII,II[9]) das Recht Alexanders auf Vergeltung gegen das der Leute Parmenions ausgespielt, jedoch ist bei Rudolf von Ems der Strafcharakter der Tötung Parmenions deutlicher herausgearbeitet, indem seine Tat immer wieder benannt wird. Obwohl die Leute des Parmenion diesen Strafcharakter eindeutig anerkennen, scheint die dem *râche*-Mechanismus innewohnende Gefahr einer Kette von Gewalthandlungen noch nicht gebannt. Wie bei Curtius Rufus (VII,II[10]) verlässt sich Alexander nicht auf den Gewaltverzicht, sondern trennt die Leute Parmenions von ihrem bisherigen Heer (vv. 20524-33). Zusätzlich wird gesagt, dass Alexander auch Cleander und seinen Leuten anordnet, sich zu entfernen:

ouch hiez er Clêandern	Auch befahl er [sc. Alexander] Cleander,
daz er und alle sîne man	dass er und alle seine Leute
sich von jenen schieden dan,	sich von jenen [sc. den Leuten Parmenions] entfernten,
daz dehein unminne	damit dann kein Hass
mit vîentlîchem sinne	mit feindlicher Gesinnung
sich durch den zorn hüebe dâ.	aus der Empörung entstünde.
	(vv. 20534-39)

Ausgeschlossen werden soll die mögliche Entstehung einer latenten Feindschaft, wie sie sich typischerweise nach einer nicht vollzogenen Rachehandlung entwickelt (Smail 2001: 90-92). Ganz hat die Straflogik hier also nicht Oberhand gewonnen.

Von der Absicht des Dimnus, Alexander zu töten, über die von Alexander angeordneten Tötungen des Dimnus und des Parmenion bis hin zu der von den Leuten des Parmenion gewünschten Vergeltung benennen die Urheber als Handlungsziel jeweils das *rechen*, das meist situativ näher bestimmt wird. Während bei Dimnus eine große Diskrepanz zwischen der subjektiven und der objektiven Einschätzung der Legitimität seiner *râche* besteht, wird die Legitimität der *râche* Alexanders an Parmenion vom Erzähler nicht ausdrücklich in Frage gestellt und auf der Handlungsebene sogar von Parmenions Leuten anerkannt. Dabei scheint

---

[20] Der Bezug von *ez* in v. 20441 ist nicht ganz eindeutig: Werden hypothetisch die Konsequenzen bei einer zu Unrecht ausgeführten Vergeltung thematisiert („wenn wir uns anders verhielten') oder der Fall, dass Parmenion unschuldig wäre („wenn die Sachlage anders wäre')? Auf jeden Fall wird aber bekräftigt, dass angesichts der als erwiesen geltenden Schuld Parmenions ein Verzicht auf *râche* geboten ist.

für sie ausschlaggebend zu sein, dass die Schuld Parmenions für sie unzweifelhaft ist, während die königliche Gerichtsgewalt nicht explizit erwähnt ist.[21] Das Beispiel der von Alexander nach dessen Befragung angeordneten Tötung des Dimnus zeigt aber, dass auch eine quasi-gerichtliche Verurteilung als *rechen* bezeichnet werden kann. Auffällig an den Befunden im Alexanderroman Rudolfs von Ems ist es, dass die im *Deutschen Rechtswörterbuch* formulierte Bedingung, dass eine Bestrafung von einer anderen Instanz als dem Geschädigten angeordnet werden müsse, nicht erfüllt ist. Gewiss ist Hochverrat ein Sonderfall, da der Herrscher als Gerichtsherr selbst betroffen ist, aber das Beispiel erweist, dass *râche* und Recht unter bestimmten Bedingungen ineinander fallen können.

râche Gottes

Anders als es die kategorischen Aussagen zur göttlichen Strafgewalt im *Deutschen Rechtswörterbuch* vermuten lassen, verschmelzen im Alexanderroman Rudolfs von Ems die Rollen des Geschädigten und Rechtsverfolgers auch dann, wenn es um göttliche *râche* geht, die insbesondere im Hinblick auf den christlichen Gott thematisiert wird. Das Geschehen im *Alexander* Rudolfs von Ems wird vom Erzähler zu Beginn explizit in einer vorchristlichen Zeit angesiedelt, in der die meisten Menschen Götzen angebetet hätten; nur die Juden seien der Lehre Gottes gefolgt (vv. 279-98). Trotzdem ist das Wirken des christlichen Gottes im Text sehr präsent, da die Herrschaft Alexanders heilsgeschichtlich eingeordnet wird (Schmitt 2003), ja er sogar als Werkzeug Gottes agiert (Schnell 1969: 126-28). Das geschieht nicht unbedingt mit Alexanders Wissen, jedoch zeichnet er sich durch eine vom Erzähler positiv hervorgehobene Ehrerbietung gegenüber seinen Göttern (‚sîne gote'; v. 4788) aus, denen er zum Dank für sein weltliches Glück Opfer darbringt (vv. 4787-810).[22]

Den Perserfeldzug Alexanders charakterisiert der Erzähler ausdrücklich als *râche*-Handeln des (christlichen) Gottes:

---

[21] Vgl. dagegen ein von Möbius (1993: 93-101) erörtertes Beispiel aus der *Kaiserchronik* (vv. 5889-996) dafür, dass schon im 12. Jahrhundert ein Plädoyer für die Gerichtsgewalt erfolgen konnte: Eine Witwe verlangt von Kaiser Trajan, den Mörder ihres Sohnes ausfindig zu machen und vor Gericht zu stellen. Der Angeklagte rechtfertigt sich damit, dass der Sohn der Witwe seinen Bruder erschlagen habe und ihm deshalb Genugtuung schuldig gewesen sei. Der Kaiser erkennt jedoch die Begründung nicht an, sondern entgegnet, der jetzt Angeklagte habe zu ihm kommen sollen, als sein Bruder erschlagen worden sei, denn die Römer hätten ihn, den Kaiser, zum Richter ernannt. Das Gericht verhängt ein Todesurteil gegen den Angeklagten.

[22] In seinen Gebeten werden – gerade an heilsgeschichtlich bedeutsamen Stellen – auch monotheistische Formeln verwendet. Vgl. dazu Schnell (1969: 156-67); Seidl / Zimmermann (2011: 349-59) (mit weiterer Literatur).

Got selbe wolde **rechen**	Gott selbst wollte
an der vorworhten heidenschaft	an den verfluchten Heiden
sînen zorn mit der kraft	seinen Groll ‚rächen' mithilfe der Stärke,
diu mit hôher wîsheit	die zusammen mit großer Klugheit
an Alexandern was geleit	Alexander verliehen war
und die er im gap durch daz	und die er [sc. Gott] ihm gegeben hatte,
er im **ræche** sînen haz.	damit er [sc. Alexander] ihm für seinen Zorn Genugtuung verschaffe.
	(vv. 12894–900)

zorn und *haz* sind hier offenbar als gerechtfertigte Gesinnungen des anthropomorph gedachten Gottes zu verstehen, nicht als negativ besetzte Emotionen (wie in der Lehrrede des Aristoteles).[23] Das legt jedenfalls die allgemeine Erklärung des *râche*-Mechanismus in den folgenden Versen nahe. Danach resultiert die *râche* Gottes nicht aus einer ‚persönlichen Befindlichkeit', sondern ist die Konsequenz eines Normverstoßes: der Nichtbeachtung von Gottes Geboten:

Swer wider Gotes gebote lebt	Wer das Gebot Gottes nicht beachtet
und wider sîne hulde strebt	und sich nicht um seine Gunst bemüht
und im des niht ze **buoze** stât	und ihm dafür keine Wiedergutmachung leistet
durch sînen süntlîchen rât,	wegen des eigenen sündhaften Entschlusses,
dem tuot er ie etewaz	dem wird er [sc. Gott] immer irgendetwas zufügen,
dâ mit er an im **richet** daz.	womit er das an ihm ahndet.
sus rach Alexanders kraft	So verschaffte Alexanders Stärke
Got an der grôzen heidenschaft	Gott Genugtuung gegenüber den Heiden
und sînen wol verdienten vluoch.	und [erfüllte] dessen voll und ganz gerechtfertigten Fluch.
	(vv. 12901-09)[24]

Daneben wird auch auf eine alternative Form des Ausgleichs von Unrecht verwiesen, die den *râche*-Automatismus aufbrechen kann: die *buoze* als Wiedergutmachung,

---

[23] Zum gerechten *zorn* Gottes vgl. Grubmüller (2003), der auf der Grundlage der von ihm untersuchten Texte *haz* eine ausschließlich negative Bewertung zuschreibt. Wenn sich die ‚feindselige gesinnung' (BMZ; Lexer) jedoch gegen etwas Schlechtes richtet, kann sie sogar aus der Liebe zum Guten resultieren (zum Konzept des ‚gerechten Hasses' vgl. Throop 2010: 192).

[24] An dieser Stelle ist *heidenschaft*, das im *Alexander* auch politisch-territorial zur Bezeichnung von ‚Barbaren' verwendet wird, christlich-religiös aufgeladen (vgl. dazu Seidl / Zimmermann 2011: 337-42). Zu einer entsprechend grundsätzlichen Parallelstelle in *Barlaam und Josaphat* (vv. 15241-49) vgl. Wisbey (1969: 44-45). Für den Erzähler des Alexanderromans ist die Ahndung gegen Gott gerichteten Handelns eine solche Selbstverständlichkeit, dass er eigens erklärt, dass Gott den sündigen Salomon um Davids willen verschont, sich dann aber an dessen Geschlecht ‚gerächt' habe (vv. 16135-42).

die vom Schädiger ausgeht. In dieser Entgegensetzung wird das *rechen* auf die strafende Form des Ausgleichs eingeengt, die so vonstatten geht, dass dem Täter etwas angetan wird.

Trotzdem dürfte der Ausgleichscharakter der *râche*-Aktion im Vordergrund stehen, wie schon in der alttestamentarischen Tradition. Wenn Gott im Alten Testament als direkt in die Ahndung von Unrecht involviert gezeichnet ist, tauchen wiederholt Wörter mit der Wurzel *nqm* auf, die in der *Vulgata* mit *vindicta* oder *ultio* übersetzt sind und im Neuhochdeutschen – nicht zuletzt in der Nachfolge Luthers – häufig mit ‚Rache' wiedergegeben werden. Treffender wäre im Neuhochdeutschen wohl ‚Vergeltung' (Stolz 2003: 84-86), wobei der alttestamentarische Gott diese Vergeltung als königlicher Richter ausübt und sie insofern als gerechte Bestrafung interpretiert werden kann (Peels 1995: 266). Im Alten Testament ist der Gedanke der Wiederherstellung eines gestörten Gleichgewichts dominant, d.h., es steht weder die Befindlichkeit des Täters noch die des Geschädigten im Vordergrund (Keller / Reicke 1966: 1878). Dagegen wird im Alexanderroman Rudolfs von Ems immer wieder unterstrichen, dass durch die Ahndung von Unrechtshandlungen gegen Gott auch ein Ausgleich für dessen persönliche Betroffenheit geschaffen wird. So begegnet bei der Vorausschau auf die Zerstörung Jerusalems durch die Römer die Formel, dass eine *Kränkung* Gottes durch *râche* ausgeglichen werde:

[...]	[...]
ez stuont lange zît	Er [sc. der Tempel der Samariter] stand lange Zeit,
bis nâch der Gotes ûfvart	bis nach Christi Himmelfahrt
Jerusalêm zerbrochen wart,	Jerusalem zerstört wurde,
dô si Romære brâchen,	als die Römer sie [sc. die Stadt] vernichteten
und Gotes anden **râchen**.	und Gottes Kränkung rächten.

(vv. 10018-22)

In der Darstellung des Alexanderromans bleibt unklar, ob die Römer den Feldzug, der im Mittelalter unter dem Namen *vindicta salvatoris* (‚Rache des Heilands') bekannt war (Buc 2006: 459-67), bewusst zur Vergeltung des Todes Jesu führen, so wie es etwa im *Evangelium Nicodemi* Heinrichs von Hesler (vv. 4195-207) der Fall ist, oder ob sie aus anderen Motivationen heraus handeln. Dass es bei Umsetzung göttlicher *râche* durch Menschen zu Diskrepanzen zwischen subjektiver und objektiver Motivation kommen kann, wird im Alexanderroman an anderer Stelle ausdrücklich formuliert. Als Alexander den Samaritern Privilegien, die er den Juden gewährt hatte, verweigert, weil sie sich von den Juden distanziert hatten (vv. 10023-50), handelt er als Werkzeug Gottes, wie der Erzähler erklärt:

die hâten beidenthalp verlorn,	Die [sc. die Samariter] hatten überall verloren,
den künc, ir ê und Got verkorn.	den König, ihr Gesetz und Gott missachtet.
daz **rach** Alexander Gote,	Dafür verschaffte Alexander Gott Genugtuung,
er wart genant von Gotes gebote	er wurde nach Gottes Willen
Gotes geisel, wan er **rach**	Geißel Gottes genannt, denn er ahndete alles,
swaz Gote unrehte dô beschach.	was Gott da an Unrecht zugefügt wurde.
durch daz was er ûz gesant,	Dafür war er ausgesandt,
daz Gote **ræche sîne hant**	dass seine Hand für Gott das Unrecht ahndete
daz unreht an verworhter diet,	an dem verfluchten Volk,
diu sich von Gotes gelouben schiet.	das sich vom Glauben an Gott abgewandt hatte.
	(vv. 10051-60)[25]

Der Erzählerkommentar wird in der Forschung oft herangezogen, um das Ineinanderwirken von Gottes und Alexanders Handeln zu belegen, ist doch Alexander ausdrücklich als ‚Geißel Gottes' bezeichnet.[26] In den folgenden Versen wird jedoch das Verhältnis von Gott und demjenigen, der die *râche* unwissentlich ausführt, auch in Bezug auf Alexander problematisiert, indem auf die Eigenmotivation des Ausführenden verwiesen wird:

vil manger Got **richet**	So mancher verschafft Gott Vergeltung
an dem der Gote brichet	an dem, der Gott gegenüber
sîne lêre und sîn gebot,	dessen Regeln und Gebote bricht,
dem es doch wênec danket Got.	dem es jedoch Gott nicht dankt,
als Alexander geschach	wie es Alexander widerfuhr,
der gotes zorn und anden **rach**	der Gott für seine Empörung und Kränkung Genugtuung verschaffte
und ez doch nie getet durch in	und es doch keineswegs um seinetwillen tat,
wan durch sînes lobes gewin,	sondern um selbst Ruhm zu gewinnen

---

[25] In dem Vers 10053 (‚daz **rach** Alexander Gote') ist *rechen* mit Akkusativ der Sache konstruiert (Alexander übt in seinem Handeln Vergeltung dafür, dass die Samariter Gott verschmäht haben). Mit dem Dativ der Person (*Gote*) ist angegeben, dass er es für Gott tut, der hier als Geschädigter aufgefasst ist, wenn gesagt wird, dass Alexander einen Ausgleich dafür schafft, was Gott an Unrecht geschehen sei. Wie aus den folgenden Versen deutlich wird, bedient sich Gott Alexanders Hand, um seinen Unwillen (*zorn*) zu zeigen und gleichzeitig seine Gefolgsleute zu belohnen: ‚Got von dem ellenthaften man / sînen knehten vride gewan, / die im wâren undertân. / sînen zorn liez er gân / von sîner hant übr alle die / sich von im gebrâchen ie.' (vv. 10061-66).
[26] Vgl. z.B. Schnell (1969: 126-27); Wisbey (1969: 41-46); Weber (2012: 184-87). Dazu, dass auch andere Figuren im *Alexander* als Werkzeuge Gottes agieren, vgl. außerdem Seidl / Zimmermann (2011: 342-44).

und daz Got sîn wunder	und damit Gott seine Wunderkraft
zeicte an im besunder.	an ihm in besonderer Weise zeigte.
	(vv. 10067-76)[27]

Zwar heißt es in den folgenden Versen dann wieder, dass Alexander, für den Unwillen Gottes einen Ausgleich schaffend (,**Rechende** den Gotes zorn', v. 10077), von Land zu Land gezogen sei, so wie ihn Gott ausgesandt habe (vv. 10077-80), aber es wird doch eine Diskrepanz zwischen der Funktion und der Motivation seines Handelns markiert.[28] Für die Bedeutung des Verbs *rechen* in diesem Kontext hat die Konstellation die Konsequenz, dass es nur den *de facto* geschaffenen Ausgleich für Unrecht bezeichnet.

râche als Recht?
Die Analyse von *râche*-Belegstellen im Alexanderroman Rudolfs von Ems ließe sich fortsetzen, aber bereits jetzt sollte deutlich geworden sein, dass im Text Bemühungen vorhanden sind, über die Handlungsführung, Figurenreden oder explizite Erzählerkommentare verschiedene Arten von *râche* voneinander zu differenzieren und auf diese Weise Konfliktlösungsmodelle zu hierarchisieren. Eine Spezifizierung ist jeweils nötig, weil *râche* im Alexanderroman sowohl eine Reaktion auf persönlich erlittenes Leid bezeichnen kann (wie bei Dimnus) wie auch den Vorgang des Ausgleichs objektiv geschehenen Unrechts (wie bei der Bestrafung der Samariter durch Alexander). Für die positive oder negative Bewertung von *râche* scheint der Charakter der ursprünglichen Gewalttat wichtiger zu sein als die Frage, von wem *râche* ausgeübt werden darf. Die Legitimität von *râche* wird im Alexanderroman danach bestimmt, ob eine Vergeltung für ein tatsächlich bestehendes Unrecht erfolgt. Das kann auch der Fall sein, wenn derjenige, der Vergeltung übt, persönlich involviert ist, jedenfalls wenn er gleichzeitig für die Rechtsordnung verantwortlich ist. Das heißt, dass die saubere Unterscheidung zwischen einer ,horizontalen' und einer ,vertikalen' Ahndung von Unrecht, wie sie das *Deutsche Rechtswörterbuch*

---

[27] Die Andeutung in v. 10071, dass Gott Alexander seinen Einsatz nicht gedankt habe (vgl. dazu Wisbey 1969: 97-98), ist angesichts der Tatsache, dass Alexander bei Rudolf von Ems als von der *sælde* begünstigt dargestellt wird (vgl. dazu zuletzt Kragl 2013: 17-25), überraschend. Jedoch ist für den (im unvollendeten Werk Rudolfs fehlenden) Schluss der Handlung ein Abstieg anzunehmen, sowohl wegen der Quellen als auch wegen der Einordnung in die *translatio imperii* (vgl. Kragl 2013: 31-37). Wisbey (1969: 64) hält es für möglich, dass für Alexanders Ende eine ähnliche Begründung gegeben worden wäre wie für den Tod Parmenions, dass er sich nämlich zu sehr erhoben habe. Tatsächlich könnte die in v. 10074 genannte Ruhmsucht in diese Richtung weisen.

[28] Auch im *Rolandslied*, wo explizit für den christlichen Gott gekämpft wird, handeln die Figuren oft aus einer irdischen Motivation heraus, der Verwandtenrache, allerdings wird sie dort auf christlicher Seite mit dem Kampf für die Sache Gottes verbunden (Möbius 1993: 119-42).

vornimmt, sich nicht mit den Textbefunden in Einklang bringen lässt. Umso schwieriger ist es, in Rudolfs Alexanderroman den Strafcharakter des Handelns zu sichern, weil oft nicht festzulegen ist, ob die primäre Motivation für das Handeln der Täter-Opfer-Ausgleich oder die Rechtsordnung ist.

Unmissverständlich führt der Text in der Parmenion-Episode vor, dass ein Rache-Mechanismus durch die Ausdeutung der Tötung Parmenions als Strafe zu einem Ende gebracht wird. Im Alexanderroman wird also demonstriert, wie Gewalt durch Straflogik einerseits domestiziert, andererseits aber entfesselt werden kann, da auch Strafaktionen jenseits formalrechtlicher Beschlüsse als legitim dargestellt werden.[29] Die Konsequenzen einer solchen Argumentation ließen sich auch außerhalb des Textes über die Zeiten hinweg verfolgen, insbesondere bei der Rechtfertigung von Gewaltakten als Strafe für die Beleidigung Gottes oder des Propheten.[30]

Wie an der Schilderung des Schicksals von Dimnus als Verräter abzulesen ist, kann auch eine Bestrafung, die auf eine Verurteilung zurückgeht, mit *rechen* bezeichnet werden. Entsprechende terminologische Schnittstellen zwischen Rache und gerichtlicher Bestrafung sind für mittellateinisch *ultio* und *vindicta* ebenfalls zu beobachten (Throop 2011: 11-12).[31] Im *Codex Iustinianus*, der Eingang in das im Mittelalter rezipierte *Corpus iuris civilis* gefunden hat, findet sich sogar die Formulierung *leges ulciscuntur* [die Gesetze rächen]; gemeint ist also eine Vergeltung, die von persönlichen Emotionen frei ist (C. I. 9, 9, 20; Rivière 2006: 35).

Von dieser Beobachtung aus lässt sich ein Bogen zu den eingangs zitierten kulturtheoretischen Überlegungen René Girards schlagen: Die Ergebnisse der Fallstudie zum Alexanderroman Rudolfs von Ems weisen interessante Parallelen zu Girards Hypothese auf, dass das Gerichtswesen keine Aufhebung der Rache darstelle. Girard (1972: 29) argumentiert, bereits der Ausdruck *Privatrache* impliziere, dass es sich bei einer gerichtlichen Verurteilung um eine Art öffentliche Rache handele. Signifikant sei vor allem, dass das Gerichtswesen die Rache auf eine einzige Vergeltungsmaßnahme begrenze. Gewiss wären – wie bei seiner These

---

[29] Vgl. dazu in Bezug auf ‚Rache' grundsätzlich Bernhardt 2014: 57: ‚Ebenso wie der Verweis auf Rache dazu dienen kann, gewaltförmige Handlungen zu legitimieren, wird er auch umgekehrt dazu verwendet, um bestimmten Handlungen ihre Legitimität abzusprechen. Die politische Rhetorik macht sich hier eine Ambivalenz zunutze, die daraus resultiert, dass der moralische Status der Rache und ihr Verhältnis zu Recht und Unrecht nicht nur zwischen verschiedenen Gesellschaften, sondern häufig auch innerhalb ein- und derselben Gesellschaft auf unterschiedliche Weise aufgefasst werden kann.'

[30] Vgl. das gängige Argumentationsschema, nach dem die Kreuzzüge als Ausgleich für das Gott durch Unglauben zugefügte Unrecht legitimiert werden (Throop 2011).

[31] Für einzelne Texte des römischen und des kanonischen Rechts lässt sich das Bedeutungsspektrum jeweils genauer bestimmen (vgl. zu *vindicta* im Römischen Recht Rivière 2006: 31–33; zu *vindicta* [in Abgrenzung zur Buße] im *Decretum Gratiani* Kéry 2006: 257-64). Im kanonischen Recht wird die Liebe zur Rache als Beweggrund für das Strafen zurückgewiesen, wobei die Rache teilweise ebenfalls mit *vindicta* bezeichnet ist (vgl. Kéry 2006: 298-301).

der Eindämmung der Blutrache – historische Differenzierungen nötig, schon allein im Hinblick auf die Kategorien der Privatheit und der Öffentlichkeit (z.B. Freise 2004). Außerdem müsste man das Konzept der *vindicta publica*, das zum Beispiel im gelehrten Recht des 16. Jahrhunderts nachzuweisen ist (Schnyder 2010: 96), zurückverfolgen.[32] Auf der Grundlage der semasiologischen Untersuchung eines Einzeltextes, wie sie hier praktiziert wurde, lässt sich wiederum das Verhältnis von Rache und Gerichtswesen nicht allgemein erfassen. Was eine solche Textanalyse aber leisten kann, ist die Diskursivierung dieser Grundfrage in einer konkreten historischen Konstellation aufzuschlüsseln. Aus der Art, wie im *Alexander* des Rudolf von Ems die Bedeutungen von *râche* und *rechen* jeweils kontextuell festgelegt werden, ist abzuleiten, dass für die impliziten Rezipienten kein grundlegender Widerspruch zwischen *râche* und Recht bestanden hat; das Verhältnis war aber offenbar im Einzelfall erst zu klären.

Mit dem Nachweis der Koexistenz von heute als konträr empfundenen Bedeutungen von *râche*, die alle durch den Aspekt des Ausgleichs von Unrecht verbunden sind, soll die diachrone Entwicklung, die schließlich zu einer Unterscheidung zwischen *râche* und Recht geführt hat, nicht in Abrede gestellt werden.[33] Punktuell fassbar scheint eine Veränderung des Wortgebrauchs von *râche* bei der Umarbeitung der Schilderung des Prozesses gegen Genelun im *Rolandslied* durch den Stricker zu sein.[34] In dessen *Karl* sagt Karl der Große ausdrücklich, er wolle, obwohl er Genelun zu Recht feind sei, nicht *nâch vîentlîcher râche* (v. 11647) gegen ihn vorgehen, sondern die Fürsten in Anwesenheit der Verwandten Geneluns urteilen lassen.[35] Im *Rolandslied* tut Karl dagegen zornig seinen Willen zur *râche* kund (vv. 8771-84), als ihn die Verwandten Geneluns um Gnade bitten (vv. 8755-70).[36] Dementsprechend ist das Rachedenken an dieser Stelle einer archaischen Rechtsvorstellung zugeordnet worden (Schmidt-Wiegand 1986: 7). Nach dem Text des *Rolandsliedes* hatte Karl allerdings kurz zuvor

---

[32] Zum Konzept der ‚Rache des Staates' in der späten römischen Republik und der frühen Kaiserzeit vgl. Rivière (2006: 31-42).
[33] Hyams (2010b: 214-17) geht davon aus, dass sich die konzeptionelle Unterscheidung zwischen Rache und Bestrafung im europäischen Raum erst im Hochmittelalter herausgebildet habe. Aus heutiger Perspektive stellt sich das Wort *râche* polysem dar, während man in den hochmittelalterlichen Texten eher mit Kontextvarianz zu rechnen hat.
[34] Die Prozesshandlung ist unter rechtshistorischen Aspekten intensiv diskutiert worden, auch weil Genelun sich auf das Fehderecht beruft (vgl. zusammenfassend Hoffmann 2001: 353-60; vgl. auch Möbius 1993: 142-48). Für einen Vergleich der Prozesshandlung im *Rolandslied* und in Strickers *Karl* vgl. Brandt (1981: 138-150).
[35] ‚Swie ich im von schulden vîent bin, / ine wil niht rihten über in / nâch vîentlîcher râche. / ich wil die vürsten zâche / urteiles über in frâgen / vor allen sinen mâgen'. (vv. 11645–50). Indem er seine persönliche Feindschaft außer Acht lassen will, verhält sich Karl der Richterethik gemäß (vgl. Drüppel 1981: 290-96).
[36] ‚man scol ez iemer ze mære sagen, / daz wirz an im gerochen haben, / unz an der werlte ende' (vv. 8779-81).

verkündet, er wolle nach den Gesetzen über Genelun Recht sprechen (vv. 8752–54).[37] Ob das tatsächlich nur eine bloße Beteuerung ist, müsste unter Berücksichtigung der gesamten Prozesshandlung diskutiert werden.[38] Vor dem Hintergrund der obigen Ausführungen scheint es jedoch nicht ausgeschlossen, dass die *râche* im Richten nach den Gesetzen besteht. Der Zorn Karls wäre dann nicht als Unbeherrschtheit zu verstehen, vor der Richter allgemein gewarnt werden; es wäre vielmehr eine Form des ‚gerechten Zorns' eines Herrschers, die sogar bei persönlicher Betroffenheit legitim ist.[39] In Strickers *Karl* hätte sich demnach nicht so sehr die Semantik von *râche* verändert, eher die Einschätzung der persönlichen Involviertheit.[40] Dass die *râche* durch das Attribut ‚feindlich' spezifiziert wird, dient sicherlich zur Betonung dieser Involviertheit; zugleich könnte sie darauf hindeuten, dass *râche* in Strickers *Karl* wie im etwa zeitgleich entstandenen *Alexander* Rudolfs von Ems noch nicht automatisch mit persönlicher Feindschaft verbunden sein muss, sondern kontextuell festgelegt wird. Dafür spricht auch, dass die letztendliche Bestrafung Geneluns durch Vierteilung vom Erzähler mithilfe des Wortes *rechen* als Ausgleich für den *mort* an Roland bezeichnet wird.[41] Die semantischen Spielräume, die sich im Alexander Rudolfs von Ems für *râche* und *rechen* beobachten lassen, sind also kein Einzelfall.

---

[37] ‚[...] / ich frâge urtaile / alsô die phachte tihten, / sô wil ich über in richten.' Zur rechtshistorischen Einordnung dieser Aussage vgl. Schulz (1998).
[38] Vgl. Janz (2001: 326): ‚Karl unterstellt sich dem Recht zwar verbal, tatsächlich jedoch sucht er es in seinem Sinne bzw. im Sinne seines göttlichen Auftrags zu manipulieren, indem er es seinem Racheplan ein- und unterordnet.'
[39] Vgl. Warnungen in Sprichwörtern vor dem Zorn beim Richten (TPMA, IX, 1999: 294 [s.v. ‚RICHTEN', 4.5]; XIII, 2001 [s.v. ‚ZORN', 1.3.3]) und insbesondere eine (in v. 12559 beginnende) Passage in *Der welsche Gast* Thomasins von Zerklaere, in der *zorn* beim Richten als *râche* negativ beurteilt wird: ‚swer mit zorne rihten wil, / der schendet sîn gerihte vil, / wan ez gerihte niht heizen sol: / ez mac râche heizen wol. / swer sich richet amme gerihte, / der ist gar ein bœsewiht / unde tuot niht daz er sol, / wan er durchz reht niht rihtet wol'. (vv. 12563–70).
[40] Im Ansatz ist hier eine Bedeutungsentwicklung zu erkennen, die dazu geführt hat, dass ‚Rache' in der germanistischen Mediävistik zuletzt nicht rechts-, sondern emotionshistorisch untersucht worden ist (Baisch / Freienhofer / Lieberich 2014).
[41] ‚swen nu der mort erbarme, / der an Ruolande geschach, / der hœre hie wie man in rach' (vv. 12136–38). Auch die Benennung des Ausgleichs für subjektiv empfundenes Unrecht als *rechen*, wie sie bei der Rede des Dimnus im *Alexander* vorliegt, lässt sich in Strickers *Karl* nachweisen, wo Genelun seine Taten als legitime *râche* zu stilisieren versucht (v. 11736).

Zitierte Literatur

Primärliteratur

Barlaam und Josaphat. Mit einem Anhang aus Franz Söhns, Das Handschriftenverhältnis in Rudolfs von Ems' 'Barlaam', hg. von Franz Pfeiffer, mit einem Nachwort und einem Register von Heinz Rupp (Leipzig: G.J. Göschen'sche Verlagshandlung, 1843). Photomechanischer Nachdruck. Deutsche Neudrucke, Reihe: Texte des Mittelalters (Berlin: De Gruyter, 1965)

Das Evangelium Nicodemi von Heinrich von Hesler, hg. von Karl Helm, Bibliothek des Litterarischen Vereins in Stuttgart, 224 (Tübingen: Litterarischer Verein in Stuttgart, 1902; repr.: Hildesheim/New York: Olms, 1976)

Galteri de Castellione Alexandreis, hg. von Marvin L. Colker, Thesaurus mundi, 17 (Padua: Antenore, 1978)

Kaiserchronik. Trierer Silvester. Annolied, hg. von Edward Schröder, Monumenta Germaniae Historica. Scriptores, 8 / Monumenta Germaniae Historica, 1 (Hannover: Hahn, 1895)

Karl der Grosse von dem Stricker, hg. von Karl Bartsch, Bibliothek der gesammten deutschen National-Literatur von der ältesten bis auf die neuere Zeit, 35 (Quedlinburg/Leipzig: Gottfr. Basse, 1857). Photomechanischer Nachdruck. Mit einem Nachwort von Dieter Kartschoke, Deutsche Neudrucke, Reihe: Texte des Mittelalters (Berlin: De Gruyter, 1965)

Das Rolandslied des Pfaffen Konrad. Mittelhochdeutsch/Neuhochdeutsch. Durchges. und bibliograph. aktualisierte Ausg., hg. von Dieter Kartschoke, Reclams Universal-Bibliothek, 2745 (Stuttgart: Reclam, 2011)

Der Wälsche Gast des Thomasin von Zirclaria, hg. von Heinrich Rückert, Bibliothek der gesammten deutschen National-Literatur, 30 (Quedlinburg/Leipzig, Gottfr. Basse, 1852). Photomechanischer Nachdruck. Mit einer Einleitung und einem Register von Friedrich Neumann, Deutsche Neudrucke, Reihe: Texte des Mittelalters (Berlin: De Gruyter, 1965)

Quintus Curtius Rufus, *Historiae Alexandri Magni. Geschichte Alexanders des Großen. Lateinisch/Deutsch*, hg. von Felicitas Olef-Krafft und Peter Krafft, übersetzt von Felicitas Olef-Krafft, Herausgegeben, kommentiert und mit einem Nachwort versehen von Felicitas Olef-Krafft und Peter Krafft, Reclams Universal-Bibliothek, 19813 (Stuttgart: Reclam, 2014)

Rudolf von Ems, *Alexander*, *Ein höfischer Versroman des 13. Jahrhunderts*, hg. von Victor Junk, 2 Bde., Bibliothek des literarischen Vereins in Stuttgart, 272, 274 (Leipzig: Hiersemann, 1928/29; repr. Darmstadt: Wissenschaftliche Buchgesellschaft, 1970)

Sekundärliteratur

Baisch, Martin, Evamaria Freienhofer und Eva Lieberich (Hg.). 2014. *Rache – Zorn – Neid. Zur Faszination negativer Emotionen in der Kultur und Literatur des Mittelalters*, Aventiuren, 8 (Göttingen: V&R unipress)

Barthélemy, Dominique, François Bougard und Régine Le Jan (Hg.). 2006. *La vengeance 400–1200*, Collection de l'École Française de Rome, 357 (Rome: École Française de Rome)

Bartsch, Karl. 1965 [1857]. Siehe oben unter *Karl der Grosse von dem Stricker*

Beck, Heinrich. 2003. 'Rache', in *Reallexikon der germanischen Altertumskunde*. Von Johannes Hoops. Zweite, völlig neu bearb. und stark erw. Auflage, hg. von Heinrich Beck, Dieter Geuenich und Heiko Steuer. Vierundzwanzigster Band (Berlin/New York: De Gruyter), S. 45-47

Bernhardt, Fabian. 2014. 'Was ist Rache? Versuch einer systematischen Bestimmung', in Baisch / Freienhofer / Lieberich 2014, S. 49-71

BMZ: Benecke, Georg Friedrich, Wilhelm Müller und Friedrich Zarncke. 1854-1866. *Mittelhochdeutsches Wörterbuch* (Leipzig: Hirzel; repr. Stuttgart: Hirzel 1990ff.)

Brandt, Rüdiger. 1981. '*erniuwet*'. *Studien zu Art, Grad und Aussagefolgen der Rolandsliedbearbeitung in Strickers 'Karl'*, Göppinger Arbeiten zur Germanistik, 327 (Göppingen: Kümmerle)

Buc, Philippe. 2006. 'La vengeance de Dieu: De l'exégèse patristique à la Réforme ecclésiastique et la Première Croisade', in Barthélemy / Bougard / Le Jan 2006, S. 451-86

Buck, Timothy. 1968. '*Zuht, râche* und *versuochunge*. Nochmals zum Begriff ‚Strafe' im Armen Heinrich', *Euphorion*, 62: 311-16

Cölln, Jan. 2002. '*werdekeit*. Zur literarischen Konstruktion ethischen Verhaltens und seiner Bewertung in Rudolfs von Ems *Alexander*', in Mölk 2002, S. 332-57

Deppermann, Arnulf. 2007. *Grammatik und Semantik aus gesprächsanalytischer Sicht*, Linguistik – Impulse und Tendenzen, 14 (Berlin/New York: De Gruyter)

Drüppel, Hubert. 1981. *Iudex Civitatis. Zur Stellung des Richters in der hoch- und spätmittelalterlichen Stadt des deutschen Rechts*, Forschungen zur deutschen Rechtsgeschichte, 12 (Köln/Wien: Böhlau)

DRW: Preußische / Heidelberger Akademie der Wissenschaften (Hg.). 1912ff. *Deutsches Rechtswörterbuch. Wörterbuch der älteren deutschen Rechtssprache* (Weimar: Böhlau)

Eulenstein, Julia, Christine Reinle und Michael Rothmann (Hg.). 2013. *Fehdeführung im spätmittelalterlichen Reich. Zwischen adeliger Handlungslogik und territorialer Verdichtung*, Studien und Texte zur Geistes- und Sozialgeschichte des Mittelalters, 7 (Affalterbach: Didymos)

Freise, Fridrun. 2004. 'Einleitung. Raumsemantik, Rezeptionssituation und imaginierte Instanz – Perspektiven auf vormoderne Öffentlichkeit und Privatheit', in *Offen und verborgen. Vorstellungen und Praktiken des Öffentlichen und Privaten in Mittelalter und früher Neuzeit*, hg. von Caroline Emmelius et al. (Göttingen: Wallstein), S. 9-32

Gellike, Christian. 2001. 'Was heißt strafen?', *ZRG GA*, 118: 385-86

Girard, René. 1972. *La Violence et le sacré* (Paris: Grasset)

Grubmüller, Klaus. 2003. 'Historische Semantik und Diskursgeschichte: *zorn, nît und haz*', in *Codierungen von Emotionen / Emotions and Sensibilities in the Middle Ages*, 1, hg. von Stephen C. Jäger und Ingrid Kasten, Trends in Medieval Philology (Berlin/New York: De Gruyter), S. 47-69

Hilgendorf, Eric, und Jürgen Weitzel. 2007. *Der Strafgedanke in seiner historischen Entwicklung. Ringvorlesung zur Strafrechtsgeschichte und Strafrechtsphilosophie* (Berlin: Duncker & Humblot)

Hoffmann, Werner. 2001. 'Genelun, der *verrâtaere*', *Zeitschrift für deutsche Philologie*, 120: 345-60

Holzhauer, Antje. 1997. *Rache und Fehde in der mittelhochdeutschen Literatur des 12. und 13. Jahrhunderts*, Göppinger Arbeiten zur Germanistik, 639 (Göppingen: Kümmerle)

Hyams, Paul R. 2010a. 'Was There Really Such a Thing as Feud in the High Middle Ages?', in Throop / Hyams 2010, S. 151-75

—. 2010b. 'Neither Unnatural nor Wholly Negative: The Future of Medieval Vengenace', in Throop / Hyams 2010, S. 203-20

Isenmann, Eberhard. 2013. 'Warum wurde die Fehde im römisch-deutschen Reich seit 1467 reichsgesetzlich verboten? Der Diskurs über Fehde, Friede und Gewaltmonopol im 15. Jahrhundert', in Eulenstein / Reinle / Rothmann 2013, S. 335-474

Janz, Brigitte. 2001. 'Genelun: »den armen Iudas er gebildot«. Verrat und Verräter im deutschsprachigen *Rolandslied*', in *Verführer. Schurken. Magier*, hg. von Ulrich Müller und Werner Wunderlich, Mittelalter-Mythen, 3 (St. Gallen: UVK, Fachverlag für Wissenschaft und Studium), S. 317-29

Jendorff, Alexander. 2013. 'Fehde oder Mord? Gerichtliche und außergerichtliche Argumentationsstrategien als Adeligkeitsdiskurs am Beispiel des Prozesses des Mainzer Kurfürsten gegen Barthold von Witzingerode 1574/75', in Eulenstein / Reinle / Rothmann 2013, S. 313-34

Junk, Viktor. 1928. Siehe oben unter Rudolf von Ems

Keller, C. A., und Bo Reicke. 1966. 'Strafe', in *Biblisch-Historisches Handwörterbuch*, hg. von Bo Reicke und Leonhard Rost (Göttingen: Vandenhoeck & Ruprecht), S. 6687-92

Kéry, Lotte. 2006. *Gottesfurcht und irdische Strafe. Der Beitrag des mittelalterlichen Kirchenrechts zur Entstehung des öffentlichen Strafrechts*, Konflikt, Verbrechen und Sanktion in der Gesellschaft Alteuropas. Symposium und Synthesen, 10 (Köln: Böhlau)

Kluge, Friedrich. 2011. *Etymologisches Wörterbuch der deutschen Sprache*. Bearbeitet von Elmar Seebold. 25. durchges. und erw. Aufl. (Berlin: De Gruyter)

Kragl, Florian. 2013. 'König Alexanders Glück und Ende in der höfischen Literatur des deutschen Mittelalters im Allgemeinen und bei Rudolf von Ems im Besonderen', *Archiv für das Studium der neuen Sprachen und Literaturen*, 165/250: 7-41

Krämer-Seifert, Silke, und Manfred Kern. 2003. 'Parmenio', in *Lexikon der antiken Gestalten in deutschen Texten des Mittelalters*, hg. von Manfred Kern und Alfred Ebenbauer, unter Mitwirkung von Silke Krämer-Seifert (Darmstadt: Wissenschaftliche Buchgesellschaft), S. 476-77

Lexer, Mathias. 1869-1878. *Mittelhochdeutsches Handwörterbuch*, 3 Bde (Leipzig: Hirzel; repr. Stuttgart: Hirzel, 1992)

Lienert, Elisabeth. 2001. *Deutsche Antikenromane des Mittelalters*, Grundlagen der Germanistik, 39 (Berlin: Erich Schmidt)

—. 2018. ‚Idealisierung und Widerspruch. Zur Figurenkonstition von Rudolfs von Ems *Alexander*', in *Rudolf von Ems*, hg. von Norbert Kössinger et al., ZfdA Beihefte (Stuttgart: Hirzel)

Möbius, Thomas. 1993. *Studien zum Rachegedanken in der deutschen Literatur des Mittelalters*, Europäische Hochschulschriften, 1: 1395 (Frankfurt a.M.: Lang)

Mölk, Ulrich (Hg.). 2002. *Herrschaft, Ideologie und Geschichtskonzeption in Alexanderdichtungen des Mittelalters*, Veröffentlichung aus dem Göttinger Sonderforschungsbereich 529 ‚Internationalität nationaler Literaturen', Serie A: Literatur und Kulturräume im Mittelalter, 2 (Göttingen: Wallstein)

MWB: Mainzer Akademie der Wissenschaften und der Literatur, und Akademie der Wissenschaften zu Göttingen (Hg.). 2013 ff. *Mittelhochdeutsches Wörterbuch*, überarbeitete Bandauflage (Stuttgart: Hirzel)

Nowakowski, Nina. 2014. 'Alternativen der Vergeltung. Rache, Revanche und die Logik des Wiedererzählens in schwankhaften mittelhochdeutschen Kurzerzählungen' in Baisch / Freienhofer / Lieberich: 2014, S. 73-100

Peels, H.G.L. 1995. *The Vengeance of God. The Meaning of the Root NQM and the Function of the NQM-Texts in the Context of Divine Revelation in the Old Testament*, Oudtestamentische studien, 31 (Leiden: Brill)

Reinle, Christine. 2013. 'Einleitung', in Eulenstein / Reinle / Rothmann 2013, S. 9-24

Renz, Tilo. 2012. *Um Leib und Leben. Das Wissen von Geschlecht, Körper und Recht im Nibelungenlied*, Quellen und Forschungen zur Literatur- und Kulturgeschichte, 71 (305) (Berlin/Boston: De Gruyter)

Rivière, Yann. 2006. 'Pouvoir impérial et vengeance. De *mars ultor* à la *diuina uindicta* (Ier–IVe siècle ap. J.-C.)', in Barthélemy / Bougard / Le Jan 2006, S. 7-42

Schlee, Günther, und Bertram Turner. 2008. 'Einleitung: Wirkungskontexte des Vergeltungsprinzips in der Konfliktregulierung', in *Vergeltung. Eine interdisziplinäre Betrachtung der Rechtfertigung und Regulation von Gewalt*, hg. von Günther Schlee und Bertram Turner (Frankfurt a.M.: Campus), S. 7-47

Schmidt-Wiegand, Ruth. 1986. 'Prozeßform und Prozeßverlauf im ‚Rolandslied' des Pfaffen Konrad. Zum Verhältnis von Dichtung und Recht im Mittelalter', in *Recht, Gericht, Genossenschaft und Policey. Studien zu Grundbegriffen der germanistischen Rechtshistorie. Symposion für Adalbert Erler*, hg. von Gerhard Dilcher und Bernhard Diestelkamp (Berlin: Erich Schmidt), S. 1-12

Schmitt, Stefanie. 2002. 'Alexander *monarchus*. Heilsgeschichte als Herrschaftslegitimation in Rudolfs von Ems *Alexander*', in Mölk 2002, S. 290-331

Schnell, Rüdiger. 1969. *Rudolf von Ems. Studien zur inneren Einheit seines Gesamtwerks*, Basler Studien, 41 (Bern: A. Francke)

Schnyder, Sibylle. 2010. *Tötung und Diebstahl. Delikt und Strafe in der gelehrten Strafrechtsliteratur des 16. Jahrhunderts*, Konflikt Verbrechen und Sanktion in der Gesellschaft Alteuropas. Fallstudien, 9 (Köln/Weimar/Wien: Böhlau)

Schulz, Monika. 1998. '‚Was bedürfen wir nu rede mere?' Bemerkungen zur Gerichtsszene im Rolandslied', *Amsterdamer Beiträge zur älteren Germanistik*, 50: 47-72

Schumann, Eva. 2008. 'Buße', in *Handwörterbuch zur deutschen Rechtsgeschichte*, 2., völlig überarb. und erw. Aufl., hg. von Albrecht Cordes et al., ab 9. Lieferung Christa Bertelsmeier-Kierst als philologischer Beraterin (Berlin: Erich Schmidt), Sp. 789-95

Schützeichel, Rudolf. 2012. *Althochdeutsches Wörterbuch*, 7., durchges. und verb. Aufl. (Berlin/Boston: De Gruyter)

Seidl, Stephanie, und Julia Zimmermann. 2011. 'Jenseits des Kategorischen. Konzeptionen des ‚Heidnischen' in volkssprachigen literarischen und chronikalischen Texten des 13. Jahrhunderts', in *Integration und Desintegration der Kulturen im europäischen Mittelalter*, hg. von Michael Borgolte und Bernd Schneidmüller (Berlin: Akademie-Verlag), S. 325-81

Smail, Daniel. 2001. 'Hatred as a Social Institution in Late-Medieval Society', *Speculum*, 76: 90-126

Stolz, Fritz. 2003. 'Rache', in *Theologische Realenzyklopädie*, hg. von Gerhard Müller, XXVIII (Berlin/New York: De Gruyter), S. 82-88

Thomas, Konrad. 2011. 'René Girard: Ein anderes Verständnis von Gewalt', in *Kultur. Theorien der Gegenwart*, hg. von Stephan Moebius und Dirk Quadflieg, 2. erweiterte und aktualisierte Auflage (Wiesbaden: VS Verlag für Sozialwissenschaften), S. 425-38

Throop, Susanna A. 2010. 'Zeal, Anger and Vengeance. The Emotional Rhetoric of Crusading', in Throop / Hyams 2010, S. 177-201

—. 2011. *Crusading as an Act of Vengeance, 1095–1216* (Farnham: Ashgate)

—. und Paul R. Hyams (Hg.). 2010. *Vengeance in the Middle Ages. Emotion, Religion and Feud* (Farnham: Ashgate)

TPMA: Kuratorium Singer der Schweizerischen Akademie der Geistes- und Sozialwissenschaften (Hg.) 1995-2002. *Thesaurus proverbiorum medii aevi. Lexikon der Sprichwörter des romanisch-germanischen Mittelalters*, begr. von Samuel Singer, 13 Bde (Berlin/New York: De Gruyter)

Walliczek, Wofgang. 1992. 'Rudolf von Ems', in *Die deutsche Literatur des Mittelalters – Verfasserlexikon.* Begr. von Wolfgang Stammler, fortgeführt von Karl Langosch. 2., völlig neu bearbeitete Auflage unter Mitarbeit zahlreicher Fachgelehrter hg. von Kurt Ruh zusammen mit Gundolf Keil, Werner Schröder, Burghart Wachinger, Franz Josef Worstbrock. Redaktion: Christine Stöllinger-Löser, VIII (Berlin/New York: De Gruyter), Sp. 322-45

Weber, Regine. 2012. *Die Inszenierung der Divina Providentia im Œuvre Rudolfs von Ems* (Hofkirchen: Tobias Weber Musik & Buch Verlag)

Weidenbusch, Waltraud. 2005. 'Überlegungen zu Möglichkeiten und Grenzen einer historischen Pragmatik', in *Historische Pragmatik und historische Varietätenlinguistik in den romanischen Sprachen*, hg. von Angela Schrott und Harald Völker (Göttingen: Universitätsverlag Göttingen), S. 101-12

Weitzel, Jürgen. 2007. 'Der Strafgedanke im frühen Mittelalter', in Hilgendorf / Weitzel 2007, S. 21-35

Willoweit, Dietmar. 2007. 'Rache und Strafe, Sühne und Kirchenbuße. Sanktionen für Unrecht an der Schwelle zur Neuzeit', in Hilgendorf / Weitzel 2007, S. 37-58

Wisbey, Roy. 1969. *Das Alexanderbild Rudolfs von Ems*, Philologische Studien und Quellen, 31 (Berlin: Erich Schmidt)

WMU: Kirschstein, Bettina, and Ursula Schulze (Hg.). 1991-2010. *Wörterbuch der mittelhochdeutschen Urkundensprache*. Auf der Grundlage des ‚Corpus der altdeutschen Originalurkunden bis zum Jahr 1300' unter Leitung von Bettina Kirschstein und Ursula Schulze erarb. von Sibylle Ohly und Peter Schmitt, Veröffentlichungen der Kommission für Deutsche Literatur des Mittelalters der Bayerischen Akademie der Wissenschaften (Berlin: Erich Schmidt)

3

'und wolt iuch hân gebezzert mite':
Keie, Cunneware and the Dynamics of Punishment

Annette Volfing
University of Oxford

The challenge of distinguishing punishment from revenge – and other forms of retributive, vindictive or otherwise hostile behaviour – is a central problem within the philosophy of law. Robert Nozick has proposed a list of criteria which cohere broadly with modern everyday usage, in which revenge tends to be viewed negatively and punishment neutrally to positively (Nozick 1983: 366–68).[1] Punishment is normally thought of as being inflicted in accordance with an accepted set of values; it addresses an objective wrong rather than a personal slight; it is focussed on the future rather than on the past, and may sometimes be construed as being for the long-term benefit of the person being punished; it is not predicated on emotional response; and, being calibrated to scale of the wrong, has a set limit. If these conditions are met, a punitive measure should ideally enable a return to normal, stable relations, rather than triggering cycles of further retaliation (which would be the pattern associated with revenge). Nonetheless, it is difficult to formulate a definition that eliminates all ambiguity: as Leo Zaibert points out in his critique of Nozick's approach, literary texts often focus precisely on the grey areas that undercut the neatness of Nozick's distinctions:

> One obvious way to attempt to refute the thesis that punishing and taking revenge are different activities would be to point to the numerous fictional examples where the 'two phenomena' seem perenially intertwined. Does Othello punish Desdemona or does he take revenge upon her for what he thought was her betrayal? Is the Count of Monte Cristo punishing or taking revenge on the malefactors who attempted to ruin his life? Does Lazarillo de Tormes really take revenge (as he claims) on the blind man who had cruelly abused him for so long, or is he in fact punishing him? Does Michael Kohlhaas seek to take revenge or to punish as he roamed Saxony in pursuit of those who did him wrong?
> (Zaibert 2006: 71)

---

[1] See Zaibert (2006: 74).

To Zaibert's list of literary examples, a medievalist might readily add figures from the *Nibelungenlied*, probing not only the nature of Kriemhild's long-term plotting against her relatives, but also that of Hildebrand's final action: does he kill Kriemhild in order to avenge the death of Hagen and the other Burgundians, or to punish her for an extreme form of gender transgression? Whilst the debate between Nozick and Zaibert attempts to rise above cultural specificity (whilst focusing on the modern English uses of the terms 'punishment' and 'revenge'), the inclusion of medieval examples would be complicated by particular cultural assumptions, not only about the value of retributive action (the term 'râche' is wider in its range and generally more positively connotated than the Modern English 'revenge'), but also about gender roles and the framework within which any cross-gender conflict might be worked out.[2] Whereas the quest for revenge implies a certain equality between the parties, punishment characteristically insists on hierarchical difference: kings punish their subjects, adults punish children, and men punish women. Within literature, one may also speak metaphorically about the author or narrator punishing his characters, in the sense that he has the power to shape events in such a way that wrong-doers undergo appropriate suffering.

In Wolfram's *Parzival*, motivations of punishment and revenge intermingle in a particularly complex way in the sequence of events arising from Keie's beating of Cunneware. This is made most apparent at the point when Parzival finally jousts with Keie. Here, the narrator specifies that the single blow leading to the fracture of Keie's arm and leg combines two separate functions – to mix the metaphors, one could even speak of Parzival killing two birds with one stone:

> sus galt zwei bliwen der gast:
> daz eine leit ein maget durch in,
> mit dem andern muoser selbe sîn.
> 295.25-28

[Thus the stranger avenged two beatings: a maiden had suffered the one because of him and he himself had had to abide the other.][3]

In so far as the blow is related to Keie's assault on Cunneware, it may be regarded as punitive. It certainly fits most of Nozick's criteria: it addresses a wrong done to a defenceless individual rather than a personal slight to Parzival himself; it coheres with the collective values of the time; and it effectively closes off the sequence of events because it is regarded as commensurate with the original offence – as

---

[2] See the contribution by MANUWALD in this volume.
[3] Translations from Wolfram's *Parzival* are by Hatto (1980) and translations from Chrétien's *Le Conte du Graal (Perceval)* by Kibler (1991). Other translations are my own.

Cunneware herself goes on to affirm, Parzival has done enough (306.4: 'genuoc'). From that point on, only Keie himself regards the matter as unresolved – and is still sulking in Book XIII because Gawan views the situation differently (675.10–12). However, Parzival's blow also serves as a form of personal revenge, not only because Keie has just made a big hole in his shield, but also because Keie's vehement response to Cunneware's prophetic laughter may be interpreted as a slight (199.7: 'laster') to Parzival's honour.[4] Of course, the fact that Parzival strikes the blow whilst in a trance problematizes the question of motivation, but his subsequent conversation with Gawan (304.13-21) makes it quite clear that he was in any case determined to fight Keie on these two accounts.

Whereas Parzival is able to combine revenge and punishment with harmonious efficiency, the conflict is initially triggered by Keie's misguided decision to mete out punishment where none was due – a decision that can be explained in terms of his inability to distinguish between an objective wrong and a source of personal irritation. Keie's behaviour towards Cunneware has been aligned by Elisabeth Lienert with various other acts of unlawful violence against women recorded within the text, such as the rapes perpetrated by Meljakanz and Urjans (Lienert 2002). Nonetheless, the beating of Cunneware differs from these other violations on account of Keie's conviction that he has acted justly, properly and within the boundaries of his authority.

Keie is of course a stock figure within Arthurian romance and an audience familiar with *Iwein* would expect him to discredit himself with some form of inappropriately churlish behaviour.[5] As Werner Röcke has shown, Girard's scapegoat-model can usefully be applied to explain the function of Keie's behaviour in *Iwein* (Röcke 2001: 347-55). On this account, the ideal of equality ('Parität') at the Arthurian court is threatened by widespread competitive tension between the knights. As Keie is the only one to articulate this tension, his spiteful outbursts enable the others to unite in cohesive disapproval of Keie, who is metaphorically driven out for the wrongs of the whole community. However, notwithstanding the increasing social isolation of Keie in *Parzival*, Röcke concedes that this model works less well for Wolfram's text, given that Keie resorts to actual violence, rather than merely voicing the sorts of inappropriate feelings that everybody is secretly harbouring: 'In

---

[4] On the question of whether Cunneware's 'lachen' should be understood as as a gesture of laughing or of smiling, see Fritsch-Rößler (1997: 75-79). Kühn (1994: I, 255), translates 'lachen' as 'lächeln'. For the prophetic nature of Cunneware's 'lachen', see Seeber (2010: 137-39 and 152-56); Philipowski (2003); Huber (1998); Fritsch-Rößler (1997); Erfen (1994); Green (1982: 67).

[5] On Keie within Arthurian romance, see Däumer (2011); Emmelius (2010: 31-51); Schonert (2009); Baisch (2003); Scheuble (2005: 313-27); Röcke (2001); Wenzel (2001); Volkmann (1995); Classen (1988); Haupt (1971).

Wolframs Roman also ist Keies Fehltritt nicht Teil einer rituellen Reglementierung oder gar Abschwächung, sondern ganz im Gegenteil Ausgangspunkt neuer Gewalt.' [In Wolfram's romance, Keie's error does not form part of a process of regulating, or even reducing, violence, but on the contrary becomes a springboard for fresh violence] (Röcke 2001: 359). In favour of the scapegoat model, one might point to the theoretical possibility of Cunneware's laughter having caused widespread offence amongst the Arthurian knights who are disgruntled at her endorsement of Parzival and accordingly harbour hostility towards her. On that account, Keie might indeed be interpreted as scapegoat, eventually paying the price for doing precisely what everybody else secretly have liked to do. However, nothing is said in the text to support the idea of such communal resentment, either of Cunneware or of Parzival. The rest of the Arthurian court is clearly puzzled by Parzival, rather than threatened; and nobody else makes any reference, however mild, to the idea of Cunneware having behaved inappropriately or of her laughter having been more widely interpreted as a slur on the rest of the court.

Rather than viewing Keie's actions primarily in anthropological terms (i.e. as being driven by a perceived need for a scapegoat figure within this particular society), the reading proposed in this article will therefore focus on the steward as a flawed, but psychologically credible figure whom the courtly world struggles to accommodate. This psychological reading is by no means intended to argue against the obvious structural importance of the Keie-Cunneware episode for marking the stations of Parzival's career: on the contrary, these structural aspects will regularly be foregrounded in the discussion of the episode. Similarly, the psychological reading, according to which the assault on Cunneware constutitues a manifestation of personal pique, does not stand in outright oppostion the scapegoat model as outlined above. Its aim is simply to show that in addition to structural and (possible) anthropological considerations, the episode also works as the delineation of a personal – and very credible – interpersonal conflict which is ultimately not about Parzival himself. Instead, the episode hinges on the questions of Keie's 'right' to exercise poor judgment, Cunneware's 'right' to nurture grievances, and the swiftness with which the roles of transgressor and victim may be reversed.

Keie's behaviour presents a social and ethical challenge, not only for the Arthurian court, but also for the narrator. On the one hand, the narrator immediately condemns the attacks, making it clear that Keie has acted *ultra vires*:

> sîns slages wær im erteilet niht
> vorem rîche ûf dise magt,
> diu vil von friwenden wart geklagt.
> 152.14-16

[His right to strike this maiden, whose friends were so very sorry for her, would not have been upheld before the Emperor.]

Keie is also described as foolish (152.1) and as having acted whilst in the grip of emotions (152.13: 'in zorne wunders vil geschiht.' [Anger leads to great excess]). On the other hand, the narrator not only shows very little sympathy for Cunneware, but also goes out on a limb to rehabilitate Keie in a lengthy *laudatio* in which the steward is praised for the zeal and rigour with which he maintains standards at court and prevents the unworthy from gaining access (296.14–297.29). As will be argued below, this surprising narratorial stance may be explained by reference to the cold war developing between Keie and Cunneware after the beating and to Keie's increasing social isolation. Although the Arthurian court takes no formal measures against Keie, the steward's increasing embarrassment and awkwardness is sufficient for the narrator to construe him, rather than Cunneware, as the victim of an unduly hostile stance. One may even discern a possible analogy between this narrator's handling of Keie and the shift in narratorial sympathy towards Hagen in the *Nibelungenlied*. Of course, events unfurl on a much smaller scale than in the *Nibelungenlied*; Cunneware may be slow to forget, but she is no Kriemhild, and apart from Keie's unfortunate horse, nobody dies as part of Keie's come-uppance. Common to both texts, however, is the pattern according to which the narrator initially expresses consternation at the great wrong done to a woman, but then moves towards a position of overt support for the perpetrator.

It should be noted that Keie attacks not only Cunneware, who had sworn not to laugh until the arrival of the worthiest knight of all, but also the mute Antanor, who suddenly becomes able to speak up in support of Cunneware's prophecy. Both victims are in some sense subordinate to Keie (Cunneware by virtue of her sex and Antanor by virtue of his non-aristocratic rank). Cunneware, however, is socially distinguished and has powerful relations; partly for this reason, and partly because the public beating of a lady is more shocking and/or titillating, her plight is given much greater attention, both by the narrator and by the other characters, than that of Antanor. Antanor himself is delighted to have been 'avenged' by Parzival, asking:

> sît irz der mich rach,
> und Cunnewâren de Lalant?'
> 307.24-25

[Was it you who avenged me and Cunneware de Lalant?]

Parzival's own focus, however, only extends as far as Cunneware, and even she was not on the top of his to-do list. In any case, Antanor's prophetic role is subordinate to to that of Cunneware.

That Cunneware's laughter should serve as the starting-point for a protracted period of psychological tension is paradoxical, in so far as Katharina Philipowski has described it as a purely symbolic gesture that tells us absolutely nothing about Cunneware's inner life at that particular moment (Philipowski 2003: 23).[6] The function of that laughter is purely to mark out Parzival's future greatness and the narrative remains deliberately hazy about the background to Cunneware's prophetic calling. It is not clear how Cunneware gains her insight or what kinds of choices were involved: was she never able to laugh, did she lose the capacity to laugh at some specific point, or did she make an active decision to refrain from laughing until the right moment? Should her response to Parzival be considered voluntary or involuntary? What is it that enables her to recognize great but unfulfilled potential?[7] In any case, the kind of symbolic laughter with which she reveals her knowledge has nothing to do with ordinary mirth. In particular, it should be stressed that Cunneware is not laughing at Parzival because she finds his appearance amusing. Similarly, Keie does not punish her on account of her apparent mockery of a guest, or because he disapproves of female laughter more generally. Keie is fully aware of the special, symbolic nature of Cunneware's laughter; what he explicitly objects to is the way in which she singles out Parzival after having withheld her laughter from numerous excellent knights (152.7-152.12). He effectively interprets Cunneware's prophetic insight as an insult to himself and all of the other conventionally successful knights. As Waltraud Fritsch-Rößler sums up:

> Cunneware wird nicht bestraft, weil sie gelacht hat. Es wäre voreilig, ja verfehlt, Keies Sanktionen vor dem Hintergrund lachfeindlicher Dogmen zu interpretieren. Es gibt im Text keinen dezidierten Beleg dafür, daß Keie Cunneware schlägt, weil sie – gar noch als Frau – lacht. Die Schläge resultieren ausschließlich aus der vermeintlichen Verhöhnung des Ritterstandes.
> (Fritsch-Rößler 1997: 84)

> [Cunneware is not punished because she laughed. It would be premature, even misguided, to interpret Keie's sanction in the context of precepts against laughter. There is nothing in the text to suggest that Keie strikes Cunneware simply because she, a woman, dares to laugh. The blows are purely the result of the presumed mockery of the knightly order.]

Furthermore, it seems plausible to credit Keie with longer-term feelings of irritation towards Cunneware's prophetic stance. After all, it is he, not Cunneware, who is

---

[6] By contrast, Däumer (2011: 107-08) associates Cunneware's laughter with the mockery to which Keie himself is often subjected within the genre.

[7] Fritsch-Rößler (1997: 77-82) addresses these questions in detail. Note Kingrun's view that Cunneware's laughter comes from 'herzen sinne' (221.22) [divining [...] in her heart].

responsible for assessing the worthiness of newcomers to the Arthurian court. In the version by Chrétien de Troyes, this aspect emerges more strongly. Here, the steward assaults the court jester, not for backing up the prophecy of the maiden (as Antanor backs up Cunneware in her specific endorsement of Parzival), but simply for having previously affirmed the maiden's prophetic capacity:

> Quant la pucele ferue ot,
> an sa voie trova un sot
> lez une cheminee estant,
> si le bota el feu ardant
> del pié par corroz et par ire
> por ce que li soz soloit dire:
> 'Ceste pucele ne rira
> jusque tant que ele verra
> celui qui de chevalerie
> avra tote la seignorie.'
>   1051-60

[After slapping the maiden he turned back and saw a court jester standing beside the fireplace; he kicked him into the roaring fire because he was furiously angry at having often heard the jester say: 'This maiden will not laugh until she has seen the man who will be the supreme lord among all knights'.][8]

Whereas Wolfram's Keie is no wiser or more temperate than his French counterpart, he is more articulate in his dealings with Cunneware and specifically presents the beating as punitive, in the sense of aiming to correct a supposed failing on her part:

> iwerm werdem prîse
> ist gegebn ein smæhiu letze:
> ich pin sîn vängec netze,
> ich soln wider in iuch smiden
> daz irs enpfindet ûf den liden.
>   152.1-6

[You have dismissed your good name with contumely: but I am the net that retrieves it. I shall hammer it back into you so that you feel it in your bones.]

The metaphor of the 'vängec netze' not only works on the abstract level of catching Cunneware's fallen honour, but also complements the preceeding description of the way in which Keie seizes Cunneware to hold her in place for the beating:

---

[8] Chrétien is cited from Chrétien de Troyes, *Le Conte du Graal (Perceval)*, ed. Félix Lecoy (1972). The English translation is from Chrétien's *Le Conte du Graal (Perceval)* by Kibler (1991).

> ir lange zöpfe clâre
> die want er umbe sîne hant,
> er spancte se âne türbant.
> ir rüke wart kein eit gestabt:
> doch wart ein stap sô dran gehabt,
> unz daz sîn siusen gar verswanc,
> durch die wât unt durch ir vel ez dranc.
> 151.24-30

[He wound her long tresses round his hand and clenched her without a door-hinge. Her back was taking no oath, yet a staff was so applied to it that its weight sank through clothes and skin till its swishing died away.]

Furthermore, with its emphasis on tightness of grip, it echoes the much earlier metaphor in which the narrator styles himself as a pair of clenching tongs (114.14: 'habendiu zange') in his anger against the woman whom he regards as having behaved inappropriately towards him. Like Keie, the narrator views the assessment of masculine, knightly worth as a very serious matter. It should also be remembered that despite the narrator's initial disapproval of Keie's uncontrolled rage, his own intertextual challenge to Hartmann shows that he feels no compunction himself at threatening women with metaphorical violence in the interests of ensuring the proper recognition of male prowess.[9] In this case, the narrator urges Hartmann to treat the newcomer Parzival well,

> anders iwer frouwe Enîde
> unt ir muoter Karsnafide
> werdent durch die mül gezücket
> unde ir lop gebrücket.
> 143.29-144.2

[Otherwise your lady Enite and her mother Karsnafide will be dragged through the mill and their reputations lowered!]

Cunneware is, of course, absolutely right in her assessment of Parzival's potential, but only Parzival himself can prove that, and at the time of the beating, he is not yet in a position to be able to vindicate her. The fact that the Arthurian court does nothing to address Keie's scandalous behaviour may be explained partly as a way of focussing audience expectations on Parzival's future achievements. The debâcle also has the function of demonstrating Parzival's capacity for compassion – although, as already noted, Cunneware is not always of paramount concern to

---

[9] For the wider context of the apostrophe to Hartmann, see Wand-Wittkowski (1989: 23–30).

him. When Parzival defeats Kingrun, for example, he initially asks him to submit to Gurnemanz; and then, as a second choice, to Condwiramurs. Cunneware is only offered as a third choice in response to Kingrun's protests about the first two. Similarly, Clamide is initially instructed to submit to Gurnemanz. Only Orilus is immediately directed to seek out Cunneware.

However, even if nobody other than Parzival can ultimately demonstrate the correctness of Cunneware's assessment, the Arthurian court could arguably have upheld her right to express a point of view about future potential without being physically assaulted. One problem lies, as already suggested, with the prophetic nature of Cunneware's laughter: prophecy is inherently provocative in that it claims a form of authority that transcends ordinary hierarchies of class and gender – and for that reason, it cannot afford to be wrong. Another problem relates to the flawed nature of the Arthurian court: a small society in which everybody has firm opinions about the behaviour of everybody, but where there are no structures in place to enforce the common values or to ensure the protection of the vulnerable. In the immediate aftermath of the beatings, life therefore goes on exactly as normal, with Cunneware, Antanor and Keie forced to co-exist, in close proximity and under the glare of public scrutiny. It is in the context of this claustrophobic setting that narratorial sympathy shifts more openly from Cunneware to Keie, demonstrating how the roles of authority figure and underdog, of aggressor and victim, are constructions that can easily be manipulated.

Over a period of time, Parzival defeats the three knights – Kingrun, Clamide and Orilus – and sends each of them to the Arthurian court, with instructions to submit to Cunneware. This piece of narrative patterning involves regular repetition of the circumstances of Keie's assault: first, Parzival tells each of the knights what happened to the maiden who laughed, and then, as Parzival does not provide the name of the maiden, each knight in turn has to go through the details again once he reaches court in order to be directed to the right person. Furthermore, Orilus makes a formal complaint to Artus (again setting out the facts) and reiterates these same facts in a lament addressed to Cunneware. Finally, Parzival himself repeats the story to Gawan, vowing revenge, unaware that he has already defeated Keie whilst entranced by the three drops of blood. On the one hand, this repetition of the key events ensures the audience's recollection of the incident and suggests to them that Keie's come-uppance must be imminent – even if Wolfram dispenses with Chrétien's device of the letting fool articulate and repeat the prediction of precisely how the steward will be made to suffer (i.e. with a broken arm and broken leg). On the other hand, in Wolfram's text, the structured repetition of the facts also has the effect of lessening their original impact: the beating is shocking the first time that it is recounted, but after hearing about it a few times, the listener or reader might easily react with the kind of shoulder-shrug response given to a grievance that has been aired rather too often. This in turn may also be seen to lessen the sympathy for Cunneware. Although she does not speak directly about her suffering at any point until the arrival of Parzival (305.27-306.5), the cumulative effect of the repetition in the speeches of the other protagonists is to create a false impression that Cunneware herself has complained extensively about Keie's misdemeanour.

Keie reacts differently to each of the three knights, but the overall effect is to demonstrate his sense of unease – and increasing social isolation – at the situation, notwithstanding the failure of the Arthurian court to take any formal measures against him.

With the arrival of Kingrun, Keie's strategy is to try to build on a presumed bond with his colleague and opposite number from another court. Kingrun is the steward at Brandigan, and Keie asks for his help with an unpromising plan to mollify Cunneware by cooking her some pleasingly thick 'krapfen':

> [']du Clamîdês scheneschlant,
> wirt mir dîn meister [=Parzival] nimmer holt,
> dîns amts du doch geniezen solt:
> der kezzel ist uns undertân,
> mir hie unt dir ze Brandigân.
> hilf mir durch dîne werdekeit
> Cunnewâren hulde umb krapfen breit.'
>   206.26-207.2

> [my Lord Seneschal of Clamide! Though I may never win your subduer's favour, you shall profit from your high office. For we are Lords of the Cauldron, I here and you there in Brandigan. By your noblesse, help me with large pancakes to win Cunneware's good graces.]

Whilst this does imply acknowledgement on the part of Keie that he owes something to Cunneware, the idea that a helping of fried food might cancel out a prolonged public beating is preposterous:

> die Tatsache, daß er zum symbolischen Gesten nicht in der Lage ist (Keie glaubt, Cunneware durch süßes Gebäck [*crâpfen*, 207,2]) versöhnen zu können, [...] nähert Keies Status fast schon dem von Primaten an.'
>   (Fritsch-Rößler 1997: 97, n. 33)

> [The fact that he is unable to make symbolic gestures (Keie believes that he will be able to mollify Cunneware with sweet confectionary [*crâpfen*, 207,2]) [...] almost reduces Keie's status to that of a primate.]

Furthermore, the gesture of sending an inadequate or inappropriate gift is in itself an aggressive strategy: it not only belittles the suffering of the victim, but – assuming that the recipient of the gift refuses to take on the awkward and unwelcome burden of gratitude – it also provides the perpetrator with with a pretext for casting himself in a victim role. An unappreciated or unaccetable gift may therefore serve as a device to remove the victim from her moral high ground and to create a false equality between the two parties, each being supposedly guilty of having injured the other.

There is conceivably a sexual innuendo in the reference to 'krapfen' – particularly to thick, broad ones. In that case, Keie may just be making a misogynist joke to his male colleague, without ever intending actually to cook any for Cunneware. It is also possible that Keie does send her some real 'krapfen', in addition to making a private joke to Kingrun that undercuts any impression of genuine regret. Or it may be that 'krapfen' really are the very best that Keie can come up with in the way of conciliatory measures. In any case, the narrator points out that this represents the absolute limit of Keie's penance: 'er bôt ir anders wandels niht' [He offered her no other amends] (207.4).

With the arrival of Clamide, Keie shifts tactics, opting for a more openly aggressive stance of self-justification, whilst as the same time entrenching himself further in the victim-role. Wolfram uses this episode to spell out just how closely Cunneware is forced to interact with Keie, despite his treatment of her: when Clamide arrives, Cunneware and Ginover are eating together, with Keie in attendance. This physical proximity – and the resulting transparency of any body language – adds tension to the very different ways in which they experience the news of Parzival's latest triumph:

> Keie ouch vor dem tische stuont,
> aldâ im wart diz mære kuont.
> der widersaz im ein teil:
> des wart frou Cunnewâre geil.
>   218.17-20

[Keie was standing by the table and heard what had been said. It gave him a perceptible shock, which delighted Lady Cunneware.]

The 'des' [which] in line 218.20 appears to refer specifically to the preceding line ('der widersaz im ein teil' [It gave him a perceptible shock]): whilst Cunneware would in any case have rejoiced at Parzival's defeat of Clamide, she is presented as being particularly pleased with the way in which Keie is discomfited by the news. The text does not elaborate on the way in which her state of mind (i.e. of feeling 'geil' [delighted]) is reflected in sound or gesture, but the audience might readily contrast her current mocking stance with the purely celebratory nature of the prophetic laughter that greeted Parzival. Even if she does not now laugh or gloat out loud, her opponent is left in no doubt of regarding her state of mind.

Keie retaliates with a speech that one could almost describe as his Hagen-moment, by reference to the scene in the *Nibelungenlied* in which Hagen rests Sifrit's sword on his legs and speaks openly to Kriemhild of what he did to her husband.[10] Here, Keie too may to some extent be seen to take defiant ownership of his past action:

> ich tetz durch hoflîchen site
> und wolt iuch hân gebezzert mite:
> dar umbe hân ich iwern haz.
> 218.25-27
>
> [I did what I did for the sake of courtly standards and with intent to improve your manners, for which I now suffer your ill will.]

However, unlike Hagen, Keie mingles his defiance with more defensive strategies: his self-justification and implied claim to victimhood are predicated on the presumption that Cunneware has no grounds for persisting in her 'haz' [ill will] when he was only doing his job. In other words, the relationship is reconfigured to suggest that he, not she, is the victim of unauthorized punishment.

With the arrival of Orilus, Keie alters his approach yet again. Whilst he would presumably have known all along that Cunneware's brother Orilus is a fierce and proud knight, the actual presence of this knight at court causes him to withdraw altogether from public view. With a newly acquired sense of tact, he realises that the Cunneware (and her brother) might prefer to be served by somebody other than himself and accordingly asks Kingrun to take his place:

> Kei bat Kingrûnen
> Orilus dienn an sîner stat.
> 278.28-29
>
> [Keie asked Kingrun to wait on Orilus in his stead.]

Silent skulking has thus become his last resort, after the failure of his previous stances (gift-giving; defiance; self-justification and self-pity). There is also the possibility that Keie is genuinely frightened of reprisals from Orilus. Konrad von Würzburg's *Heinrich von Kempten* recounts a situation in which a steward strikes

---

[10] See Hagen's defiant affirmation of his (mis-)deed in *Nibelungenlied* 1787.1

an aristocratic child for misbehaving at table; however, the child's guardian (the eponymous Heinrich) then retaliates by killing the steward with a club. This story makes the point that it is potentially dangerous for stewards to take action against well-connected individuals, even in cases of clear-cut transgressions against courtly etiquette.

In the aftermath of Keie's attacks on Cunneware and Antanor, public opinion grows increasingly critical of him. After the arrival of Clamide,

> dô sprâchens alle gelîche,
> beide arm und rîche,
> daz Keie hete missetân.
> 222.7-9

[High and low, they all agreed that Keie had misbehaved.]

Orilus' public complaint to Artus makes things even worse, with Keie experiencing 'niwen haz' [animosity of a new intensity] from all the knights and ladies at Plimizœl (277.1-3). Not even Kingrun feels much respect for him, despite the bonds of collegiality; although willing to step in to wait on Orilus, Kingrun also comments privately to Clamide on the irony of the fact that, given Parzival's string of victories, the Arthurian court has in fact increased its renown as a consequence of Keie's stupidity:

> sol Artûs dâ von prîs nu tragn,
> daz Kai durch zorn hât geslagen
> ein edele fürstinne,
> diu mit herzen sinne
> ir mit lachen hât erwelt
> der âne liegen ist gezelt
> mit wârheit für den hôhsten prîs?
> 221.19-25

[Is Arthur now to reap the glory because Keie in his anger struck a noble princess when she, divining it in her heart, laughed, and so chose the man who is held in all truth to be the most illustrious of all?]

In this increasingly critical environment, only the narrator comes out in support of Keie. Initially this support is indirect, in so far as he refuses to dwell on the steward's humiliation and instead makes a point of moving the narrative on as quickly as possible. After reporting in 222.7-9 that the whole court now condemns Keie's action, he effectively hurries the audience past this painful point in the narrative:

die sule wir diz mære lân,
und komens wider an die vart.
                    222.10-11

[But let us leave this and return to where we were.]

This matches an earlier comment made in the context of Keie's attempt to mollify Cunneware with the 'krapfen':

er bôt ir anders wandels niht.
die rede lât sîn, hœrt waz geschiht
dâ wir diz mære liezen ê.
                    207.3-5

[He offered her no other amends. But let that pass, and hear how it continues where we left the story.]

Again, lines 207.4 and 207.5 serve as an indirect defence of Keie, discouraging any further reflection on the question of whether Keie was wrong not to offer her further amends or compensation.

As the public criticism intensifies, the narrator becomes more explicit in his support for Keie. He commends Keie's decision to stand aside from table-service as being motivated by 'zuht' [propriety] (279.6), and ascribes his earlier loss of control to 'unsælde' [ill-luck] (279.4):

Keie durch daz sîn dienst liez:
unsælde ins fürsten swester hiez
ze sêre âlûnn mit eime stabe:
durch zuht entwiech er diens abe
                    279.2-5

[The reason why Keie relinquished serving Orilus was that he had been prompted by his ill-luck to thrash that prince's sister too energetically with his stave. It was his sense of propriety that made him yield this service.]

In other words, even as Keie is praised for a rather feeble attempt at damage-limitation, his direct responsibility for the original transgression is played down through the ascription of agency to an abstract personification.

The narrator's support for the underdog Keie may also be invoked as the motivation behind his puzzling criticism of Cunneware as 'lôs' (284.12).[11] The context for this comment is the misunderstanding that results from Parzival's love-

---

[11] Hatto (1980) translates this term as 'flighty'; however, this article will argue against such an understanding of it.

trance. Cunneware's page mistakes the immobile hero for an aggressor and seeks to rouse the entire camp against him:

> als gein einem æhtære
> schupfterz volc hin ûz an in:
> er wolt im werben ungewin.
>   284.8-10
>
> [He called out the retinue and set them on to him, meaning to do him harm as though he were an outlaw.]

The narrator notes that the creation of this hostile and unnecessary din reflects badly on the courtly standing of the page: 'sîne kurtôsîe er dran verlôs' [He thereby lost all claim to being thought courtly] (284.9). However, this criticism of the page is immediately relativized by a barbed narratorial comment directed against Cunneware: 'lât sîn: sîn frouwe was ouch lôs' (284.12).[12]

This comment is clearly not complimentary, although there is some lack of clarity as to what exactly the narrator means.[13] One line of interpretation takes the line as an imputation of sexual impropriety (i.e. suggesting that Cunneware is in some sense 'loose' or morally lax). However, as the narrative itself gives little basis for this view, it only makes sense as an expression of the inadequate (and lustful) narrator's wishful thinking.[14] Another line of interpretation links the term 'lôs' back to Cunneware's pivotal moment of laughter, arguing that – notwithstanding the prophetic and exceptional nature of that laughter – she is now being criticized for lacking the self-control required of courtly women. Elisabeth Lienert in particular argues that the narrator is suddenly, and unreasonably, invoking the discourses of 'Frauenerziehungslehren' [manuals of female good behaviour] as promulgated by Thomasin von Zerklaere and in the *Winsbeckin* (Lienert 2002: 236). The point of comparison would then be that the page and Cunneware are equally uncontrolled in their generation of noise – albeit with the key difference that the page's noise results from his failure to recognize Parzival, whilst Cunneware's laughter was triggered precisely by the accuracy of her recognition. However, as noted earlier, Keie's objection was to not to female laughter *per se*, but to the particular prophetic context.

Instead of treating 'noisy response to Parzival' as the key point linking Cunneware and the page, it might be more productive to focus on 'hostility' as the common

---

[12] Hatto (1980): 'Yet no matter, his lady, too, was flighty.'
[13] 'Lôs' can have positive connotations ('fröhlich, freundlich, anmutig') as well as neutral ('frei, ledig') and negative ones ('leichtfertig, durchtrieben, verschalgen, frech'); see Lexer (1872-78: II, 1956).
[14] Nellmann (1994: II, 605), with parallels; similarly Nellmann (1994: II, 655, commenting on 424.4). For the lustfulness of the narrator, see also Nellmann (1973: 14).

denominator. This reading will involve treating 'lôs' not as a self-standing adjective, but rather as one with a genitive object, implied in this case by the quality 'kurtôsîe' [courtliness] mentioned in the previous line.[15] The analogy would then work as follows: the page loses his 'kurtôsîe' because of his unkind and inappropriate attempt to make Parzival suffer 'ungewin' [harm] – whether this attempt was particularly noisy is relatively unimportant. Similarly, Cunneware is said to have become 'lôs' (i.e. deficient) in 'kurtôsîe', not because she laughed in the first place, but because she subsequently maintained a stance of wishing 'ungewin' on Keie – and rejoicing (becoming 'geil') at his embarrassment. Her state of 'haz' may not be backed up by specific action, but it contributes to Keie's sense of social exclusion – and passive aggression is never very gracious. The irony is that at the point when Keie struck Cunneware (presenting himself as the safety-net designed to catch her renown), she really was entirely faultless, but by the time that his come-uppance is imminent, her punitive stance has, according to the narrator, led precisely to such a slippage in her 'kurtôsîe'. Keie, by contrast, has meanwhile been praised for his 'zuht' [propriety] in standing down from table service. The key term 'kurtôsîe' also recurs shortly afterwards in *laudatio* of Keie, when the narrator reassures his audience that Keie would willingly serve anybody in possession of that quality:

> an swem diu kurtôsîe
> unt diu werde cumpânîe
> lac, den kunder êren,
> sîn dienst gein im kêren.
>   297.1-4

[Those who were truly well-bred and genuinely companionable he always served and honoured.]

This declaration strengthens the case for thinking that anybody hostile to Keie must indeed be lacking in 'kurtôsîe'.

The reader may well wonder how Cunneware could possibly have been expected to behave better than she actually does: she does not rant or complain; does not incite men to fight on her behalf; and does not attempt to take legal action. However, she is also less forgiving than the two other victims of male domination – Jeschute and Enite – to whom she is linked genealogically and intertextually (Draesner 1993: 247-48). Unlike Cunneware, these two women both prove themselves to be astonishingly free from any resentment towards their male oppressors. Jeschute in particular is remarkable for the way in which she, 'diu senfte süeze wol getân' [the sweet gentle

---

[15] See Lexer (1872-78: II, 1956): 'befreit, beraubt von, mit gen.'

lovely woman], goes straight from her bony nag into the bath-tub, and from the bath-tub to Orilus' bed (273.15-17). There is of course a significant difference between Cunneware and the two other women, in that these are tormented by the man whom they love. Nonetheless, the motif of undeserved female suffering remains the common denominator – and the common test of character. All three women are listed positively as equal paragons of female beauty in 187.14-15, at a point in the story that comes after the beating of Cunneware, but before we have heard about her sustained coldness towards Keie. However, once the narrative focus shifts back to the tensions of the Arthurian court, it becomes clear that Cunneware differs from the two others in her disposition towards nurturing grievances.

Parzival is a text that places extraordinary moral demands on some of its characters. If Kriemhild had simply remained in a state of frosty passivity, neither Hagen nor, presumably, the narrator of the *Nibelungenlied* would have been particularly concerned; but for Wolfram's narrator, female 'haz' is problematic and transgressive, even when it does not translate into direct action. For Chrétien's narrator, it is not only natural, but also commendable that the maiden should remain angry with the man who struck her. Indeed, her stance is evaluated by reference to masculine norms:

> De la bufe que ele ot prise
> estoit ele bien respassee,
> mes oblïee ne passee
> la honte n'avoit ele mie,
> que mout est malvés qui oblie,
> s'an li fet honte ne leidure.
> Dolors trespasse et honte dure
> an home viguereus et roide,
> et el malvés muert et refroide.
> 2896-904

[She had recovered fully from the pain of the slap but she had not overcome or forgotten the insult, for only a coward overlooks it when he is shamed or insulted: pain passes and shame endures in a sturdy and healthy man, but cools and dies in a coward.]

By contrast, Wolfram's narrator has a particular agenda concerning the normativity of womanly 'triuwe' [loyalty] (Volfing 2004) and consequently expects his female characters to respond to ill-treatment with unflappable acceptance and forgiveness. Nonetheless, the bar is also set very high for some male characters: Parzival himself is subjected to serious criticism (intra- and extra-diegetically) for nothing more than having maintained the wrong inner stance at a given moment in the Grail Castle, whilst other get away scot-free with serious criminal acts.

This being said, the *laudatio* of Keie represents a moment of extreme and combative partisanship, from which the narrator effectively backs down as the narrative progresses. As noted above, Keie's final appearance in the text is not a glorious one: whilst everybody else has moved on by Book XIV, he is still nurturing a grievance against Gawan for not avenging the blows inflicted on him by Parzival. By contrast, Cunneware's star rises with the progression of the text, to such an extent that in the catalogue of female suffering at the end of Book VI, she is placed alongside Jeschute in a two-fold example of honour restored: 'ir bêder scham hât prîs genomn' [Their humiliation has turned to high renown] (337.22).

It is, however, noteworthy that Cunneware should not allowed to reach this state of renown without undergoing more suffering. Cunneware's weeping marks the first public response to Parzival's disgrace: 'Cunnewâr daz êrste weinen huop' [The first to weep [...] was Cunneware] (319.12; see Seeber 2010: 154). Whilst her tears at this point stand in most obvious structural opposition to her earlier prophetic laughter, serving to mark out the stations of Parzival's career, one may also see an opposition between this unhappiness and her earlier state of feeling 'geil'. Unlike the first opposition, which operates on a symbolic level, this secondary opposition relates directly to the construction of Cunneware as a psychologically credible individual whose emotional reaction is motivated by a mixture of compassion with Parzival and intense personal disappointment at having her sense of triumph snatched away so soon. With these tears, the narrator himself constructs a low-key but poignant punishment for Cunneware that fulfils most of the criteria outlined at the start of this paper: it is predicated on hierarchical inequality, it aims to correct a fault in the victim, and it serves to restore normal social relations.[16] Only after having been made to weep in this way is Cunneware once again worthy of being mentioned in the same breath as the ever-compliant Jeschute.

---

[16] The tears of Orgeluse in 602.18 may be interpreted in a similar way: by making her weep at the point when Gawan tumbles into 'Li gweiz prelljus', Wolfram is arguably not only demonstrating her capacity for love and compassion, but also punishing her for her previous unkind and exploitative behaviour.

Works Cited

Primary Sources

Chrétien de Troyes, *Le Conte du Graal (Perceval)*, ed. Félix Lecoy, Les Classiques Français du Moyen Age, 2 vols (Paris: Editions Champion, 1972)

Chrétien de Troyes, *The Story of the Grail (Perceval)*, in *Arthurian Romances*, trans. William W. Kibler (London: Penguin, 1991), pp. 381-494

Konrad von Würzburg, *Heinrich von Kempten; Der Welt Lohn; Das Herzmære*, ed. Edward Schröder, trans. into modern German by Heinz Rölleke, Reclams Universal-Bibliothek, 2855 (Stuttgart: Reclam, 1965)

Das Nibelungenlied, ed. Ursula Schulze, trans. into modern German by Siegfried Grosse, Reclams Universal-Bibliothek, 18914 (Stuttgart: Reclam, 2010)

Wolfram von Eschenbach, *Parzival*, ed. Karl Lachmann, revisions and commentary by Eberhard Nellmann, trans. into modern German by Dieter Kühn, Bibliothek des Mittelalters, 8/1-2, 2 vols (Frankfurt a. M.: Deutscher Klassiker Verlag, 1994)

Wolfram von Eschenbach, *Parzival*, trans. A.T. Hatto (London: Penguin, 1980)

Secondary Sources

Baisch, Martin. 2003. '*Welt ir: er vervellet; / Wellent ir; er ist genesen!* Zur Figur Keies in Heinrichs von dem Turlin 'Diu Crône'', in *Aventiuren des Geschlechts: Modelle von Männlichkeit in der Literatur des 13. Jahrhunderts*, ed. Martin Baische, Hendrikje Haufe, Michael Mecklenburg, Matthias Meyer and Andrea Sieber, Aventiuren, 1 (Göttingen: V & R unipress), pp. 149-73

Classen, Albrecht. 1988. 'Keie in Wolframs von Eschenbach *Parzival*: "Agent Provocateur" oder Angeber?', *Journal for English and Germanic Philology*, 87: 382-405

Däumer, Matthias. 2011. 'Truchsess Keie: Von Mythos eines Lästermauls', in *Artusroman und Mythos*, ed. Friedrich Wolfzettel, Cora Dietl and Matthias Däumer, Schriften der Internationales Artusgesellschaft, 8 (Berlin: De Gruyter), pp. 69-108

Draesner, Ulrike. 1993. *Wege durch erzählte Welten: intertextuelle Verweise als Mittel der Bedeutungskonstitution in Wolframs 'Parzival'*. Mikrokosmos, 36 (Frankfurt a. M.: Peter Lang)

Emmelius, Caroline. 2010. *Gesellige Ordnung: literarische Konzeptionen von geselliger Kommunikation in Mittelalter und Früher Neuzeit*, Frühe Neuzeit, 139 (Berlin: De Gruyter)

Erfen, Irene. 1994. 'Das Lachen der Cunneware: Bemerkungen zu Wagners *Parsifal* und Wolframs *Parzival*', in *Sprachspiel und Lachkultur: Beiträge zur Literatur- und Sprachgeschichte, Rolf Bräuer zum 60. Geburtstag*, ed. Angela Bader, Annemarie Eder, Irene Erfen and Ulrich Müller, Stuttgarter Arbeiten zur Germanistik, 300 (Stuttgart: Heinz), pp. 69-87

Fritsch-Rößler, Waltraud. 1997. 'Lachen und Schlagen. Reden als Kulturtechnik in Wolframs *Parzival*', in *Verstehen durch Vernunft: Festschrift für Werner Hoffmann*, ed. Burkhardt Krause, Philologica Germanica, 19 (Vienna: Fassbaender), pp. 75-98

Green, D. H. 1982. *The Art of Recognition in Wolfram's 'Parzival'* (Cambridge: Cambridge University Press)

Hatto, Arthur. 1980. See above under Wolfram von Eschenbach, *Parzival*

Haupt, Jürgen. 1971. *Der Truchsess Keie im Artusroman: Untersuchungen zur Gesellschaftsstruktur im höfischen Roman*, Philologische Studien und Quellen, 57 (Berlin: Erich Schmidt)

Huber, Christoph. 1998. 'Lachen im höfischen Roman: Zu einigen komplexen Episoden im literarischen Transfer', in *Kultureller Austausch und Literaturgeschichte im Mittelalter: Kolloquium im Deutschen Institut Paris, 16.-18.3.1995*, ed. Ingrid Kasten, Werner Paravicini and René Pérennec, Beihefte zu Francia, 43 (Sigmaringen: Jan Thorbecke), pp. 345-58

Kibler, William W. 1991. See above under Chrétien de Troyes, *The Story of the Grail (Perceval)*

Kühn, Dieter. 1994. See above under Wolfram von Eschenbach, *Parzival*

Lexer, Matthias. 1872-78. *Mittelhochdeutsches Handwörterbuch*, 3 vols (Leipzig: Hirzel)

Lienert, Elisabeth. 2002. 'Zur Diskursivität der Gewalt in Wolframs 'Parzival'', in *Wolfram von Eschenbach – Bilanzen und Perspektiven: Eichstätter Kolloquium 2000*, ed. Wolfgang Haubrichs, Eckart C. Lutz and Klaus Ridder, Wolfram-Studien, 17 (Berlin: Erich Schmidt), pp. 223-45

Nellmann, Eberhard. 1973. *Wolframs Erzähltechnik: Untersuchungen zur Funktion des Erzählers* (Wiesbaden: Steiner)

—. 1994. See above under Wolfram von Eschenbach, *Parzival*

Nozick, Robert. 1983. *Philosophical Explanations* (Cambridge, MA: Harvard University Press)

Philipowski, Katharina. 2003. 'Das Gelächter der Cunnewâre', *Zeitschrift für Germanistik* N. F., 13: 9-25

Röcke, Werner. 2001. 'Provokation und Ritual: Das Spiel mit der Gewalt und die soziale Funktion des Seneschall Keie im arthurischen Roman', in *Der Fehltritt: Vergehen und Versehen in der Vormoderne*, ed. Peter von Moos and Klaus Schreiner, Norm und Struktur, 15 (Cologne: Böhlau), pp. 343-61

Scheuble, Robert. 2005. *mannes manheit, vrouwen meister: Männliche Sozialisation und Formed der Gewalt gegen Frauen im Nibelungenlied und in Wolframs von Eschenbach Parzival*, Kultur, Wissenschaft, Literatur, 6 (Frankfurt a. M.: Peter Lang)

Schonert, Christiane. 2009. *Figurenspiele: Identität und Rollen Keies in Heinrichs von dem Türlin 'Crône'*, Philologische Studien und Quellen, 217 (Berlin: Erich Schmidt)

Seeber, Stefan. 2010. *Poetik des Lachens: Untersuchungen zum mittelhochdeutschen Roman um 1200*, Münchener Texte und Untersuchungen zur deutschen Literatur des Mittelalters, 140 (Berlin/New York: De Gruyter)

Volfing, Annette. 2004. '*Welt ir nu hæren fürbaz?* On the Function of the Loherangrin-episode in Wolfram von Eschenbach's *Parzival*', *Beiträge zur Geschichte der deutschen Sprache und Literatur*, 126: 65-84

Volkmann, Berndt. 1995. '*Costumiers est de dire mal*: Überlegungen zur Funktion des Streites und zur Rolle Keies in der Pfingstfestszene in Hartmanns Iwein', in *bickelwort und wildiu mære: Festschrift für Eberhard Nellmann zum 65. Geburtstag*, ed. Dorothee Lindemann, Berndt Volkmann and Klaus-Peter Wegera, Göppinger Arbeiten zur Germanistik, 618 (Göppingen, Kümmerle), pp. 95-108

Wand-Wittkowski, Christine. 1989. *Wolfram von Eschenbach und Hartmann von Aue: literarische Reaktionen auf Hartmann im 'Parzival'* (Herne: Verlag für Wissenschaft und Kunst)

Wenzel, Franziska. 2001. 'Keie und Kalogrenant: Zur kommunikativen Logik höfischen Erzählens in Hartmanns *Iwein*', in *Literarische Kommunikation und soziale Interaktion: Studien zur Institutionalität mittelalterlicher Literatur*, ed. Beate Kellner, Ludger Lieb and Peter Strohschneider, Mikrokosmos, 64 (Frankfurt a. M.: Peter Lang), 89-109

Zaibert, Leo. 2006. *Punishment and Retribution* (Aldershot: Ashgate)

4

Sünder, Prediger, Dichter: Rollenspiele im *Beichtlied* Oswalds von Wolkenstein

Andreas Kraß
Humboldt-Universität zu Berlin

Michel Foucault illustriert in seinem Buch *Überwachen und Strafen* (Foucault 1994: 251-94) die Entstehung der modernen Disziplinargesellschaft am Prinzip des Panoptikons. Gemeint ist damit eine Gefängnisarchitektur, die von einem Wachtturm aus, der in der Mitte eines kreis- oder sternförmigen Gebäudes steht, einen allumfassenden Blick in die offenen Zellen erlaubt. Die Vorstellung des Panoptikons kann auch hilfreich sein, um die zentrale Pointe des *Beichtlieds* Oswalds von Wolkenstein zu erfassen. Oswald inszeniert sich einerseits als Sünder, der, nach einem Blick in den Beichtspiegel, vor den Priestern ein umfassendes Geständnis seiner Fehltritte ablegt und sich so der kirchlichen Disziplinarmacht unterwirft. Andererseits nimmt er zugleich die Rolle des Dichters ein, der die Systematik der Sündenkataloge souverän überblickt, in den komplexen Strophenbau seines Liedes einpasst und somit poetisch diszipliniert. So spielt Oswald ein doppeltes Spiel im Spannungsfeld von Strafe und Strophe: Er konterkariert die Selbstunterwerfung in der Rolle des Sünders mit der Selbstüberhöhung in der Rolle des Dichters.

Rollenspiele
Der Musikwissenschaftler Walter Salmen folgte der Einladung Oswald von Wolkenstein, die Ich-Aussagen seiner Lieder als autobiographische Zeugnisse zu lesen. Aus dem sogenannten *Beichtlied*, in dem sich Oswald bezichtigt, alle Sünden begangen zu haben, die aus christlichen Sündenkatalogen bekannt sind, zog Salmen den Schluss, dass der tirolische Liederdichter am Ende seiner Tage den irdischen Freuden abgeschworen habe: ‚In sich gekehrt, Abschied nehmend von einem erlebnisreichen Lebenswandel gab er seinem Gesange anstelle der früher betonten *‚kurzweil'* den moralisierenden Zweck, zu *‚lern ... vil hoveleut und mangen ungewissen mensch'*. Der Vanitas-Gedanke ergriff ihn; aller frühere Sängerglanz zählte nun nicht mehr, denn der nahende Tod nimmt alle Erdenfreuden zurück' (Salmen 1974: 244). Lambertus Okken schloss sich dieser Auffassung

an. Die namentliche Selbstnennung des Wolkensteiners sei ‚nur als Bestandteil religiöser Kontexte belegt' und gehöre daher ‚in die Tradition der christlichen Demutsformel'; dieser Sachverhalt verbiete es, ‚in der Namenformel einen diesseitig orientierten Autorenstolz zu bemerken' (Okken 1974: 214). Kein ‚Sängerglanz', kein ‚Autorenstolz' also im *Beichtlied* Oswalds von Wolkenstein? Regina Toepfer gelangt in einem Beitrag zu den autobiographischen Elementen in Oswalds Liedern zu einem anderen Schluss. Sie wertet die Selbstnennungen als ‚Indiz für ein ausgeprägtes Selbstbewusstsein des Dichters' und als ‚Ironiesignal'. Oswald spiele mit dem Kontrast zwischen seiner turbulenten Biographie und der moralischen Rolle des Predigers, die er im *Beichtlied* einnehme: ‚Ausgerechnet dem Wolkensteiner hat Gott den Rat erteilt, andere zur Beichte zu führen' (Toepfer 2013: 236). Es sei ganz unwahrscheinlich, dass der Dichter alle Sünden, die er sich in seinem Lied vorwerfe, tatsächlich begangen haben könne. Folglich seien in diesem und anderen Liedern Oswalds von Wolkenstein zwei Rollen auseinanderzuhalten, die letztlich unvereinbar sind: die Rolle des *Sünders* und die Rolle des *Predigers*. Indem Oswald von einer Rolle in die andere hinübertrete, mache er das Rollenspiel als solches performativ sichtbar: ‚Nicht nur das umfangreiche Register, die Anzahl und Vielfalt der Sünden lassen meines Erachtens Zweifel an einer autobiographischen Auslegung aufkommen, vielmehr verbietet die divergierende Rollenzuschreibung innerhalb des Textes eine Gleichsetzung von historischem Autor und Sprecher-Ich. Indem der Bußprediger aus der Rolle des Sünders tritt, wird offenbart, dass es sich um die literarische Inszenierung eines erbaulich-katechetischen Rollenspiels handelt' (Toepfer 2013: 236).

Im Folgenden möchte ich mich Regina Toepfers Thesen zum Rollenspiel des Autors anschließen und sie um einen weiteren Aspekt ergänzen. Mir scheint, dass zu den Rollen des Sünders und Predigers, die Oswald in seinem *Beichtlied* einnimmt, noch eine dritte hinzutritt, nämlich die Rolle des Dichters. Das Lied impliziert meines Erachtens eine poetologische Reflexion, die das Selbstverständnis des Autors charakterisiert. Bei meinen Beobachtungen gehe ich zunächst von der Komposition des Liedes aus. Dieses umfasst drei Teile und fünf Abschnitte. Der erste Teil ist eine Apostrophe an den Priester, mit der das Lied beginnt und schließt. Der zweite Teil ist die Aufzählung der Sünden, die zunächst *en detail* erfolgt und dann summarisch wiederholt wird. Der dritte Teil thematisiert die Rolle des Sängers vor seinem Publikum. Das Lied weist somit eine geschachtelte Struktur auf:

A	1. Einleitende Apostrophe an den Priester: Reue (I, 1-8)
B	2. Detailliertes Sündenbekenntnis (I, 9 - V, 4)
C	3. Selbstthematisierung als Sänger (V, 5-12)
B	4. Summarisches Sündenbekenntnis (VI, 1-7)
A	5. Abschließende Apostrophe an den Priester: Bitte (VI, 8-12)

Mit dieser Einteilung folgt das Lied dem Aufbau des christlichen Beichtrituals und des mittelalterlichen Beichtgebets, das vom Gläubigen eine Erklärung der Reue (vgl. Abschnitt 1), ein Bekenntnis der Sünden (vgl. Abschnitte 2 und 4) und eine Bitte um Vergebung (vgl. Abschnitt 5) verlangt (vgl. Bruchhold 2010: 506-34).[1] Der dritte Abschnitt fällt aus diesem Zusammenhang heraus, denn er stellt keinen liturgischen, sondern einen poetologischen Sprechakt dar. Entscheidend ist, dass die Wiederholungen der Teile A und B, also die Abschnitte 4 und 5, vom Zentrum des Liedes, also der Selbstthematisierung des Sängers, geprägt sind (C). Sowohl im summarischen Sündenbekenntnis als auch in der abschließenden Apostrophe an den Priester schwingt die poetologische Reflexion weiter mit. Neben der Komposition des Liedes ist auch die Komposition der Strophen relevant. Das Lied folgt der Form der Kanzone. Die Strophen teilen sich in einen Aufgesang, der aus zwei gleich gebauten Stollen besteht, und einen Abgesang. Im vorliegenden Lied umfasst jede dieser Partien vier Verse. Die Einteilung der Strophen in drei gleich große Abschnitte disponiert eine entsprechende Gliederung auf inhaltlicher Ebene.

Der Sünder

Der Sprecher beginnt und beschließt das Lied in der Rolle des Sünders. Die betreffenden Partien sind jeweils durch explizite Anreden an den Priester markiert: ‚eu, priester' (I, 1) und ‚o priester' (VI, 8). Der Aufgesang der ersten Strophe ist der Rolle des Sünders vorbehalten. Im ersten Vers weist sich der Sprecher als Sünder aus, indem er das *Mea culpa* spricht: ‚Mein sünd und schuld'. Die Selbstanklage richtet sich an den Priester, der als Stellvertreter Gottes angesprochen wird: ‚an stat, der alle ding vermag' (I, 2). Die Umschreibung Gottes als Allmächtiger impliziert, dass er auch die übergroße Sünde des Sprechers zu vergeben vermöchte. An der Kommunikationssituation der Beichte sind folglich drei Parteien beteiligt: der Sprecher, der Priester und Gott. Sie formieren eine Hierarchie, in der Gott oben, der Sünder unten und der Priester in der Mitte steht. Als Spender des Beichtsakraments ist der Priester dem Sünder übergeordnet; zugleich ist er Gott untergeordnet, dessen Stelle er vertritt. Im dritten und vierten Vers bringt der Sprecher zum Ausdruck, in welcher Haltung er beichten will: unbeschönigt (‚grob'), offenherzig (‚lauter'),

---

[1] Bruchhold erwähnt das *Beichtlied* Oswalds von Wolkenstein nur am Rande (2010: 17, Anm. 34).

zerknirscht („schamrot'), gottesfürchtig („vorchtlich'), andächtig („durch andacht') und reuevoll („nasser augen'). Damit beweist der die reuige Haltung, derer es für die Wirksamkeit der Beichte bedarf. Die asyndetische Häufung der Adverbien lenkt die Aufmerksamkeit nicht nur auf die Reue des Sprechers, sondern auch auf den Akt des Sprechens selbst. So kündigt sich bereits die Rolle des Dichters an, die später in den Vordergrund tritt. In den nächsten vier Versen (dem zweiten Stollen) versichert der Sprecher die Erfüllung weitere Bedingungen für eine wirksame Beichte: zum einen den Vorsatz, dass er künftig nicht mehr sündigen wolle (I, 5-6: ‚Und hab ein fürsatz, nimmermer / mit vleiss zu sünden, wo ich ker'), zum anderen die Freiwilligkeit der Beichte (I, 7: ‚diemüetiklich mit willen'). Diese Verse sind nicht mehr an den Priester, sondern an Gott selbst (I, 7: ‚herr') gerichtet, der somit als eigentlicher Adressat der Beichte ausgewiesen wird.

In den letzten fünf Versen der Schlussstrophe wendet sich der Sprecher erneut an den Priester, um nach abgelegtem Sündenbekenntnis Gnade (VI, 8: ‚hulde') und Vergebung (VI, 10: ‚ablas') zu erbitten. Er verknüpft diese Bitten mit Erinnerungen an die sieben Sakramente (VI, 9: ‚Durch hailikait der siben gab') und acht Seligkeiten (VI, 11: ‚acht sälikait ir nempt mir ab'), von denen schon im Sündenbekenntnis die Rede war. Der Priester soll also an jenen Gaben und Werten festhalten, die der Sprecher missachtet hat. Dies ist umso bemerkenswerter, als der Sprecher in der vierten Strophe bekennt, dass er das Sakrament der Priesterweihe entehrt habe: ‚Den priester ich smäch' (IV, 5). Der Sprecher hofft auf Vergebung des Priesters, den er zuvor geschmäht hat. Man könnte meinen, dass sich die Versündigung gegen das Sakrament der Priesterweihe in der Vielzahl der Sünden verliere, aber das ist nicht der Fall. Sie steht, wie sich gleich zeigen wird, genau in der Mitte des Sündenbekenntnisses. Man kann also festhalten, dass das Verhältnis zwischen Sprecher und Priester gestört ist und diese Störung durch die zentrale Position im Sündenbekenntnis in den Vordergrund gerückt wird. Hier zeichnet sich eine gewisse Rivalität ab, die noch deutlicher wird, wenn der Sprecher von der Rolle des Sünders in die Rolle des Predigers hinübertritt. Im letzten Vers nennt der Sprecher das Ziel seiner Beichte: die Erneuerung der geistlichen Liebe zu Gott, die er mit der Metapher des Brennens umschreibt. Auch diese Schlusswendung hat es in sich, wie ebenfalls noch zu zeigen sein wird.

Der Prediger
In der Rolle des Sünders ordnet sich der Sprecher dem Priester unter, in der Rolle des Predigers tritt er zu ihm in Konkurrenz. Der Rollenwechsel wird in der ersten Strophe in der Weise vorbereitet, dass der Sprecher den Adressaten wechselt. Der Aufgesang der ersten Strophe beginnt mit einer Apostrophe an den Priester und

endet mit einer Apostrophe an Gott. Im Abgesang der ersten Strophe setzt das umfangreiche Sündenbekenntnis ein, das zwei Partien umfasst: das Bekenntnis des Einzelsünden und die summarische Zusammenfassung. Das Bekenntnis wird als persönliche Beichte vorgestellt; insofern verbleibt der Sprecher in der Rolle des Sünders. Doch weist die systematische Vollständigkeit der aufgezählten Sündengruppen darauf hin, dass es sich nicht um eine individuelle, sondern eine exemplarische Beichte handelt, die den Charakter eines Beichtspiegels aufweist (Jones 1980). Im summarischen Teil wird die katechetische Systematik aufgedeckt, die nicht weniger als neun Sündenkategorien und 64 Einzelsünden umfasst:

1. Zehn Gebote (I, 9 - II, 7; vgl. VI, 1: ‚die zehen pot')
2. Sieben Todsünden (II, 8-12; vgl. VI, 2: ‚die siben todsünd')
3. Neun ‚fremde' Sünden (III, 1-4; vgl. VI, 3: ‚die fremden sünd')
4. Sieben Werke der Barmherzigkeit (III, 5-8; vgl. VI, 5: ‚Die hailigen werch der parmung')
5. Vier ‚rufende' Sünden (III, 9-12; vgl. VI, 7: ‚vier rueffend sünd')
6. Sieben Gaben des Heiligen Geistes (IV, 1-4; vgl. VI, 6: ‚die gab des hailgen gaistes')
7. Sieben Sakramente (IV, 5-8; vgl. VI, 9: ‚siben gab')
8. Acht Seligkeiten (IV, 9-12; vgl. VI, 11: ‚acht sälikait')
9. Fünf Sinne (V, 1-4; vgl. VI, 7: ‚fünf sinn')

Die Sündengruppen korrespondieren weitgehend mit der Gliederung der Strophen. Jeder Strophenabschnitt (Stollen, Abgesang) nimmt eine Kategorie auf. Die Zahl 64 betrifft nicht nur die Zahl der Einzelsünden, sondern auch die Zahl der Verse. Das Lied umfasst sechs Strophen mit je zwölf Versen, also insgesamt 72 Verse. Der Aufgesang der ersten Strophe bildet, wie bereits gezeigt wurde, eine Einheit, die dem Sündenbekenntnis vorausgeht. Nach Abzug der acht Verse des Aufgesangs bleiben 64 Verse übrig. Diese gliedern sich zwar in weitere Abschnitte, doch wird das Prinzip des Sündenbekenntnisses bis zum Schluss durchgehalten, denn die summarische Aufzählung der Sündenkategorien reicht bis in die Vergebungsbitte am Schluss des Liedes hinein (VI, 9: sieben Sakramente; VI, 11: acht Seligkeiten). Die Zahl der Einzelsünden entspricht also der Zahl der Verse, in denen die Sünden thematisiert werden. Die gezählte Frömmigkeit des Liedes findet ihre Entsprechung in der Zählung der Verse. Die Missachtung der Priesterweihe (wie auch des Ehesakraments) wird in der Mitte der 64 Verse thematisiert, die auf die Einleitung folgen, nämlich in Vers 33 (IV, 5). Auf diese Weise wird die Konkurrenz zwischen Sprecher und Priester markiert. Wenn der Sprecher zunehmend von der beichtenden Rolle des Sünders in die katechetische Rolle des Predigers wechselt, greift er gewissermaßen in die Kompetenzen der Priester ein. Das Sündenbekenntnis schlägt in eine Sündenlehre um, die im summarischen Teil, der die Systematik aufdeckt und benennt, in den Vordergrund tritt.

Zunächst liegt der Akzent noch auf der Rolle des Sünders. Die Systematik wird verdeckt, indem die Kategorien vorerst nicht benannt und die zugehörigen Sünden in aufgelockerter Weise präsentiert werden. Jeglicher Schematismus wird vermieden. So werden die Verfehlungen gegen die Zehn Gebote, die das Sündenbekenntnis eröffnen, in abweichender Reihenfolge dargeboten (Jones 1980: 641-43; Wachinger 2007: 385; Bruchhold 2010: 562-69). Zwar zielt der erste Vers auf das erste (I, 9: ‚An dem gelauben zweifel ich') und der zweite auf das zweite Gebot (I, 10: ‚pei gotes namen swer ich vast'), sodass das Muster des Dekalogs erkennbar wird, doch richten sich die nächsten Verse schon auf das vierte Gebot (I, 11-12: ‚mein vater und mueter erenrich / vertragen hab mit überlast'). Im weiteren Verlauf löst sich die Ordnung auf. Das nächste Verspaar (das erste der zweiten Strophe) greift das siebte, fünfte und neunte Gebot auf, präsentiert sie aber nicht nacheinander, sondern in verschränkter Form. Der erste Vers handelt vom Rauben, Stehlen und Töten (II, 1: ‚Raub, stelen, töten ist mir gach'), der zweite nennt in umgekehrter Reihenfolge die zugehörigen Objekte: Leib, Ehre und Besitz (II, 2: ‚leib, er und guet'). Das Paar *leib/töten* verweist auf das Tötungsverbot, das Paar *guet/raub* auf das Diebstahlverbot, das Paar *er/stelen* auf das Verbot, die Ehre des Nächsten zu verletzen, indem man dessen Frau begehrt. Mit ihrem dreigliedrigen Parallelismus weisen diese Verse ein eigenes kompositorisches Gepräge auf, das die Reihenfolge der Zehn Gebote in den Hintergrund treten lässt. Die nächsten Verse ergänzen nacheinander das dritte (II, 3: ‚banveir, vast tuen ich ungemach'), achte (II, 4: ‚falsch zeugknus füegt mir eben') und zehnte Gebot (II, 5: ‚Spil, fremder hab wird ich nicht vol'). Das sechste Gebot (Ehebruch) fehlt, wird aber im Kontext der sieben Sakramente nachgereicht (IV, 5: ‚mein e zerbrich'). Es folgen zwei abschließende Verse, die den Bezugsrahmen verlassen. In den Sünden der Zauberei, Lüge und Untreue (II, 6: ‚zoubri, lug, untreu') mögen noch einmal das erste, achte und neunte Gebot anklingen und die Sünden des Verrats und der Brandstiftung (II, 7: ‚verräterschaft, brand') mögen noch das Gewicht der Zehn Gebote haben – sie lassen sich diesen aber nicht mehr zuordnen.

Das Variationsprinzip setzt sich fort. Der zweiten Gruppe, den sieben Todsünden, sind fünf Verse gewidmet (Jones 1980: 643-44; Wachinger 2007: 385; Bruchhold 2010: 547-54). Der erste nennt die erste Todsünde, nämlich die Hoffart: ‚hochvertig ist mein leben' (II, 8). Der zweite nimmt die vierte Todsünde vorweg, nämlich den Geiz: ‚Von geitikait ich selten rue' (II, 9). Der dritte fasst drei Verfehlungen zusammen, von denen nur die zweite und dritte den Todsünden zugehören: Spott, Zorn und Unkeuschheit (II, 10: ‚spot, zoren, unkeusch ist mir kunt'). Die nächsten beiden Verse sind jeweils zweigliedrig gebaut. Der erste gliedert die Todsünde der Unmäßigkeit in zwei Aspekte: ‚überessen, -trinken spat und frue' (II, 11); der zweite präsentiert die Todsünden der Trägheit und des Neids als Paar und illustriert sie mit Tiervergleichen: ‚träg, neidig als der esel und hund' (II, 12).

Die dritte Gruppe umfasst die neun ‚fremden' Sünden, d.h. die Mitwirkung an Sünden, die von anderen ausgeführt werden (Jones 1980: 644-45; Wachinger 2007: 385; Bruchhold 2010: 560-62):[2] 1. Befehlen einer Sünde (*iussio*), 2. Raten zu einer Sünde (*consilium*), 3. Einwilligen in eine Sünde (*consensus*), 4. Loben einer Sünde (*palpo*), 5. Verstecken von Sündern (*recursus*), 6. Beteiligung an einer Sünde (*participans*), 7. Verschweigen einer Sünde (*mutus*), 8. Duldung einer Sünde (*non obstans*) und 9. Verhehlen einer Sünde (*non manifestans*). Oswald drängt sie in vier Versen zusammen. Zunächst bildet er parataktisch formulierte Sündenpaare. Der erste Vers vereint die erste (III, 1: ‚Die sünd ich haiss') und zweite (‚die sünd ich rat') Sünde, der zweite Vers die vierte (III, 2: ‚die sünd ich lieb')[3] und fünfte (‚und leich ir stat') Sünde. Dann zieht er mehrere Sünden syntaktisch zusammen, indem er sie auf die Satzglieder verteilt. So verschränkt der dritte Vers die dritte (III, 3: ‚günstlich') und achte (‚nicht understen die tat') Sünde, der vierte die sechste (III, 4: ‚tailhaft'), siebte (‚an [...] melden') und neunte (‚rüglichs').

Die vierte Gruppe zielt auf die sieben Werke der Barmherzigkeit (Jones 1980: 645-46; Wachinger 2007: 385; Bruchhold 2010: 544-47). Der erste Vers ist einem einzelnen Werk gewidmet: dem Bekleiden der Nackten (III, 5: ‚Den blossen hab ich nie erkennt'). Der zweite Vers fasst zwei verwandte Werke zusammen: das Speisen der Hungernden und Tränken der Dürstenden (III, 6: ‚armen durst, hungers nicht gewent'). Der dritte Vers reiht schlagwortartig die übrigen Werke: den Besuch der Kranken, das Begräbnis der Toten, die Befreiung der Gefangenen und die Beherbergung der Fremden (III, 7: ‚krank, tot, gevangen, ellend hend'). Der vierte Vers verweist zusammenfassend auf die prinzipielle Unbarmherzigkeit des Sprechers: ‚kain barmung nicht mag velden' (III, 8).

Die fünfte Gruppe umfasst die vier ‚rufenden' Sünden, d. h. eklatante Störungen der sozialen Ordnung (Jones 1980: 645; Wachinger 2007: 385; Bruchhold 2010: 541-42). Ihnen wird jeweils ein Vers und ein Satz eingeräumt. Die erste Sünde entspricht dem fünften Gebot: ‚Unschuldigs bluet vergossen han' (III, 9), die zweite

---

[2] Meine Zuordnung weicht von der von Jones (1980) vorgeschlagenen teilweise ab. Wachinger (2007) veranschlagt vier statt neun fremde Sünden.

[3] Wachinger (2007) bietet hier die Lesart des Textzeugen B (‚die sünd ich tuen'), übersetzt aber die Lesart des Textzeugen A (‚die sünd ich lieb'), für die er sich in der ersten Auflage seiner Ausgabe entschieden hatte und der ich hier folge (Wachinger 1992: 80).

besteht in der Bedrückung der Armen: ‚die armen leut beswär ich ser' (III ,10); die dritte zielt auf die Sodomie (im Sinne von Homosexualität): ‚ich kenn die sünd von Sodoman' (III, 11), die vierte meint die Vorenthaltung zustehenden Lohns: ‚verdienten lon nit halb gewer' (III, 12).

Die sechste Gruppe nennt die sieben Gaben des Heiligen Geistes, gegen die sich der Sprecher vergangen hat (Jones 1980: 645-46; Wachinger 2007: 385; Bruchhold 2010: 555-56). Oswald fasst sie in einem einzigen, über vier Verse reichenden Satz zusammen. Als Stilmittel verwendet er das Asyndeton und die anaphorische Wiederholung des Adjektivs *götlich* bzw. des Genitivattributs *gots*. Die genannten Gaben sind *weishait* (*sapientia*), *vernunft* (*intellectus*), *kunst* (*scientia*), *rat* (*consilium*), *sterk* (*fortitudo*), *inbrunst* (*pietas*), *vorcht* (*timor Dei*). Außerdem werden Gunst (*gunst*), Liebe (*lieb*) und Güte (*güet*) angeführt, die auf weitere Aspekte der *pietas* verweisen.

Die siebte Gruppe behandelt die sieben Sakramente (Jones 1980: 646; Wachinger 2007: 386; Bruchhold 2010: 557-58). Priesterweihe und Ehe werden in einem Vers zusammengefasst (IV,5: ‚Den priester ich smäch, mein e zerbrich'), ebenso Taufe und Firmung (IV, 6: ‚mein touf und firmung übersich'). Der Eucharistie ist ein eigener Vers gewidmet (IV, 7: ‚gots leichnam ich nim unwirdiklich'). Beichte und Krankensalbung werden wieder in einem Vers zusammengezogen (IV,8: ‚ölung, beicht, buess tuet mir ande'). Die synonyme Doppelformel *peicht* und *puess* hebt dasjenige Sakrament hervor, das Sujet des *Beichtlieds* ist.

Bei den Verfehlungen gegen die acht Seligkeiten trifft der Sprecher eine Auswahl (Jones 1980: 646-47; Wachinger 2007: 386; Bruchhold 2010: 558-60). Er bekennt, dass er mit Armut hadert (IV, 9: ‚Unwillig armuet') und weder Gerechtigkeit (IV, 10: ‚gots recht'), Barmherzigkeit (IV, 11: ‚an barmherzikait'), Sanftmütigkeit (IV, 12: ‚ich hass nach gunst mit zoren') noch Herzensreinheit (IV, 9-10: ‚übelhait / treib ich durch zeit verloren') übt. Die Seligkeiten der Trauer, Friedfertigkeit und Verfolgung werden nicht mehr genannt.

Der Sündenkatalog schließt mit dem Missbrauch der fünf Sinne (Jones 1980: 647-48; Wachinger 2007: 386; Bruchhold 2010: 542-44): Sehen und Hören (V, 1: ‚Mein sehen, hören süntlich brauch'), Riechen und Schmecken (V, 2: ‚mein kosten, smecken lustlich slauch'), Tasten (V, 3 f.: ‚mein greifen [...] verdauch / unfrüchtiklich dem herren'). Dem Tastsinn werden noch das Gehen und Denken (V, 3: ‚gen, gedenk') hinzugefügt, die nicht zu den fünf Sinnen zählen.

Während Oswald den Sündenkatalog der Strophen I bis V in poetisch aufgelockerter Weise in einer exemplarisch zu verstehenden Ich-Rolle darbietet, deckt Strophe VI mit der summarischen Auflistung der Sündenkategorien das katechetische Prinzip der Musterbeichte auf. Das Lied bietet beides: strenge

Systematik und geschmeidige Umsetzung, Traditionstreue und eine rhetorische Variationskunst, die mit Kürzungen und Erweiterungen, Umstellungen und Verdichtungen sowie dem Wechsel lakonischer und elaborierter Passagen arbeitet.

Der Dichter
Die ambitionierte Poetik des Liedes folgt Regeln, die sich der Dichter selbst auferlegt hat. Die erste Regel besteht in der Wiedergabe von 64 Sünden in 64 Versen, die nur bei eingehender Textlektüre sichtbar wird, aber dennoch ein wesentliches poetisches Gestaltungselement darstellt. Die zweite Regel geht aus der Kanzonenform hervor. Oswald nutzt sie in der Weise, dass er den Sündengruppen je einen Strophenabschnitt (Stollen, Abgesang) zur Verfügung stellt. Ob eine Kategorie nun vier, fünf, sieben, acht oder neun Sünden umfasst: die Zahl der Verse ist in den meisten Fällen auf vier begrenzt (Ausnahmen sind die Umsetzung der Zehn Gebote in elf Versen und der sieben Todsünden in fünf Versen). Eine weitere Regel ergibt sich aus dem gewählten Reimschema. Der Aufgesang besteht aus Dreireimen und Schweifreim (*aaab cccb*), der Abgesang aus Kreuzreimen (*dede*). In den Stollen des Aufgesangs sind also Formulierungen erforderlich, die entsprechende Reimhäufungen erlauben. Wie dies gelingt, zeigt das Beispiel der sieben Geistesgaben. Zwei Gaben, *scientia* und *pietas*, werden mit den reimenden Wörtern *kunst* und *inbrunst* wiedergegeben; als drittes Reimwort tritt *gunst* hinzu, eine Tugend, die über das traditionelle Repertoire der Geistesgaben hinausgeht (IV, 1-3).

Die anspruchsvolle Formkunst des Liedes verweist auf den Dichter, nicht aber schon auf die Dichterrolle. Beides ist zu unterscheiden. Der Dichter ist der empirische Autor, der Text und Melodie des Liedes komponiert, die Dichterrolle hingegen die Selbstrepräsentation des Dichters als Dichter im Text. Die Rolle des Dichters, die über die Rollen des Sünders und Predigers hinausgeht, bringt sich in der fünften Strophe explizit zur Geltung (V, 5-12):

> Der himel und erd beschaffen hat,
> und was dorinne wonlich stat,
> der gab mir Wolkenstainer rat,
> aus beichten solt ich leren
> Durch mein gesangk vil hoveleut
> und mangen ungewissen mentsch,
> die sich verierren in der heut,
> recht als zu Behem tuent die gens.

Alle drei Sprecherrollen werden in dichter Folge genannt: die Rolle des beichtenden Sünders (V, 8: ‚aus beichten'), des predigenden Lehrers (V, 8: ‚solt ich leren') und des Liederdichters (V, 9: ‚Durch mein gesangk'). Oswald nutzt die Opposition von Singen und Sagen, um die Differenz der Rollen zu markieren. Als Sünder und Prediger spricht er (I, 3: ‚das sag'), als Dichter singt er. Ein wichtiges Signal ist bereits die einleitende Periphrase Gottes als Schöpfer. Zum einen erinnert sie an die Umschreibung Gottes als Allmächtiger in der ersten Strophe. Während dort der Priester als Stellvertreter Gottes angesprochen wird, nimmt der Sprecher hier für sich in Anspruch, von Gott dazu berufen worden zu sein, als Lehrer vor die Hofgesellschaft zu treten wie der Priester vor die Gemeinde. Damit wird die Konkurrenz zwischen Dichter und Priester deutlich verschärft. Zum anderen ist entscheidend, welche Periphrasen der Sprecher wählt. Wenn Gott mit Bezug auf den Priester als Allmächtiger umschrieben wird, so impliziert dies, dass der Stellvertretene mächtiger sei als sein Stellvertreter. Wenn er mit Bezug auf den Dichter als Schöpfer umschrieben wird, so impliziert dies, dass der Dichter selbst ein Schöpfer sei, nämlich Schöpfer des Gedichts. Auch die Wendung ‚was dorinne wonlich stat' kann als poetologische Metapher verstanden werden, denn es ist ja die Aufgabe des Dichters, eine Form zu finden, die dem Inhalt eine angemessene Wohnstatt bietet.

Wie aber verhält es sich mit dem merkwürdigen Bild der böhmischen Gänse, mit dem Oswald sein Publikum umschreibt und das er durch den gewagten Reim *gens/mentsch* stützt? Es ist Forschungskonsens, dass damit die Hussiten gemeint sind, die Anhänger des als Priester und Prediger wirkenden Theologen Jan Hus, der beim Konstanzer Konzil als Ketzer hingerichtet wurde (Jones 1980: 648; Wachinger 2007: 386; Wellmann 1974: 336-37). Die als Gänse umschriebenen Hussiten werden als Beispiel für jene Menschen angeführt, die in ihrem Glauben verunsichert sind (V, 10: ‚ungewissen'). Die Verunsicherung im Glauben wird mit einer Wendung umschrieben (V, 11: ‚die sich verierren in der heut'), die man mit der Redewendung wiedergeben kann, dass man ‚sich in seiner Haut nicht wohl fühle'. Soll mit diesen Anspielungen eine makabre Analogie zwischen dem Prediger auf dem Scheiterhaufen und den Gänsen im Backofen evoziert werden? Wenn dem so ist, wird man auch das am Schluss des Liedes platzierte Bild der brennenden Gottesliebe einbeziehen müssen. Dann hätte Oswald (was ihm wohl zuzutrauen wäre) eine böse Pointe gesetzt, die aus dem metaphorischen Kurzschluss zwischen dem verbrannten Prediger, den gegrillten Gänsen (als Bild für die verunsicherten Gläubigen) und dem in geistlicher Liebe glühenden Sprecher (VI, 12: ‚das ich gaistlich erzünde') resultiert. In jedem Fall stellt das Bild der böhmischen Gänse im Zusammenhang eines Beichtlieds einen Stilbruch dar, der einen komischen Effekt erzielt. Insofern ist Dirk Joschko zuzustimmen, der lakonisch feststellt: ‚Den persönlichen Ernst läßt das Lied allerdings vermissen' (Joschko 1985: 151). Das

Rollenspiel des Liedes beruht auf der Abfolge von Sünder, Prediger und Dichter. Obwohl der Sprecher am Ende in die Rolle des Sünders zurückkehrt, bleibt doch die Rolle des Dichters präsent, der den scheinbaren Ernst seines Beichtlieds durch eine bizarre Anspielung ruiniert.

Autorkonzept
Die Geste des spätmittelalterlichen Beichtlieds tritt deutlicher hervor, wenn man sie mit einer hochmittelalterlichen Novelle vergleicht, die ein ähnliches Thema gestaltet. Auch im *Gregorius* Hartmanns von Aue trifft man die paradoxe Vorstellung an, dass der größte Sünder die größte Gnade empfängt, wenn er nur die größte Buße übt. Im Falle des Beichtlieds ist es aber nicht eine fiktive Figur, an der dieser Zusammenhang demonstriert wird, sondern der Autor selbst. Oswald verwischt die Grenze zwischen Dichtung und Wahrheit, indem er sich als *Wolkenstainer* einbringt und in der ersten Person spricht. Wenn er behauptet, dass er maximale Schuld auf sich geladen habe (nämlich alle Sünden, die die Systematik der christlichen Moraltheologie aufzuweisen hat), und hinzufügt, dass Gott ihn eben wegen der Totalität seiner Sünden als Prediger auserwählt habe, so sind dies ironische Fiktionalitätssignale, die noch einmal die Aufmerksamkeit auf den Autor lenken. Diese Signale verweisen aber nicht mehr auf den Autor als Sünder (also die fingierte Autobiographie), sondern auf den Autor als Dichter (also die poetologische Selbstbestimmung). Oswald setzt ein angeblich von Gott beglaubigtes Gleichheitszeichen zwischen den größten Sünder, den größten Prediger und den größten Dichter. Die Demut des Sünders ist der Hochmut des Dichters.

Die Fähigkeit zur Sünde findet ihren Widerhall in der Fähigkeit zum Dichten. Die auktoriale Kompetenz, die der Dichter für sich in Anspruch nimmt, kommt in den komplexen poetischen Spielregeln zum Ausdruck, die er sich in seinem Lied auferlegt, um sie mühelos zu erfüllen. Auch für diesen Sachverhalt kann man eine Parallele anführen, nämlich den Mönch von Salzburg, der in seinem Marienlied *Das Goldene Abc* ebenfalls seine poetische Schöpferkraft in Szene setzt (Kraß 2014). Beide Liederdichter nutzen und überbieten traditionelle Formen und Systeme, um ihre poetische Meisterschaft zu beweisen. Beide Liederdichter ordnen sich dem Schöpfergott unter, um zugleich ihre eigene Schöpferkraft als Dichter zur Schau zu stellen.

Bei Oswald tritt noch die Konkurrenz zwischen Dichter und Priester hinzu. Er misst sich mit der Autorität der Priester, die er zunächst anerkennt (in der Exposition des Liedes), dann sabotiert (im Hinweis auf die Schmähung des Sakraments der Priesterweihe), dann für sich selbst in Anspruch nimmt (in der Rolle des von Gott bestellten Bußpredigers) und schließlich ironisch unterläuft (durch die Anspielung auf Hus und die Hussiten). Was Oswald in seinem *Beichtlied* treibt, grenzt an Blasphemie. Die abschließende Bitte, dass er in geistlicher Liebe entbrennen möchte, ist eine sarkastische Inversion der Strafe, die den Ketzer auf dem Scheiterhaufen erwartet. Oswald spielt mit den Rollen des Sünders, Predigers, Dichters, und der Spieleinsatz ist hoch. Man wird dieses Spiel vielleicht als Indiz verstehen können für den Wandel des literarischen Autorkonzepts, der sich im Übergang vom Spätmittelalter zur frühen Neuzeit vollzieht. Oswald stellt sich einerseits in die Tradition des mittelalterlichen Dichters, wenn er überlieferte Formen und Inhalte aufgreift, um sie neu zu gestalten. Er weist andererseits auf ein frühneuzeitliches Autorverständnis voraus, wenn er sich mit poetischen Ambitionen, prekären Rollenspielen und ironischen Brüchen von den zitierten Traditionen emanzipiert.

Zitierte Literatur

Primärliteratur

Oswald von Wolkenstein, *Lieder*. Auswahl. Hg., übersetzt und erläutert von Burghart Wachinger (Stuttgart: Reclam, 1992) [Wachinger 1992]

Oswald von Wolkenstein, *Lieder*. Ausgewählte Texte hg., übersetzt und kommentiert von Burghart Wachinger, Melodien und Tonsätze hg. und kommentiert von Horst Brunner (Stuttgart: Reclam, 2007) [Wachinger 2007]

Hartmann von Aue, *Gregorius*. Hg. von Burghart Wachinger, Altdeutsche Textbibliothek, 2 (Berlin: de Gruyter, 2011)

Sekundärliteratur

Bruchhold, Ullrich. 2010. *Deutschsprachige Beichten im 13. und 14. Jahrhundert. Editionen und Typologien zur Überlieferungs-, Text- und Gebrauchsgeschichte vor dem hintergrund der älteren Tradition*, Münchener Texte und Untersuchungen zur deutschen Literatur des Mittelalters, 138 (Berlin: de Gruyter)

Foucault, Michel. 1994. *Überwachen und Strafen. Die Geburt des Gefängnisses*, übersetzt von Walter Seitter, suhrkamp taschenbuch, 2271 (Frankfurt am Main: Suhrkamp)

Kraß, Andreas. 2014. 'Das *Goldene Abc*. Spiel und Ernst in einem Marienlied des Mönchs von Salzburg', in *Spiel und Ernst. Formen – Poetiken – Zuschreibungen. Zum Gedenken an Erika Greber*, hg. von Dirk Kretzschmar et al., Literatura, 31 (Würzburg: Ergon), S. 125-37

Jones, George F. 1980. 'Oswald von Wolkenstein's *Mein Sünd und Schuld* and the *Beichtlied* Tradition', in *Oswald von Wolkenstein*, hg. von Ulrich Müller, Wege der Forschung, 526 (Darmstadt: Wissenschaftliche Buchgesellschaft), S. 241-55

Joschko, Dirk. 1985. *Oswald von Wolkenstein. Eine Monographie zu Person, Werk und Forschungsgeschichte*, Göppinger Arbeiten zur Germanistik, 396 (Göppingen: Kümmerle)

Okken, Lambertus. 1974. 'Oswald von Wolkenstein: Lied Nr. 44. Wortschatz Untersuchung', in: *Oswald von Wolkenstein. Beiträge der philologisch-musikwissenschaftlichen Tagung in Neustift bei Brixen 1973*, hg. von Egon Kühebacher, Innsbrucker Beiträge zur Kulturwissenschaft. Germanistische Reihe, 1 (Innsbruck: Institut für Deutsche Philologie der Universität Innsbruck), S. 182-218

Salmen, Walter. 1974 'Die Musik im Weltbilde Oswalds von Wolkenstein', in *Oswald von Wolkenstein. Beiträge der philologisch-musikwissenschaftlichen Tagung in Neustift bei Brixen 1973*, hg. von Egon Kühebacher, Innsbrucker Beiträge zur Kulturwissenschaft. Germanistische Reihe, 1 (Innsbruck: Institut für Deutsche Philologie der Universität Innsbruck), S. 237-44

Töpfer, Regina. 2013. 'Oswald von Wolkenstein und sein Sprecher-Ich. Poetisches Spiel mit autobiographischen Elementen in den Liedern Kl 3, 33 und 39', in *Oswald von Wolkenstein im Kontext der Liedkunst seiner Zeit*, hg. von Ingrid Bennewitz und Horst Brunner unter Mitarbeit von Maria Wüstenhagen, Jahrbuch der Oswald von Wolkenstein-Gesellschaft, 19 (Wiesbaden: Reichert), S. 225-40

Wellmann, Hans. 1974. '"Ain burger und ain hofman". Ein "Ständestreit" bei Oswald von Wolkenstein?', in *Oswald von Wolkenstein. Beiträge der philologisch-musikwissenschaftlichen Tagung in Neustift bei Brixen 1973*, hg. von Egon Kühebacher, Innsbrucker Beiträge zur Kulturwissenschaft. Germanistische Reihe, 1 (Innsbruck: Institut für Deutsche Philologie der Universität Innsbruck), S. 332-43

5

Legal Process and Fantasies of Torture: Reality and Imagination in Oswald von Wolkenstein

Almut Suerbaum
University of Oxford

Imprisoned by a woman: poetic allegory versus historical fact
Oswald von Wolkenstein is an unusual figure in more than one way, and anyone who has read even a few lines of his poetry will remember the forceful first person persona and the strong, seemingly autobiographical presence. Moreover, we are in the unusual position of being able to contrast that literary 'I' of the songs with an attested historical figure about whose career, possessions, promotion and law suits we know a great deal – especially now that the monumental five-volume edition of the 'Lebenszeugnisse' by Anton Schwob is complete.

Legal processes play a significant part in Oswald's literary as well as his historical persona, and his oeuvre therefore offers interesting material for considering the literary uses to which legal and especially penitential images are put. Through the available records, his participation in court cases and legal disputes is well documented at virtually all stages of his life. At the same time, these historical records provide an important subtext to his literary œuvre, in which one of the most intriguing motifs is that of captivity. Oswald explores this theme in a number of songs which lament his imprisonment at the hands of a merciless woman who holds him captive, inflicting pain and torture. The most famous of these, 'Durch abenteuer tal und berg' (Kl 26),[1] plots the stages of an adventurous life, although it also reveals, with considerable irony, that much of this adventure is the subject of wistful reminiscences, contrasting it with a reality where the singer is housebound. Towards the end, the singer inserts the story of his imprisonment at the hands of a cruel woman as a narrative episode:

> Die selbig red was wol mein fueg;
> mit meines buelen freund müsst ich mich ainen,
> die mich vor jaren auch beslueg

---
[1] Songs are quoted from the critical edition by Klein, as revised by Wachinger.

mit grossen eisen niden zu den bainen.
was ich der minn genossen hab,
des werden meine kindlin noch wol innen,
wenn ich dort lig in meinem grab,
so muessen si ire hendlin dorumb winden,
das ich den namen ie erkannt
von diser Hausmanninnen. (Kl 26, XII)

[That speech was my destiny; I had to make common cause with the friend of my lover, who all those years back had put irons on my lower legs. My children will feel the consequences of the love I enjoyed; when I am laid in my grave, they will wring their hands, lamenting that I should ever have known that Hausmann daughter.][2]

Use of proper names in lyric poems is unusual, and the rhetorically charged use of the proper name in this instance as the final rhyme word of the strophe exposes its significance (Spicker 2007: 47; Wittstruck 1987: 210). The exposed position displays the deliberate departure from literary convention according to which courtly love songs relate to generalizable circumstances, but refrain from specific reference and for that reason avoid use of proper names. Its prominent use in this strophe raises questions about the external reality to which the concrete name may refer. In this particular song, the specific name thus creates a tension between literary fantasies of frustrated sexual desire and torture, which literary convention suggests are topical for a lament, and a narrative of real imprisonment attributed to a specific woman. Critics had noted early on that the song moves beyond lyric convention in naming the woman responsible for inflicting such pain and humiliation (Spicker 1993: 101; Wittstruck 1987: 201). Unusually, however, the deictic gesture of pointing to a world outside the song can be related to historical records, and thus the use of the name was rendered even more significant when it was discovered that Anna, daughter of Hans Hausmann, is not only named in the song but also features in historical documents, most prominently in a lengthy court case about the possession of Burg Hauenstein, part-owned by Oswald (Schwob 1979). This use of a name in a love song differs from earlier examples: where Walther von der Vogelweide playfully closes a lover's lament by blaming his wounded heart on Hiltegunt (La 74,19), the deliberate infringement of the literary rule of anonymity is part of a literary game. By contrast, Oswald's song evokes a specific person who appears to be part of the immediate circle not only of the singer, but also of the audience. In this case, therefore, the records, unusually, place modern readers in a position which is comparable to that of contemporary audiences in that, like them, the historical

---

[2] All translations are by the author.

evidence reveals something about who Anna Hausmann was and how her legal interests collided with those of Oswald. Nevertheless, such factual knowledge of external reality contributes little to understanding the song as a literary text, or to the ways in which it is put together. It does not explain how mention of body parts eroticizes a seemingly factual account of events, nor does it account for the difference in impact between narrative voice or dream sequences. The song, with its shift from such a narrative of imprisonment to sexual fantasies of subjugation, is interesting in its move between literal and metaphorical use of notions of torture and imprisonment. Nevertheless, I propose a different focus for this paper, which will investigate the relationship between forms of self-presentation in the historical records and those in the literary oeuvre. Put differently, the focus will not be on asking whether events depicted in the songs are real, or how we know, but on the voice which speaks though the historical as well as the literary texts.

The starting point for this analysis will be some of the extant documents which allow us to plot Oswald's involvement in court cases, though the guiding questions will in the end be literary rather than historical or sociological. In the early stages of scholarly engagement with the historical records, the documentary evidence was usually used to check on the facticity or otherwise of images presented in Oswald's songs. The reasons for this are self-evident, because it is so rare that we are able to juxtapose the literary world created within works of fiction with external historical evidence. Thus it is possible to ask the kinds of questions for which the work of other poets may offer material for speculation, but no answers: how does Oswald's use of images of torture work poetically, and how does it differ from that of other poets, given that we know he was actually imprisoned? Who was the woman whom Oswald accuses and abuses as his arch-enemy? How much of what he stylizes as his role in the songs correlates with what we know of his life from external sources – and does such correlation mean that it is 'true' in the light of historical evidence? The methodological problem of such questions has become increasingly obvious, as historians have pointed out that historical records themselves are the result of conscious stylization. As a result, it is impossible to maintain the simple juxtaposition between artful literary fiction on the one hand, and simple historical fact on the other (Müller 1968; Schwob 1979; Helmkamp 2003). This paper will instead pose the questions in the other direction, starting from the legal documents which survive, and asking how they relate to the literary oeuvre. The aim will be to move beyond the simple juxtaposition of fact and fiction, or history versus literature, and to identify common strategies of self-presentation.

Historical documents versus literary fiction – a dichotomy?

It is clear from the start that in the case of Oswald von Wolkenstein, the two sides do not stand in stark contrast but are related. Literary works create a world of their own, yet a common strategy of reading is to ask how such texts refer to an external reality, or, in other words, how 'true' they are. In most cases of lyric poetry, such attempts are thwarted in more than one way – by the fact that we rarely have evidence about the life of the singer from outside the literary works, yet often also by the fact that courtly love lyric often deliberately refuses specific reference. Oswald's œuvre is unusual in that we are often in a position to assess whether references to an outside world tally with externally attested statements, i.e. whether we consider them factually true or not, in which case we assign them the status of fictional reality. Oswald himself is unusual in that even contemporary observers establish a link between the aristocrat involved in various political and legal interactions, and the poet: references to Oswald the writer in the legal documents are rare, but they exist – not just in a reference to ownership of the Innsbruck manuscript which was commissioned in his life-time and transmits his songs, preceded by an author portrait showing the one-eyed Oswald (*Lebenszeugnisse* III, 236; IV, 341), but also in an attack on the truthfulness of Oswald's statement, suggesting that he is not to be trusted because he is a poet. In the course of a legal dispute, Oswald had defended his position by publicizing a witness statement which the Landeshauptmann is said to have torn down, denouncing it as fiction. In a letter written in Hauenstein in mid May 1442, Oswald recounts this action in his own version of events:

> als ich dann v(er)nom(m)en hab wie das mein schreib(e)n als ain getichtte sach sey das sich mit warhait nym(er) eruind(e)n soll and(er)s.
> (*Lebenszeugnisse* IV, 352, p. 204)

> [when I heard how a scribe said that it was fictitious matter which would never be found to be true.]

Oswald's account of the events projects outrage at the injustice of this action, because in his view the accusation is without basis, since his witness made his declaration publicly and for all to hear. He implies that, according to legal convention, such a statement should therefore not have been called into question. Yet the wording suggests that this is more than an attack on Oswald's truthfulness, because in using the term 'ain getichtte sach' [a fictitious matter], the focus of the accusation is not the improbability of the statement, but the occupation of the writer: if he is known as a poet, then, the slur appears to suggest, he is likely to offer fabrications of his imagination rather than the truth. Unusually, the letter, in refuting the opponents and cursing them, offers a more than colourful self-reference:

wann ich dy rittn(e)r vnd alle die in woll well(e)n ee gen hell mit ein and(er) far(e)n
liescz <dem swarcz(e)n teuf(e)l hint(e)n in sein <swarcz> arsloch> ee das ich an saech
[vnd] <vn(d)> vngehortt ain sollich ged<t>ichtt von in erdenck(e)n od(er) aúff richt-
t(e)n wollt <wie wol ich súnst tichtt(e)n chann>.
(*Lebenszeugnisse* IV, 352, p. 205)

[for I would rather the Rittner and all their well-wishers all together went to hell, to creep into the black bottom of the black devil, than invent such a baseless and unheard-of fiction, for all that I am a poet.]

The manuscript of the letter bears traces of the writing process here. Multiple erasures in the curse, sharpening its offensiveness though insertion of adjectives, point to deliberate and self-aware irony: what we hear is not just the voice of the outraged aristocrat whose word has been unfairly dismissed as fiction, but also that of the inventive poet, who uses imaginative invective in order to underline his linguistic prowess. As a result, his double identity as poet and aristocrat, which had been used by his opponents as a way of undermining his credibility, becomes the strategic instrument with which to defend his honour.[3]

Most of the surviving legal documents are less colourful than this exchange. They could, of course, be used to reconstruct aspects of the legal and penal system in force in Northern Italy in the first half of the fifteenth century, along Foucauldian lines. Justice is administered by the various lords, and we can trace the way in which members of the Wolkenstein family acquire castles and the accompanying jurisdiction. Oswald himself has an active role in administering this system of justice in all its forms, since he was appointed as court judge by Duke Heinrich of Görz and Tyrol. Acting on behalf of his lord, Oswald passes judgement in a dispute between two Nuremberg burghers and a third burgher from Augsburg.[4] The account of this court case, preserved in two copies, details the significant stages of the legal proceedings, from the naming of witnesses for the defence and prosecution to the judgement and a record of its acceptance by both parties:

Ich Oswalt von Wolkenstein Ritter Bekenne offennlich mit dem brief vnd tun kund allen die den brief ansehent od(er) hórent lesen daz Ich von geschéffts wegen des Hochgeborn fúrsten . Graf Heinrichs Grauen ze Górcz vnd ze Tyrol (etc.) meins genádigen h(er)n / an heutigen tag datu(m) des briefs / Als ein gewaltig(er) gesatzter hofricht t(er) zw Lúncz an dem hofrecht gesessen bin / von solcher Stóss vnd zwitrácht wegen.
(*Lebenszeugnisse* IV, 339, p. 163)

---

[3] On the use of invective as part of a polemical disavowal of opponents, see Suerbaum (2015).
[4] The context of the case is evident from a document preserved in the archives of the city of Nuremberg: two Nuremberg merchants on their way to Venice had quarrelled with a merchant from Augsburg, which resulted in their arrest by Duke Heinrich of Görz; see *Lebenszeugnisse* IV, 310, pp. 97-99.

> [I, Oswald of Wolkenstein, Knight, proclaim publicly by means of this letter, and announce to all who see it or hear it being read out, that I, by order of His Highness, Duke Heinrich Count of Görcz and of Tyrol etc., my gracious lord, have this day, as dated in the letter, sat as the authorized court judge at Luncz, on account of such discord and strife.]

While the judgement is clearly an attempt at mediating between the positions of the two parties, we learn that both had been imprisoned for seven months (*Lebenszeugnisse* IV, 339, p. 162); other documents reveal that confessions were occasionally sought by torture – its availability as an option evident even where it is presented as rare, as in the following example, where the confession of an attempted murder is stated to have been procured 'dem merren tail an alle marter' [mostly without any form of torture]:

> All(e)n h(er)rn ritt(er)n vnd chnecht(e)n purgern gemain reich(e)n vnd armen Tún ich oswalt vo(n) wolkenstain zu wiss(e)n dye dysy gschrift an sehe(en) hór(e)n od(er) les(e)n das grozz mórtt so dan etleich vb(er) mich in ain(er) gútt(e)n stallung vnd frid(e)n auch vb(er) mein Prued(er) h(er)r mich(e)l pósleich(e)n an gelegt hab(e)n als das ein posswicht den ich in meine(r) Fankchnús yectz etwelang gehabt han vnd noch hab genant chúncz widmar dem merren tail an alle martt(er) [v(er)heb] v(er)geh(e)n vnd bechant hat vnd noch tútt vor pid(er) lautt(e)n vnd dem ich sein leb(e)n bis her dar auf gefrist vnd gefreit han.
>
> (*Lebenszeugnisse* IV, 351, p. 200–01 [May 1442])

> [I, Oswald of Wolkenstein, proclaim to all knights, knaves and burghers collectively, whether rich or poor, who may see this letter or hear it read out loud, that a miscreant named Conrad Widmar, whom I had held in my prison form some time and still hold, has now confessed, mostly without any form of torture and in front of respectable people, to the grave murder of which some had maliciously accused me and my brother, despite being of good repute and in good faith. I have therefore so far spared his life.]

What is of interest here is not the self-justification in which Oswald can point the finger at precisely those who had hitherto accused him of espionage and murder, but the passing reference to accepted standards: the confession of the real culprit is presented as reliable because it has been made in the presence of respectable witnesses and because it has been made almost without use of physical threats – clear evidence that torture is considered an acceptable means of eliciting the truth, both by Oswald and by his opponents, whom he sets out to persuade of his innocence.[5]

---

[5] A draft record of the statements made by Conrad (Kunz) Widman as made during his questioning at castle Hauenstein is preserved in *Lebenszeugnisse* IV, 350, pp. 184-99; it stresses that his confession was made 'an alle marte(er) [...] unweczwungenleich(e)n' [without any form torture [...] not under duress]

The picture which emerges in one of a legal system which considers such forms of physical violence generally acceptable, and it is clear that punishment meted out is equally severe and includes the gallows.[6] It is possible therefore to use the evidence of these documents to construct the sociological and cultural context in which Oswald the poet operates – it is a context which Foucault describes briefly as the foil against which he differentiates the superficially less violent and yet at least as repressive 'political technology' of the Enlightenment (Foucault 1977: 32-69).[7]

Self-presentation in conflict

Such readings use the well-documented case of Oswald as an example of pervading social trends and treat it as representative of wider cultural phenomena; autobiographical readings on the other hand create a sense of uniqueness. What this paper would like to offer instead is neither a biographical reading nor a general picture of the penal system in the region, but an exploration of the way in which both intersect in this particular case. Having considered the cultural context in which Oswald's references to torture operate, it will therefore be necessary now to assess how Oswald's role can be understood as one shaped by social as well as literary conventions, or, to put it differently, to ask what we can learn from the historical documents about the way in which Oswald articulates his own position.

In this context, the fact that the documents are not as sensational as a Foucault-inspired reading might make us expect is in itself revealing: the majority of the surviving historical records of Oswald's life relate not to capital crimes, but to disputes about property, from inheritance affairs to boundary disputes. The most long-drawn out of these cases concerns pasture rights on a local mountain plateau, the Ritten – and it is this dispute between two villages and their respective supporters which sparked the statement about Oswald's veracity quoted earlier. So far, the dispute has not attracted as much scholarly attention as the case against the Hausmannin – 'cherchez la femme' is perhaps still a greater magnet than 'cherchez le boeuf' – but it is at least as interesting for the purpose of assessing how Oswald himself casts and stylizes his role within the judicial system.

In order to understand the self-presentation of Oswald as litigant in the dispute, it will be necessary to sketch its rather complex turns and twists. Around 1441, the village of Ritten is accused by the family of Villanders, supported by the

---

and in the presence of named witnesses (p. 195).

[6] On the connection between knowledge and violence see Foucault (1977: 198), who describes the aim to forge a 'docile body that may be subjected, used, transformed and improved.'

[7] See Bowden, in the introduction to this volume, on the shift in interpreting somatic aspects of punishment.

Wolkensteiner, of having used pastures to which the family of Villanders held the rights; their counterclaim is that the Villanderer and Wolkensteiner unlawfully held and confiscated some of the cattle on those pastures.[8] That may seem a small issue to us, but within a farming community, the rights to pasture are an emotive issue because they concern the principles of peaceful coexistence as well as individual livelihood: because rights of pasture are governed by custom rather than legislation, circumstances may arise in which the legal position is unclear. Although the dispute has sometimes been presented as the result of a primitive or insufficient legal system, or indeed as evidence of generalized tendencies to violence, it is much better understood as revealing the friction of a system in which detailed legal codes govern some aspects of life such as court proceedings, while other aspects are established through unwritten conventions.

Schwob, in his commentary on the document, highlights that the case illustrates structural rather than personal fault-lines; that is, the dispute is very clearly not the result of Oswald's litiginous personality, but an example of the kinds of issues which arise in a system of common law with unclear or rather competing and contradictory legal claims (*Lebenszeugnisse* IV, 312, p. 103). Nevertheless, it has an interest beyond the systemic, because the surviving documents bear a personal stamp in more than one way: some of them are written by Oswald, and the majority, especially where we are dealing with drafts and copies, come from the family archive of the Wolkensteiner, which means that they have been collected and collated by Oswald or his immediate family, though a handful of documents from the other side survive in other contexts. This implies that we may be dealing with a skewed sample, but what could be considered a methodological drawback in historiographical terms may well be an advantage in literary terms, because it gives us a multi-faceted panorama of self-presentation, written from a single point of view but in a variety of genres and text-types.

Schwob's edition orders the material chronologically; the first document we have is a personal letter by Oswald to his older brother Michael. In it, he states the case: his rights have been infringed in an aggressive way by the villagers of Ritten, who have used pastures clearly marked by border stones as belonging to the village of Villanders, part of the Wolkenstein inheritance. By 1422, this dispute already has a long history – attempts at separating the areas of pasture by a wall had failed, because each side retained rights of access to meadows on the other side, and this caused tension when the village of Ritten claimed the right to allow about nine hundred oxen, required for transport on the main roads, ninety days of access to a meadow.

---

[8] For dating and a summary of the events, see Schwob's introduction to the first of several documents plotting the stages of the dispute (*Lebenszeugnisse* IV, 312, p. 102).

The village of Villanders, on the other hand, relied on hay from that meadow for winter feeding, and the period between August – when cattle are driven down to the lower-lying farms – and the onset of winter was too short to make sufficient hay. Both sides thus argue from economic necessity, but the Villanderer could claim a judgement of 1315 in their favour, and Oswald and his brother Michael, as the main landowners, defend the rights of their tenants.

The dispute escalates quickly when the Villanderer seize some of the oxen driven onto the disputed meadow for pasture; Ritten in turn appeals to Duke Friedrich of Tyrol, who requires Oswald and the Wolkensteiner to see to the restitution of the animals, but then dies, leaving the case unresolved. Oswald's letter to his brother, who is the head of the family but probably already ill, argues for concerted action to defend their and their tenants' rights. The terms he uses are defensive: 'So wolt wir das vnser von Jnn schirmen vnd retten so wir besst móch(e)n' (Lebenszeugnisse IV, 312; p.105) [thus we desired to protect what is ours from them as best we could]. This serves to project the speaker not just as the protector of a particular village, but as part of that group. Yet Oswald's statement also articulates his willingness to take action, if necessary on his own: 'so wolt ich den krieg Jn obgeschribn(er) mass / also allain auf mich lad(e)n vnd treib(e)n' (*Lebenszeugnisse* IV, 312; p. 105) [therefore, I am willing to pursue the aforementioned cause single-handedly]. This has sometimes been read as revealing Oswald's individual characteristics, although it should by now be clear that it is part of an elaborate strategy of self-presentation: the speaker is not in fact a hot-head willing to go it alone, but a skilled politician using rhetorical strategy in order to solicit his brother's alliance and support for the cause.

The next stage of the dispute bears out the need for strategic dialogue: both parties appeal to the new Duke, who offers to hear both sides in an attempt to mediate and achieve a mutually acceptable resolution (*Lebenszeugnisse* IV, 316; p. 111-13). This requires both to hold the peace and refrain from further acts of aggression. The Rittner insist on the return of the confiscated oxen, while Oswald in turn produces the confession of a hired murderer who claims to have been paid by the Rittner to kill Oswald, assisted by two 'Welsche' (foreigners, i.e. romance speakers) who procured poison from Venice. The veracity of this confession is disputed, despite the fact that it was made freely or only with minimal use of torture – as seen in the example discussed earlier. What follows is a complex wrangle; of interest here is not the political intrigue used by both parties but the shifting ground of the argument: a dispute which appeared to be simply about the use of certain pastures rapidly escalates to question judicial authority and local politics. Oswald insists on an adversarial arbitration between the two affected parties ('Schiedsgericht'), whereas the Duke offers an inquisitorial process ('Hofgericht') which Oswald refuses to attend, later claiming that he had never been notified in the proper form. In repeatedly questioning the neutrality of the judge who represents the king, and in threatening to appeal to the nobles of Tyrol, Oswald politicizes the conflict: he is part of a broader opposition within the Tyrolese nobility against the increasingly arbitrary exercise of princely and imperial power.[9] Moreover, this escalation of the conflict appears to be the result of Oswald's influence – or at least the surviving documents ascribe to him a dominant role in this process, through his repeated questioning of ducal and episcopal orders.

The documents also allow us to see differences between the protagonists. Oswald is cast as the prime mover – not because he is most affected by the dispute, but because he is rhetorically powerful; his older brother Michael on the other hand emerges as the diplomat who is concerned not to manoeuvre himself and the family into an untenable position, aiming to achieve a negotiated settlement – with the Rittner as well as with the Duke. Where Oswald's letters are often brusque or rhetorically emphatic, those of his older brother strike a more diplomatic and often conciliatory tone. Both stances are conveyed through use of rhetorical means and both are part of a strategy for handling a complex dispute in which it appears to be evident to all parties concerned that there is no simple right and wrong, for all the posturing in evidence by those who speak up for their own interests.

What does that mean for our reading of Oswald the poet? While it is tempting to psychologize, this is neither very useful nor defensible on the basis of the written material we have, because to do so would be to ignore the nature of the evidence: what we see in the letters and documents is not the result of personality, though that is the temptation in reading most autobiographical writing, but the result of careful selection and deliberate self-presentation. What is interesting in the historical records instead is the way in which they allow us to see processes of negotiation and mediation. HENRIKE MANUWALD'S contribution to this volume highlights that adversarial and inquisitorial forms of justice are two distinct models which may, nevertheless, coexist, especially in German-speaking areas.[10] This tendency is very obvious in the material presented here: overwhelmingly, parties seek negotiated settlements, and there is surprisingly little mention of punishment. In the disputes in which Oswald involves himself both as judge and as injured party, the aim is peaceful coexistence, not annihilation of the opponent. Such attempts at reconciliation –

---

[9] See *Lebenszeugnisse* IV, 384, pp. 288-91, which pleads for Sigismund, then a minor, to be allowed to return to Tyrol in order to prevent his cousin Friedrich, the regent, from incorporating Tyrol into the Empire.
[10] See MANUWALD, in this volume.

not in a Christian sense, but as forms of social interaction – point to the fact that judicial processes in the sphere in which Oswald moves are dominated by non-corporeal methods and attempts at achieving a balance of powers. Punishment, or even negotiated non-punishment, is a complex tool within a power-structure of multiple dependency between equals whose interests collide and who nevertheless form political alliances beyond their own particular interests.

Poetic self-representation

Finally, it will be necessary to relate the self-image developed within the historical documents to the picture emerging from Oswald's songs. Does what we have discovered about forms of aristocratic self-presentation in the historical records help us to understand the specific aspects of the lyric 'I'? There are a number of very different answers to this question. The conventional one is to look for biographical elements in the songs, which is more difficult for the Villanderer Almenstreit than it is for the dispute with Anna Hausmann, though it could be done: song Kl 44, 'Durch Barbarei, Arabia' might be adduced in this context, because its final strophe alludes to difficulties with the neighbours as well as with the singer's sovereign:

> Mein kurzweil die ist mangerlai,
> neur esel gesang und pfawen geschrai,
> des wünscht ich nicht mer umb ain ai.
> vast rawscht der bach neur hurlahai
> mein houbt enzwai,
> das es beginnt zu kranken,
> Also trag ich mein aigen swär;
> tëglicher sorg, vil böser mär
> wirt Houenstain gar seldn lër.
> möcht ichs gewenden an gevär,
> oder wer das wär,
> dem wolt ich immer danken.
> Mein lanndesfürst der ist mir gram
> von böser leutte neide,
> mein dienst die sein im widerzam,
> das ist mir schad und laide,
> wie wol mir susst kain fürstlich stamm
> bei meinem gueten aide,
> nie hat geswecht leib, er, guet, nam
> in seiner fürsten waide
> köstlich raide.
> Mein freund, die hassen mich überain
> an schuld, des muess ich greisen,

> das klag ich aller werlt gemain,
> den frummen und den weisen,
> darzue vil hohen fürsten rain,
> die sich ir er land preisen,
> das si mich armen Wolckenstein
> die wolf nicht lan erzaisen,
> gar verwaisen.
>
> (Kl 44, III)

[My pasttimes are many and varied – but as for asses' songs or peacock cries, I really would not wish for a penny worth's more of it. The brook with its gushing and rushing is splitting my head, so that it turns all weak and feeble. Thus I carry my very own load. Hauenstein is never empty of daily cares, many a piece of bad news. Were I able to change that easily, or if someone else could do it, I'd be eternally grateful. My feudal lord is angry with me, because evil people are envious of me. He says my services are not welcome, which hurts and pains me, since on my solemn oath no ducal house in its ducal splendour has ever inflicted any diminution in possessions, body, honour, or reputation on me. My friends all hate me without reason, which is what makes me age. I lament this to the whole world, honourable and wise people as well as many great and noble princes, who may well boast that they called the wolves to torment me and expel me.]

A biographical reading such as that of Wand-Wittkowski argues for the close link between the formulation in the song and the historical reality of conflict as documented (Wand-Wittkowski 2002: 178-91). While that may be superficially attractive, it oversimplifies the status of writing by considering it an unmediated and straightforward expression of individual personality, ignoring the complex ways in which writing is mediated through cultural conventions. Moreover, it is in danger of presenting a circular argument: knowing that the historical Oswald took certain positions does not in fact adequately elucidate the way in which isolation and lament are used by a lyric 'I' in the song, especially where some of these lines are said to refer to specific events only because critics are aware of such events from the historical documents. In many cases, it makes no difference for assessing the literary impact whether we relate the lines to an actual dispute or to an imagined possibility – what we need to understand is the way in which the final strophe of the song moves between the lament of lost social ties, and the singer's urge to set himself apart.[11]

The alternative strategy is that advocated by Spicker, who sees the lyric 'I' of the songs as essentially unconnected with the historical person Oswald. He debates,

---

[11] On the use of allusions to the Psalms in this song, see Suerbaum (2007: 65-76).

and rejects, the hypothesis that songs which contain references to 'Margarethe', the historically attested name of Oswald's wife, Margarethe of Schwangau, form a coherent group of so-called 'Ehelieder' (marriage songs), because he argues that the label, chosen on the basis of supposed reference to an external reality, obscures the considerable literary diversity of theses songs (Spicker 2007).[12] In Spicker's view, it is therefore a mere accident, of interest to historians but not to literary scholars, that we happen to know some of the things Oswald did, but what matters in order to appreciate the songs is not a knowledge of the historical author's actions, but an awareness of the literary stylization. That is methodologically safe, but perhaps also reductive, because it does not allow for any discussion about the ways in which the extraordinarily prominent first-person perspective of the songs relates to the known contours of the historical person and his way of writing in non-literary as well as literary contexts.

The study of the historical documents and their literary features suggests that the closest link between the two groups of texts, the 'I' of the letters and legal documents and the 'I' of the songs, is in fact the way in which they conceive of the relationship in which that 'I' stands with others. That relationship is, I would argue, neither entirely a literary construction, nor a straightforward representation of biographical events, but a way of negotiating between the need to belong to a group, and the articulation of conflicting or deviant views, desires or practices which set the singer as well as the aristocrat Oswald apart. The interest of the final strophe of 'Durch Barbarei, Arabia' (Kl 44) therefore lies in the way in which it moves from comic images of domestic strife to regret over political and legal isolation, and from there to a lament with biblical overtones, in which the singer presents himself as the friendless wretch exposed to the wolves, repenting of his misspent life. None of this needs to be autobiographical – but much of it, I would argue, articulates the tensions of a specific form of social existence. Oswald finds a way of expressing this tension much more sharply than contemporaries whom we see in the legal documents – yet it is the literariness of that articulation, not the biographical authenticity, which sets him apart as an artist.

In the reading of Oswald proposed here, what matters is not whether the pain inflicted by rejection is real or allegorical imprisonment, nor whether the penitence staged at the end of Kl 44 is heart-felt or a literary construction, because such questions suggest a separation between cultural practices of punishment on the one hand and literary, non-literal abstractions on the other. The voice which characterizes Oswald as a writer is instead defined by its literary quality: drawing

---

[12] See also Spicker (1993); cf. Hartmann (2004: 255-63).

on the discourse of legal dispute and punishment as well as that of penitence, it articulates a subjectivity which may experience deviance from the norm as social isolation, yet also, in laying it open, aims to reposition the subject. Oswald's 'I' is no longer just the victim of social forces meting out punishment, or complicit in 'the ritual of producing penal truth' through confession (Foucault 1977: 38), but instead asserts the right to differ, even where that difference is the source of suffering. By repositioning familiar tropes of pain and punishment, this voice thus asserts the uniqueness of the poet.

Works cited

Primary Sources

Die Lieder Oswalds von Wolkenstein, ed. Karl Kurt Klein, 4th edn, rev. by Burghart Wachinger, Altdeutsche Textbibliothek, 55 (Berlin/Boston: de Gruyter, 2015)

Die Lebenszeugnisse Oswalds von Wolkenstein: Edition und Kommentar, ed. Anton Schwob unter Mitarbeit von Karin Kranich-Hofbauer, Ute Monika Schwob and Brigitte Spreitzer, 5 vols (Vienna: Böhlau, 1999-2013)

Die mehrstimmigen Lieder Oswalds von Wolkenstein, ed. Ivana Pelnar, Münchner Editionen zur Musikgeschichte, 2 (Tutzing: Schneider, 1981)

Wachinger, Burghart (ed.). 2007. *Oswald von Wolkenstein: Lieder. Frühneuhochdeutsch / Neuhochdeutsch*, ed. Burghart Wachinger, Reclams Universal-Bibliothek, 18490 (Stuttgart: Reclam)

Secondary Sources

Foucault, Michel. 1977. *Discipline and Punish: The Birth of the Prison*, trans. Alan Sheridan (New York: Vintage Books)

Hartmann, Sieglinde. 2004. 'Oswald von Wolkenstein und Margarethe von Schwangau: ein Liebespaar?' in *Paare und Paarungen: Festschrift für Werner Wunderlich zum 60. Geburtstag*, ed. Ulrich Müller, Margarete Springeth and Michaela Auer-Müller, Stuttgarter Arbeiten zur Germanistik, 420 (Stuttgart: Heintz), pp. 255–63

Helmkamp, Kerstin. 2003. *Genre und Gender im späten Sang des Mittelalters: Die 'Gefangenschafts-' und 'Ehelieder' Oswalds von Wolkenstein*. Diss. FU-Berlin

Marold, Werner. 1995. *Kommentar zu den Liedern Oswalds von Wolkenstein*, ed. Alan Robertshaw, Innsbrucker Beiträge zur Kulturwissenschaft. Germanistische Reihe, 52 (Innsbruck: Institut für Germanistik an der Universität Innsbruck)

Müller, Ulrich. 1978. '"Dichtung" und "Wirklichkeit" bei Oswald von Wolkenstein: Aufgezeigt im Vergleich mit Altersliedern von Walther von der Vogelweide und Hans Sachs', in *Literaturwissenschaftliches Jahrbuch*, NF 19: 133-56

Schwob, Anton. 1979. *Historische Realität und literarische Umsetzung: Beobachtungen zur Stilisierung der Gefangenschaft in den Liedern Oswalds von Wolkenstein*, Innsbrucker Beiträge zur Kulturwissenschaft. Germanistische Reihe, 9 (Innsbruck: Institut für Germanistik an der Universität Innsbruck)

Spicker, Johannes. 1993. *Literarische Stilisierung und artistische Kompetenz bei Oswald von Wolkenstein* (Stuttgart: Hirzel)

—. 2007. *Oswald von Wolkenstein. Die Lieder*, Klassiker-Lektüren, 10 (Berlin: Erich Schmidt)

Suerbaum, Almut. 2007. 'Selbstinszenierung und literarische Tradition: Oswalds Lied K 31 'Der oben swebt'', in *mit clebeworten underweben: Festschrift für Peter Kern zum 65. Geburtstag*, ed. Thomas Bein and others, Kultur, Wissenschaft, Literatur, 16 (Frankfurt a.M./Oxford: Lang), pp. 65-76

—. 2010. 'Paradoxes of Performance: Autobiography in the Songs of Hugo von Montfort and Oswald von Wolkenstein', in *Aspects of the Performative in Medieval Culture*, ed. Manuele Gragnolati and Almut Suerbaum (Berlin/New York: de Gruyter), pp. 143-64

—. 2015. 'Language of Violence: Language as Violence in Vernacular Sermons', in *Polemic: Language as Violence in Medieval and Early Modern Discourse*, ed. Almut Suerbaum, George Southcombe and Benjamin Thompson (Farnham: Ashgate), pp. 125-48

Wachinger, Burghart. 1987. 'Oswald von Wolkenstein', in *Verfasserlexikon*, 2nd ed., VII (Berlin: de Gruyter), cols 134-69

—. 1991. 'Autorschaft und Überlieferung', in *Autorentypen*, ed. Walter Haug and Burghart Wachinger, Fortuna vitrea, 6 (Tübingen: Niemeyer), pp. 1-28

—. 1999. 'Liebeslieder vom späten bis zum frühen 16. Jahrhundert', in *Mittelalter und frühe Neuzeit: Übergänge, Umbrüche und Neuansätze*, ed. Walter Haug, Fortuna vitrea, 16 (Tübingen: Niemeyer), pp. 1-29.

Wand-Wittkowski, Christine. 2002. 'Topisches oder biographisches Ich? Das Lied 'Ain anefangk' Oswalds von Wolkenstein', in *Wirkendes Wort*, 52: 178-91

Wittstruck, Wilfried. 1987. *Der dichterische Namengebrauch in der deutschen Lyrik des Spätmittelalters*, Münstersche Mittelalter-Schriften, 61 (Munich: Fink)

6

Offenlich und unter ogen: Honour and Punishment in Late Medieval Urban Life

Jamie Page
University of Durham

Visions of punishment in the later Middle Ages are often drawn to its spectacular judicial manifestations: public executions involving the hanging, beheading or drowning of criminals and the brutal mutilation of their bodies are all part of the 'theatre of horror' (*Theater des Schreckens*) of late medieval and early modern justice, to cite Richard van Dülmen's evocative phrase (van Dülmen 1995).[1] Such images can also be associated with an historiographical narrative charting the slow rise of an official monopoly of the right to punish at the expense of more communal forms of justice based upon personal vengeance (Langbein 2007: 141-54). But whilst urban and royal authorities undoubtedly expanded their ability to pursue and prosecute crime considerably throughout and beyond the late Middle Ages, punishment can also be understood as a phenomenon deeply embedded in everyday life in this period, one practised in less spectacular, though highly significant ways amongst 'ordinary' people. In his recent and influential study of fourteenth-century lawsuits from Marseilles, for instance, Daniel Lord Smail reveals the extent to which the courts depended upon litigants themselves, who could inflict punishment upon adversaries by skilful use of legal procedure (Smail 2003: 1–28). For scholars of late medieval popular literature, the notion that people punished one another through violence or mockery is, of course, hardly news: the plots of genres such as the short verse *Mären* are replete with errant spouses, foolish clerics, and misbehaving servants who figure as the subjects and objects of punishment. Urban literature from this period is also frequently concerned with justice and social order, and grotesque acts of mutilation or physical abuse which echo judicial penalties are common.[2] Although such texts do not on their own constitute good evidence of

---

[1] Despite what its title implies, van Dülmen's work gives partial coverage to justice in the Middle Ages.
[2] On mutilation see Chinca (1994). Social order as a theme of late medieval popular literature is a central concern in Grubmüller (2006).

actual behaviour, they could reach a broad public, and suggest that phenomena like punishment could provide compelling entertainment.

In what follows, I bring together a selection of German legal and literary narratives to explore in depth the claim made above: namely that punishment was embedded in the everyday interactions of 'ordinary' people in late medieval urban life. I aim to demonstrate that as a conscious, though informal practice, punishment might be usefully understood as behaviour which aimed in some way to manipulate or damage the honour *(Ehre)* of another individual or group.[3] Honour was a crucially important component of personal identity in late medieval urban life, and a major influence upon norms of behaviour across social strata.[4] It can be understood in this context as a close relative of reputation, taking a cue from the Latin *fama*, the 'public talk of people and things' which overlaps semantically with the Middle and Early New High German *ere* (Fenster and Smail 2003: 1-2). The status of a person's honour was thus determined heavily by *fama* relating to them, and as I shall show here, both legal and fictional narratives depicting scenes of punishment are heavily concerned with the boundaries between the private, domestic sphere and the more public domain in which talk and rumour circulated.

I draw upon two specific types of narrative in my discussion. These constitute, firstly, a selection of fourteenth- and fifteenth-century judicial depositions from cases of slander and violence handled by the municipal council court (*Ratsgericht*) of the imperial free city of Zurich. Amongst German-speaking cities, Zurich is almost unique in presiding over a rich set of late medieval judicial archives containing witness testimony from a secular court. Beginning in 1376, the so-called *Rats- und Richtbücher* which hold the records run virtually unbroken well into the early modern period and are at their most detailed for the fourteenth and fifteenth centuries.[5] This judicial material is examined alongside two well-known *Mären*, Claus Spaun's *Fünfzig Gulden Minnelohn* and *Spiegel und Igel* (the latter an adaptation of an earlier story known simply as *Der Spiegel*), both of which depict domestic conflicts centred upon themes of punishment and revenge. Fictional texts and legal depositions offer a strong basis for comparison: as Natalie Zemon Davis showed famously in her study of sixteenth-century French supplication pleas, premodern litigants sought primarily to communicate narratives which conformed to recognizable, and thus convincing modes of storytelling (Davis

---

[3] Honour and punishment were, of course, closely related to one another in the phenomenon of *Ehrenstrafen*, whose purpose was to shame criminals through the imposition of physical penalties such as the pillory or banishment; on *Ehrenstrafen* see Schwerhoff (1993), Schmidt (1995: 64), and Wettlaufer (2010).
[4] On honour and the law, see Burghartz (1990), Schreiner and Schwerhoff (1995), and Zmora (1998).
[5] On the Zurich Ratsgericht, see Burghartz (1990), Malamud (2003), and Pohl-Zucker (2017).

1987). Fictionality was thus deeply embedded in the practice of testifying.[6] Placing these two types of narrative and their shared concerns alongside one another also allows us to look at the phenomenon of punishment in two ways: whilst legal documents demonstrate the extent to which it shaped daily life and reveals some of the categories through which it was conceptualized, fiction shows us the role it could play in the imagination.

Slander, violence and honour: punishment in the Zurich *Ratsgericht*
Zurich's surviving judicial archives make it exceptional from a legal historical perspective, although in a more general sense the city itself was largely unremarkable in the Middle Ages. Of middling size, its population numbered something close to 6000 in the fourteenth century, a figure which increased slowly throughout the fifteenth. After joining the Swiss Confederacy in 1351, Zurich was nominally part of the German Empire until the early modern period.[7] The court of the city council, known as the *Ratsgericht*, was one of several active secular courts and was staffed by council members who sat in judgment on a variety of low-level crimes such as slander, fraud, assault, and manslaughter. After 1400 the court also acquired the authority to judge capital crimes. One of its primary functions was to arbitrate conflicts concerned with honour, where a delicate balance existed between the demands of burghers' personal honour and the need to preserve the peace of the city (*Stadtfrieden*). Often, this meant that the most expedient response to crime was to facilitate reconciliation between disputing individuals or families, although towards the fifteenth and sixteenth centuries the council sought increasingly actively to discipline and punish deviant behaviour through *ex officio* actions, a trend also observed elsewhere in the late medieval West (Pohl 1999). Policing crime and encouraging moral behaviour heightened the authority and prestige of the council, and contributed to the honour of the city (*Ehre der Stadt*) in the eyes of God (Burghartz 1990: 14; Isenmann 2014: 330).

Both women and men were able to access justice in the Zurich *Ratsgericht*, although the court itself was overwhelmingly a male space: whilst women could give evidence, they appeared far less often than men and needed the presence of male supporters to do so, whilst their testimony was weighted less heavily than that of men.[8] One of the more common types of case dealt with by the court involved

---

[6] The debate over the 'truth' of premodern judicial documents and the methodological problems of their interpretation is extensive; for a recent summary of these issues and a series of compelling case studies, see Goodich (2006).

[7] For a brief, though comprehensive history of the city, see Gilomen (1995).

[8] On women in the courts in later medieval Germany see Burghartz (1991), Rublack (1998) and Malamud (2003).

complaints of insult and slander. Slander needed to have taken place in public for it to qualify as such – in other words, where other people could overhear an insult or hear gossip relating to the injured party. Most cases therefore refer to the fact that insulting words or actions had taken place 'publicly' (*offenlich*) and 'visibly' (*unter ogen*), and often the presence of witnesses was noted explicitly in comments that the offending action had taken place 'in front of honourable people' (*vor erbern luten*) or 'in front of decent people' (*vor biderben luten*). It was the presence of others, rather than simply a public location which made something 'public'; as Shannon McSheffrey has noted, 'public' and 'private' were situational as well as spatial concepts (McSheffrey 2004: 986).[9]

In common with the findings of regional studies of insult and slander across medieval Europe, patterns of invective which appear in the Zurich records were strongly gendered, and were attuned to the conventions of feminine and masculine honour (Lesnick 1991; Toch 1993; Strocchia 1998; Dean 2004; Laufenberg 2007). Women's honour was heavily predicated upon their sexual comportment, and by far the most common insults directed at female targets were those which suggested they were prostitutes.[10] In his study of slander in late medieval Bologna, Trevor Dean notes that 'insults against women took the form of naming and seeking to punish alleged "whores"' (Dean 2004: 220). Because of the official penalties which could be associated with illegal prostitution, this could be an effective way to chastise women for real or imagined sexual transgressions. In German-speaking cities, particularly towards the later 1400s, civic authorities began to undertake increasingly aggressive policies against clandestine prostitution and illicit sex which might see independent operators forced into official brothels. The brothel thus stood as a symbol of punishment, whose inhabitants could be seen as negative examples for virtuous women to avoid (Schuster 1993).

Cases from Zurich show how references to whoredom could inform a range of slanderous speech acts against women. Sometimes this simply involved the use of the word 'whore' in the midst of a dispute. Such was the case in 1394, for example, when the wife of Hans Maler complained to the council about the insults she had suffered from the wife of Rüdi Vertinger. Maler's wife told the court that after having given birth, she had been forced to go out in search of bread on account of her poverty. As a result, and to the great consternation of her neighbours, she had not

---

[9] On the concepts of public and private in this period, see also the essays in Melville and von Moos (1998), and more recently Emmelius (2004).
[10] See the comments in Roper (1994: 64) on Augsburg criminal trials, mostly later than 1500, but which also apply to the medieval period: 'For women, by contrast, honour was paradigmatically personal, dependent to a far greater degree on her sexual com-portment alone [...]. As slander cases show, the most direct way to assault a woman's honour, married or not, was to call her a whore.'

had her child baptized for several days. In response to this, she claimed, Vertinger's wife had called her 'a wicked whore and a procuress', and claimed that her husband was a pimp [si sye ein böse hůr und ein arswelberin und habe ir man verkuppelt] (Staatsarchiv Zürich, B VI, 195, fol. 270ʳ). In other cases, variants of the insult such as 'priest's whore' (also common in English slander cases) might be reported (Karras 1996: 30). In one such example from 1394, a woman named Hangenörlin claimed that another woman named Vogelin had stood outside her house at night, where she shouted 'Come out, you damned priests' whore! The priests are standing in front of the door waiting for you' [gang her us du verhite pfaffenhůrr die pfaffen stånd vor der tur und wartend din] (StaZh, B VI, 195, fol. 282ᵛ). A slightly earlier case from 1386 supplies nearly the full lexicon of common variants of the insult 'whore': here, Uli Zen Husern's wife complained to the *Ratsgericht* that Kochli's wife had called her not just a 'a wicked, damned priests' whore,' but also a 'students' whore, usurers' whore, and all the world's whore [...] and right wicked woman' [ein bôsi verhiti pfaffen hůr und schůler hůr und Ganwetschen hur und all der welt hůr [...] und ein recht bôsi frow] (StaZh, B VI, 193, fol. 34ʳ).

Were such allegations of whoredom well-founded? In most cases it seems far more likely that insults like these were used in the heat of the moment, and were not directed at real prostitutes, reflecting the fact that 'whore' was simply a default term of abuse for a female adversary.[11] Nor is it probable that women who genuinely worked as prostitutes would find officials willing to accept complaints about slander, or indeed would wish to bring themselves to the council's attention. Some instances in which women were defamed as whores do, nevertheless, make specific reference to illicit sexual behaviour. Any kind of extra-marital sexual transgression could be equated by contemporaries with prostitution, since promiscuity rather than financial exchange was considered the prostitute's most telling characteristic (Karras 1996: 27) Slander based upon accusations of adultery, for instance, might see women being described as the whore of a particular man; in one such case from 1392, Meyerin Vischerin told the court in 1392 that Bertschy Bach's wife had said that 'she was Luidmager's whore, and he rode her day and night' [si were des Luidmagers hur und er ritte si tag und nacht] (StaZh, B VI, 195, fol. 38). Women whose marriages were were in some way ambiguous might also be labelled whores. Margaret Strelet said in 1395 that Willi Östin and her mother had come to her house and 'told her that she was a whore, and that she was living with her husband whoreishly' [si wer ein hur und sessen och bi ir man in hurs wise]. In her own defence, Margaret told

---

[11] Rath (1994: 354) notes that for medieval and early modern criminal court cases, a woman committing any kind of crime might be labelled in this way because of the heavy emphasis placed on women's supposedly carnal nature.

the court that 'this was not true, and that he was her husband' [daz aber nicht war ist und daz er ir elich man ist], suggesting that the original accusation had been that her marriage was somehow invalid (StaZh, B VI 196, fol. 97^v).

A case from 1468 illustrates how individuals perceived the link between prostitution and the municipal brothel as a place of punishment for sinful women. In this instance Grette Gullerin and her daughter Elsy reported to the council an incident which had taken place as they made their way back from a companion's house after dark. They described being approached by group of men named Hanns, Cunrat Scher from Schaffhausen, and Appentzeller, who tried together to take them into a nearby brothel. When they resisted, the men called them 'priests' whores' (*pfaffenhuren*) and said that both of them should be taken to the so-called Huttly, the site in Zurich where public executions were carried out, and drowned (StaZh, B VI, 226, fol. 35^r-36^v). In this case, the men in question appear initially to have mistaken Grete Gullerin and her daughter for clandestine prostitutes touting for business after dark, and then reacted angrily to the discovery that this was not the case.[12] As independent operators, they were fit to be taken into the brothel; the men's attempt to do so can be interpreted as a form of punishment for their failure to keep to stay within their own private, domestic space as they were supposed to inhabit after dark. Another sense of the association between punishment and prostitution can be seen in a case handled by the council in 1456, in which two brothers named Eberhart reported their step-father Heini Hottinger to the court after he had beaten their mother and sister. In their testimony, the men told the court that they had confronted Hottinger, saying 'why are you beating our mother? You shouldn't beat decent women, this would be too much even for a woman in the brothel' [warumb schlechst du uns unser mütter man solt biderb frowen nit also slachen, were sy auch ein frow uff dem frowen hus es were zu vil] (StaZh, B VI, 220, fol. 91^r–92^r). In this instance, the record suggests that a prostitute could be considered a more worthy recipient of punishment than an 'honourable' woman.

For men, the picture which emerges from court records with regard to honour, slander and punishment is a little different. Whereas women's honour was predicated heavily upon their sexual conduct and primarily demanded the maintenance of chastity, in the culture of artisanal masculinity of the late medieval city, the acquisition of a respectable masculine identity depended to a large extent upon engaging in social and economic competition with other men (Karras 2003: 10). Honour was also tightly bound to a man's professional identity and his status within the craft guild hierarchy, whilst some types of work were considered explicitly

---

[12] In some cities, women who travelled at night without a light could be taken into the brothel on the assumption that they were prostitutes; see Buff (1877: 187).

dishonourable for their practitioners (Stuart 1999). These factors shaped patterns of invective, making the most common insults for men those which had to do with dishonesty, and which contained economic undertones that attacked men's roles as 'carriers of public trust' (Dean 2004: 219). Common insults in this vein which appear in the Zurich records include 'thief' (*dieb*) or 'rogue' (*schelm*). Much like 'whore', such terms of abuse were mostly used in a general rather than a specific sense against opponents. As Derek Neal has argued in the context of slander and insult in late medieval England, 'when late medieval Englishmen hurled the insult "thief" at one another [...] they did not narrowly mean "person who steals things" but "dishonestly tricky, crafty, deceptive person"' (Neal 2008: 191). A case from 1389 brought to the court by Metzi Kunczin illustrates this kind of usage neatly. She described to the council how Jo Hasenkol had insulted her and her daughter as whores, 'and said that she should tell this to her husband, the old thief, and her sons, the thieves' [ir man dem alten diep und och ir sunen den dieben] (StaZh, B VI, 194, fol. 53ᵛ). The insult contains no targeted reference to thievery, but rather shows how *dieb*, like *hur*, provided a readily available term of abuse in a moment of anger.

Other, more elaborate ways of slandering an individual man in relation to his economic standing could involve attacking his competence or fitness to work within the craft guild hierarchy of the city. In one such example from 1463, Johannes Velck brought a complaint to the court about Jacob Müller and another man named Ysenhutt. Strife had first arisen amongst the three after Velck had heard that Müller had insulted him by saying that he would never send an apprentice to work with him, because he was 'not good enough for it' [nit gnüg gut dartzu]. A confrontation had followed in the marketplace between Velck, Müller and Ysenhutt, after which the three men agreed a sworn truce known as *Stallung*.[13] As they were parting from one another, however, Velck claimed that Ysenhutt had called after him in a mocking fashion as if challenging him to a fight. Velck's complaint was based upon an accusation that Ysenhutt had breached their truce by mocking him, a dishonourable action which was liable to land the offender with a fine (StaZh, B VI 223, fol. 217ʳ).

Another, extraordinary, case from 1469 shows a more elaborate attempt to undermine a man's economic credibility. In this instance a hat-maker from Vienna named Jörg Crünberger reported that Pauly Glaser, another hat-maker from Strasbourg, had told a number of others in the trade that:

he was neither a decent man nor craftsman, because once, when he was serving with his master Hanns Dignower, he saw him take his penis in his hand and love himself

---

[13] On *Stallung*, see Pohl (2003).

with it, so that his seed came from him and fell on the ground, and once this had happened he ground it with his foot.

[er sye nit ein redlicher geselle noch handwercks genoß dann er habe von im gesehen, as er by Hannsen Dignower sinem meister gedient, das er sinen zerß in sin hend genomen, und sich selbs damit gemint hab, das im sin natur entgangen und vor im uff die erd nidgevallen und als das beschehen sye, habe er das mit dem füß vertretten.]

(StaZh, B VI, 226, fol. 378^{r-v})

This was a shocking allegation whose seriousness was emphasized by the fact that Glaser also referred to it as 'heresy' (*ketzry*). Given that both men were hatmakers, the conflict may well have arisen in the context of a rivalry between guild members. Here, the fact that only a small number of men could hope to become masters within most craft guilds could generate intense competition (Karras 2003: 109). Glaser had perhaps slandered Crünberger in order to gain retribution for some unknown offence, or perhaps hoped to undermine him as an economic rival by destroying his honour. Crünberger's complaint about this accusation suggests that his opponent was successful, at least in the short term: it states that not only had his honour been severely damaged, but also that had been forbidden to practice his trade in the wake of this shameful rumour. Having successfully mobilized a number of witnesses to speak in his defence, however, Crünberger was then able to turn the tables on Glaser. In a note following the initial record of Crünberger's complaint, the register states that Glaser had been required to make an official complaint about Crünberger to the council within a month. Rather than do so, however, he had simply fled the city.

Incidents of insults and slander such as these could function as an informal, though effective means of punishment within late medieval urban life because of the damage they could do to the honour of their targets. This could also have significant material consequences: women defamed as whores might struggle to find marriage partners, whilst men who were suspected of dishonesty might find acceptance or advancement within guild ranks difficult. The response to an insult, too, could be considered a form of punishment. A successful complaint to the court which produced a favourable verdict could see the actions of the offending party publicly censured and could result in a material punishment, usually a fine. The language of legal documents suggests that participants were well aware that a court case represented a chance to have an opponent punished by the authorities, with cases often containing requests for officials to take action, or statements that the injuries they had suffered deserved to be punished. In the aforementioned case of Johannes Velck and Ysenhutt, for instance, the written record of Velck's complaint concludes with the statement that because Ysenhutt had mocked him, he should be 'be punished for breaking *Stallung*' [für ein stallung bruch gestraft werden] (StaZh, B VI, 223, fol. 217ʳ). Although it is impossible to verify whether phrases like these represent the original speech of the complainant (a perennial problem in the study of medieval judicial documents), it at least suggests that the desire for punishment was understood implicitly to be part of the process of going to court, even if it was not always verbalized.[14] Private vengeance did not vanish as the judicial apparatus of late medieval officialdom grew; rather, as the availability of legal procedures and courts increased, individuals became adept at making use of them to pursue adversaries in court (Smail 2003: 9-13).

If insult and slander could be found at one end of a scale of offences which for which individuals sought redress at court, then acts of violence could be found at the other. A scale of actions is, in fact, a helpful image in this context: on the evidence of late medieval and early modern judicial documents, scholars have found indications that conflicts often played out in a ritualized, almost staged manner, in which participants moved upwards towards violence through recognized steps including the trading of insults and threats, sometimes the drawing of weapons, and finally the exchange of blows (Jansen 2013: 434).

Where violence is concerned, patterns of deviancy in the Zurich records show once again how conflicts were played out according to the demands of heavily gendered codes of honour. For women, most incidents handled by the court concerned attacks carried out by men, although women could certainly expect officials to respond to complaints about the violence of other females. The most common form of violence likely to be suffered by women, however, and one which was closely associated with punishment, was domestic chastisement by a husband or another male householder. Husbands had the rights to discipline their wives or daughters in order to correct sin and preserve the honour of both man and wife, and the city council was generally reluctant to interfere in instances of violence against women, whose protection was supposed to be the responsibility of male relatives (Pohl 2002: 254-55). An exception could, however, be made in cases of extreme cruelty in which a man overstepped the boundaries of acceptable chastisement by seriously injuring his wife or putting her in fear of her life.[15] One Zurich case which illustrates the kind of scenario which might bring a man to the attention of the city council concerns a certain Hans Aberlÿ, the subject of an investigation in 1465. The testimony of a neighbour, Hanns von Egre, recorded how he had been woken around the twelfth hour by a terrible noise and had asked another neighbour,

---

[14] A comprehensive discussion of the methodological issues in dealing with the records of speech in pre-modern judicial records can be found in the introduction to Goodich (2006).
[15] On domestic violence see Salisbury, Donavin & Price (2002), Dean (2004), and Wieben (2010).

Margreth Leman, what was going on. Although Margreth was unable to say, a third woman called Gebhartin told them that 'it was Aberlÿ's wife, her husband beat her, and she ran out of the house and came to her, and was very poorly' [es were die Aberlinin, die hette der man geschlagen, und die were uß dem huß gelouffen und zu ira komen, und die gehübe sy so ubel]. Although it is not clear how the case came to court, it seems plausible that one of the neighbours reported Aberlÿ to the council, which then launched its own investigation. This kind of disturbance may well have been a regular occurrence in the neighbourhood, whilst Gebhartin seems to have been motivated by sympathy for the suffering of Aberlÿ's wife's. Aberlÿ also seems to have had a poor relationship with his neighbours, as seems evident from Hans von Egre's report that after his wife had fled, he had 'cursed his neighbours with the dropsy [...] and made many other wicked oaths' [und flüchte allen sinen nachpuren das fallentubel [...] und auch [...] habe er vil böse swuren getan] (StaZh, B VI, 224, fol. 78ʳ-80ʳ).

When it came to incidents of violence involving men alone, the demands of personal honour exerted a strong influence upon the reporting of crimes. Male conflicts dominated the court business, although the 'dark number' of male-only violent episodes was undoubtedly far greater than the number which made it before the judges. This was partly because masculine honour codes impelled men to demonstrate the capability to protect themselves and to respond to provocations or attacks independently: complaining to the authorities thus risked acknowledging an inability to do so. In order to save face, a man who had been the victim of violence usually had to demonstrate that he had suffered a sneaky, underhanded attack which gave him little chance to defend himself, and which painted the perpetrator in a dishonourable light.

In one such example from 1467, a carpenter named Rudy Fry brought a complaint to the court concerning a fisherman named Heini Wunderlich, with whom he had had a dispute about a sum of money the latter owed him. When the two men had argued in the fish market after Fry had reported him to the council for failing to pay back the money at his asking, Fry claimed that after he had turned his back to leave, Wunderlich 'had followed him without him knowing, and had hit him on the head so that his hat fell onto the ground' [sye der benant Heiny Wunderlich im unwissent nachgevolgt und hab im an sin hopt geschlagen das im der hut abgevallen schier darzu herdvellig worden war] (StaZh, B VI, 225, fol. 463ʳ). Whether or not this is what actually happened, or indeed in other descriptions of conflicts like this one, describing an opponent in this manner could be way of getting even by calling into question his honour. Where Fry gave a fairly detailed description of how he had been the victim of a sneak attack, other cases relied upon stock phrases to signal dishonourable intent on the part of their adversaries. One of the most commonly used in the Zurich registers is 'by night and fog' [bey nacht und nebel]; instead of being a comment upon the time of day or weather conditions, this phrase signified the complainant's claim that whoever had attacked them had done so covertly. Successful punishment of an opponent through the court therefore required a man to demonstrate carefully how he had been the victim of treachery, a move which affirmed one's own honour and called into question that of the aggressor.[16]

der burger straft sein frauen allein: honour and punishment in popular fiction

Conflicts found in late medieval court cases find many points of comparison with the plots of late medieval popular fiction. Although surviving *Mären* are often too outlandish and grotesque to reflect directly the kind of details recounted in court documents, in thematic terms they address many of the concerns which do appear regularly, such as sexual behaviour, marital relations, justice and honour. Particular fascination appears to have been reserved for tales concerning the preservation of honour and the permeability of the boundaries between the domestic and public spheres, which do appear regularly in the latter signified in court documents by descriptors such as *vor biderben luten* or *offenlich und unter ogen*.

These concerns underpin the well-known *Mären* entitled *Fünfzig Gulden Minnelohn* by Claus Spaun and Hans Rosenplüt's *Spiegel und Igel*. Both were both written around the mid- to late fifteenth century, when the activity of the Zurich *Ratsgericht* was at its height, and circulated initially around the cities of Augsburg and Nuremberg. If legal cases supply evidence about the categories through which people thought about reputation and honour and the divisions between domestic and public life, then fiction suggests how they engaged with these imaginatively, and what about them made good entertainment, or induced anxiety.

Fünfzig Gulden Minnelohn begins when a young student arrives in a far-off town with fifty florins from his father to spend on an education. Instead of doing so, however, the student uses his money to spend the night with the beautiful wife of a well-to-do burgher he sees on the street, the encounter arranged by the maidservant of the wife who craftily recognizes his lust. When the student arrives at the wife's house that night, she shows him into the latrine to wait for her while she goes to bed as normal with her husband. During the night, however, she manages to sneak off

---

[16] When the Zurich city council began to judge cases of homicide in the fifteenth century, sneak attacks were associated with the category of 'dishonourable manslaughter' which could earn a killer the death penalty. In such cases a covert approach was assumed to demonstrate the intent to kill, as opposed to instances of 'honourable manslaughter', a category which could be applied to self-defence or to cases of justifiable provocation which could allow the offender to pay a fine to the deceased party's kin and return to the community after a period of exile; see Pohl (1999) and Pohl-Zucker (2017).

to see the student by convincing her husband that she is suffering illness. The pair have sex three times in succession, whilst the wife manages to cover up the sounds of their lovemaking by asking the husband to sing in the background.

The next day, having lost his money, the student goes about the town bemoaning his foolishness when he is overheard by a passerby – this, of course, is the same burgher betrayed by his wife the previous night. The burgher realizes at once what has happened, although rather than reacting angrily he thinks up a scheme to teach both parties a lesson. He invites the student to have a meal with him and his wife, neither of whom are expecting to see the other again. When the student duly arrives the wife reacts with silent horror to his presence, but nevertheless obeys her husband's wish that she act the good hostess. At dinner, the husband – who clearly regards the affair as a big joke – reveals that the game is up, and sets about making restitutions. Firstly he takes back the fifty florins paid to his wife in exchange for sex, and gives a small sum to the maid for her services as a procuress. Then he pays his wife the customary fee given to a prostitute for each of the three sexual encounters the previous night, and then he pays himself for providing musical entertainment for the two of them. Finally, he gives the remainder of the money to the student and sends him on his way. The text closes by noting that 'the burgher punished his wife alone' ('der burger straft sein frauen allein', 376), with the result that she remained faithful to him thereafter, and was able to keep her honour as nobody ever found out what had happened.

Fünfzig Gulden Minnelohn can be seen on the surface to depict the kind of domestic chastisement which was seen to be the privilege of husbands, and which finds occasional references in court cases. The role of punishment in the story might be read in several ways: from one perspective, in the legal context of marriage, the husband can be seen taking a pragmatic response to the discovery of his wife's adultery that echoes its treatment in ecclesiastical courts in the later Middle Ages. Although he forces the student to reimburse his wife for her sexual services, showing clearly that she has behaved as a whore, he declines to confirm this status in public. As Leah Otis-Couer has recently shown, the prosecution of adultery in the later Middle Ages often aimed at repairing the marital relationship (Otis-Couer 2009: 351). The insistence of canon law on the indissolubility of marriage and the potential for the husband's humiliation meant that partners were encouraged to negotiate a reconciliation, rather than create an ugly spectacle through the punishment of one party. In *Fünfzig Gulden Minnelohn*, public punishment of the wife would damage the honour both of the wife and and of her husband, and so produce a far worse outcome than dealing with the matter in private.

From another angle, the burgher's treatment of his wife and her lover can also be read as a validation of patriarchal authority based upon the right of senior civic men to punish both women and younger men for their sinful behaviour. This is first evident in the burgher's treatment of the student. By using some of his wealth to pay for a prostitute's services, he can be seen to affirm the license granted to young men to indulge in this kind of morally ambiguous entertainment. At the same time, however, by surprising him with an invitation to dinner in his own house, the threat of more severe punishment lurks in the background to teach the young man a lesson. This kind of patriarchal authority could be associated both with husbands, who as *paterfamilias* were responsible for the behaviour of those within their household, and with municipal officials whose role towards the later fourteenth and fifteenth centuries saw them take a greater responsibility for the regulation of the moral behaviour of city-dwellers (Schuster 2013). Women and young men could be expected to act foolishly, and the practice of good civic government aimed primarily to correct deviance and re-integrate offenders.

Punishment in *Fünfzig Gulden Minnelohn* is thus presented as a masculine prerogative which, when wielded in a benevolent fashion, could be a force upholding a patriarchal vision of social order. Restitution comes about because the boundaries between the domestic sphere and the streets are repaired by the end of the tale, preventing *fama* about the betrayal of the burgher by his wife from leaking out. More broadly, authority of the husband within the domestic sphere can be compared to that of civic rulers, whose own authority was exercised in part through judicial punishment. The benevolent attitude towards the wife and student in the tale contrast notably with the portrayal of the maidservant, however. At the end of the text, the narrator remarks in retrospect that she had been responsible for the whole affair because of her procurement [kupplerei, 385], closing the story with the hope that 'the devil give her his blessing!' [der teufel geb ir seinen segen, 388] and 'break her neck' [iren hals abprech, 390]. Her crime seems to have been her willingness to transgress freely across the public and private spheres which divide the home from the streets, where gossip and *fama* might circulate freely. This malicious mobility makes her an agent of social disorder, whilst her punishment is implied to be the most severe of all, and to take place at the hands of the devil.

Spiegel und Igel, by the Nuremberg poet Hans Rosenplüt, deals with related themes of honour, sexuality and *fama*. Rosenplüt's story is based upon an earlier tale known simply as *Der Spiegel*, extended and given alternate ending which suggests how both men and women may punish one another in managing reputation in the context of sexual transgression. Both *Der Spiegel* and *Spiegel und Igel* begin by describing the unsuccessful efforts of a servant named Herolt to seduce Demut, a maid who works alongside him in the same household. Having had his advances rebuffed by her, he comes down to the kitchen early one morning to find her asleep by the fire. He briefly considers forcing himself upon her. Worried that she could throw him into the fire, however, he decides instead to play a trick. Taking a mirror down from the wall, he places it between her legs. Demut wakes shortly, and, seeing the reflection of the flames, cries out in fear that her body and soul are burning up inside her. She calls for help, and when the master of the house arrives, he reaches between her legs and discovers the trick. He castigates Demut for her foolishness, telling her that she should have given in to his advances; now, he says, everybody will find out about Herolt's deception and ridicule her.

Rosenplüt's version adds a second part to the tale which sees Demut take her revenge. Following her humiliation in front of the other members of the household, she agrees to have sex with Herolt if he only promises not to tell anybody else about his mirror trick. He agrees, and the pair arrange a secret meeting for that night. Before he arrives at her room, however, Demut places a hedgehog between her legs. Herolt arrives, and, unaware of the trick, receives a painful shock as he tries to have sex with her. Having got even, Demut suggests that the two of them part in friendship, and never tell anybody else outside the house about what had happened. Herolt agrees, and the tale ends with the narrator adding that – just like the wife of the burgher in *Fünfzig Gulden Minnelohn* – thus was Demut was thus able to retain her honour ('also behielt die meit ire er', II, 131).

In both Spaun's and Rosenplüt's tales, the resolution of a domestic disturbance depends upon knowledge of what has happened behind closed doors never becoming public, where it could bring dishonour on one or more characters involved. Rosenplüt's addition allows him to tell a slightly different story with regard to gender: whereas *Der Spiegel* suggests that men have the ability to punish women who refuse to submit to their will, and shows how women's honour can be vulnerable to masculine aggression, *Spiegel und Igel* offers a more complex vision in which women as well as men are skilled manipulators of *fama*. Similarly to the court cases discussed above, both stories show that things truly 'matter' once they became the stuff of public knowledge – even cuckolding, one of the most shameful scenarios imaginable for the male head of a household, is rendered harmless because it remains a secret. Both stories can be understood as fantasies about the difficulties and the necessity of controlling the vitally important boundaries between public and private spheres, and thus determining the status of personal honour.

Conclusion

Punishment emerges in fictional and legal narratives as a practice embedded in everyday life, one which for ordinary people played a crucial role in guarding and maintaining honour and reputation. In this sense it was part of a set of practices connected to the management of *fama*, an important skill in late medieval urban life which facilitated social integration and cohesion (Fenster and Smail, 2003: 4). It appears in this way primarily as a conservative phenomenon, one concerned with the integrity of boundaries between private and public realms, whose transgression could be associated with dishonour. Punishment is also associated in male-authored texts with masculine authority and with the maintenance of a patriarchal vision of social order: the right to punish was reserved mostly for men, and predominantly for senior civic men. Although women could practise punishment, too, the fact that most late medieval urban records are attuned to masculine norms makes traces of their agency more challenging to recover.

Works Cited

Primary Sources

Claus Spaun, *Fünfzig Gulden Minnelohn*, in *Die deutsche Märendichtung des 15. Jahrhunderts,* ed. Hanns Fischer, Münchener Texte und Untersuchungen zur deutschen Literatur des Mittelalter, 12 (Munich: Beck, 1966), pp. 351-61

Hans Rosenplüt, *Spiegel und Igel* I and II, in *Die deutsche Märendichtung des 15. Jahrhunderts*, ed. Hanns Fischer, Münchener Texte und Untersuchungen zur deutschen Literatur des Mittelalter, 12 (Munich: Beck, 1966), pp. 124-33

Zurich, Staatsarchiv Zürich, BVI 193, 194, 195, 196, 220, 223, 224, 225, 226

Secondary Sources

Buff, Adolf. 1877. 'Verbrechen und Verbrecher zu Augsburg in der zweiten Hälfte des 14. Jahrhunderts', *Zeitschrift des Historischen Vereins für Schwaben und Neuburg*, 4: 160-231

Burghartz, Susanna. 1990. *Leib, Ehre und Gut: Delinquenz in Zürich Ende des 14. Jahrhunderts* (Zurich: Chronos)

—. 1991. 'Kein Ort für Frauen? Städtische Gerichte im Spätmittelalter,' in *Auf der Suche nach der Frau im Mittelalter: Fragen, Quellen, Antworten*, ed. Bea Lundt (Munich: Fink), pp. 49-64

Chinca, Mark. 1994. 'The Body in some Middle High German *Mären*: Taming and Maiming,' in *Framing Medieval Bodies*, ed. Sarah Kay and Miri Rubin (Manchester: Manchester University Press), pp. 187-210

Davis, Natalie Zemon. 1987. *Fiction in the Archives: Pardon Tales and their Tellers in Sixteenth-Century France*, The Harry Camp Lectures, 1985-86 (Stanford: Stanford University Press)

Dean, Trevor. 2004. 'Domestic Violence in Late-Medieval Bologna', *Renaissance Studies*, 18: 527-43

—. 2004. 'Gender and Insult in an Italian city: Bologna in the later Middle Ages', *Social History*, 29: 217-31

Dülmen, Richard van. 1995. *Theater des Schreckens. Gerichtspraxis und Strafrituale in der frühen Neuzeit*, 4th edn (Munich: Beck)

Emmelius, Caroline, et al. (ed.). 2004. *Offen und Verborgen: Vorstellungen und Praktiken des Öffentlichen und Privaten in Mittelalter und Früher Neuzeit* (Göttingen: Wallstein)

Fenster, Thelma and Daniel Lord Smail. 2003. 'Introduction', in *Fama. The Politics of Talk and Reputation in Medieval Europe*, ed. Thelma Fenster and Daniel Lord Smail (Ithaca: Cornell University Press), pp. 1-11

Gilomen, Hans-Jörg. 1995. 'Innere Verhältnisse der Stadt Zürich 1300–1500', in *Geschichte des Kantons Zürich*, I: *Frühzeit bis Spätmittelalter*, ed. Niklaus Flüeler and Marianne Flüeler-Grauwiler (Zurich: Werd), pp. 336-89

Goodich, Michael. 2006. *Voices from the Bench: The Narratives of Lesser Folk in Medieval Trials*, New Middle Ages (New York: Palgrave Macmillan)

Grubmüller, Klaus. 2006. *Die Ordnung, der Witz und das Chaos: eine Geschichte der europäischen Novellistik im Mittelalter: Fabliau, Märe, Novelle* (Tübingen: Niemeyer)

Isenmann, Eberhard. 2014. *Die deutsche Stadt im Spätmittelalter, 1250-1500: Stadtgestalt, Recht, Stadtregiment, Kirche, Gesellschaft, Wirtschaft*, 2nd edn (Cologne: Böhlau)

Jansen, Katherine L. 2013. '"Pro bono pacis": Crime, Conflict, and Dispute Resolution. The Evidence of Notarial Peace Contracts in Late Medieval Florence', *Speculum*, 88: 427-56

Karras, Ruth Mazo. 1996. *Common Women: Prostitution and Sexuality in Medieval England*, Studies in the History of Sexuality (Oxford: Oxford University Press)

—. 2003. *From Boys to Men: Formations of Masculinity in Medieval Europe* (Philadelphia: University of Pennsylvania Press)

Langbein, John H. 2007. *Prosecuting Crime in the Renaissance: England, Germany, France* (Clark, NJ: The Lawbook Exchange)

Laufenberg, Lynn Marie. 2007. 'More than Words: Gender, Gesture, Insult, and Assault in Medieval Florence', *Virginia Social Science Journal*, 42: 64–97.

Lesnick, Daniel. 1991. 'Insults and Threats in Medieval Todi', *Journal of Medieval History*, 17: 71-90

Malamud, Sibylle. 2003. *Die Ächtung des 'Bösen'. Frauen vor dem Zürcher Ratsgericht im späten Mittelalter (1400-1500)* (Zurich: Chronos)

McSheffrey, Shannon. 2004. 'Place, Space, and Situation: Public and Private in the Making of Marriage in Late-Medieval London', *Speculum*, 79: 960-90

Melville, Gert and Peter von Moos. 1998. *Das Öffentliche und Private in der Vormoderne*, Norm und Struktur, 10 (Cologne: Böhlau)

Neal, Derek G. 2008. *The Masculine Self in Late Medieval England* (Chicago: University of Chicago Press)

Otis-Couer, Leah. 2009. '*De jure novo*: Dealing with Adultery in the Fifteenth-Century Toulousain', *Speculum*, 84: 347-92

Pohl, Susanne. 1999. '"Ehrlicher Totschlag", "Rache", "Notwehr": zwischen männlichem Ehrencode und dem Primat des Stadtfriedens (Zürich 1376-1600)', in *Kulturelle Reformation: Sinnformationen im Umbruch 1400-1600*, ed. Bernhard Jussen and Craig Koslofsky, Veröffentlichungen des Max-Planck-Instituts für Geschichte, 145 (Göttingen: Vandenhoeck & Ruprecht), pp. 239-83

—. 2002. '"She was killed wretchedly and without a cause": Social Status and the Language of Violence in Zürcher Homicide Trials of the Fifteenth Century', *Acta Histriae*, 10: 247-64

—. 2003. 'Uneasy Peace. The Practice of the *Stallung* Ritual in Zürich, 1400-1525', *Journal of Early Modern History*, 7: 28-54

Pohl-Zucker, Susanne. 2017. Making Manslaughter: Process, Punishment and Restitution in Württemberg and Zurich, 1376-1700 (Leiden: Brill)

Rath, Brigitte. 1994. 'Von Huren, die keine sind...', in *Privatisierung der Triebe? Sexualität in der Frühen Neuzeit* ed. Daniela Erlach, Markus Reisenleitner and Karl Vocelka, Frühneuzeit-Studien, 1 (Frankfurt a.M.: Peter Lang), pp. 349-66

Roper, Lyndal. 1994. *Oedipus and the Devil: Witchcraft, Sexuality and Religion in Early Modern Europe* (London: Routledge)

Rublack, Ulinka. 1998. *Magd, Metz oder Mörderin: Frauen vor frühneuzeitlichen Gerichten* (Frankfurt am Main: Fischer Taschenbuch Verlag)

Salisbury, Eve, Georgiana Donavin and Merrall Llewelyn Price (eds). 2002. *Domestic Violence in Medieval Texts* (Gainesville: University Press of Florida)

Schmidt, Eberhard. 1995. *Einführung in die Geschichte der deutschen Strafrechtspflege*, 3rd edn (Göttingen: Vandenhoeck & Ruprecht)

Schreiner, Klaus and Gerd Schwerhoff (eds). 1995. *Verletzte Ehre: Ehrkonflikte in Gesellschaften des Mittelalters und der frühen Neuzeit*, Norm und Struktur, 5 (Cologne: Böhlau)

Schuster, Peter. 1993. 'Hinaus oder ins Frauenhaus. Weibliche Sexualität und gesellschaftliche Kontrolle an der Wende vom Mittelalter zur Neuzeit' in *Mit den Waffen der Justiz: zur Kriminalitätsgeschichte des Spätmittelalters und der frühen Neuzeit* ed. Andreas Blauert and Gerd Schwerhoff (Frankfurt a.M.: Fischer), pp. 17-31

—. 2013. 'Sünde und Moral im spätmittelalterlichen Europa', in *Krise und Aufbruch in der Geschichte Europas*, ed. Wolfgang Behringer, Geschichte und Kultur. Saarbrücker Reihe, 3 (Trier: Kliomedia), pp. 71-80

Schwerhoff, Gerd. 1993. 'Verordnete Schande? Spätmittelalterliche und Frühneuzeitliche Ehrenstrafen zwischen Rechtsakt und sozialer Sanktion', in *Mit den Waffen der Justiz: zur Kriminalitätsgeschichte des späten Mittelalters und der frühen Neuzeit* ed. Andreas Blauert and Gerd Schwerhoff (Frankfurt a.M.: Fischer), pp. 158-88

Smail, Daniel Lord. 2003. *The Consumption of Justice: Emotions, Publicity, and Legal Culture in Marseille, 1264-1423* (Ithaca: Cornell University Press)

Strocchia, Sharon Therese. 1998. 'Gender and the Rites of Honour in Italian Renaissance Cities', in *Gender and Society in Renaissance Italy*, ed. Judith C. Brown and Robert C. Davis (London: Longman), pp. 39-60

Stuart, Kathy. 1999. *Defiled Trades and Social Outcasts: Honor and Ritual Pollution in Early Modern Germany*, Cambridge Studies in Early Modern History (Cambridge: Cambridge University Press)

Toch, Michael. 1993. 'Schimpfwörter im Dorf des Spätmittelalters,' *Mitteilungen des Instituts für österreichische Geschichtsforschung*, 101: 311-27

Wettlaufer, Jörg. 2010. 'Schand- und Ehrenstrafen des Spätmittelalters und der Frühneuzeit – Erforschung der Strafformen und Strafzwecke anhand von DRW-Belege', in *Das deutsche Rechtswörterbuch: Perspektiven*, ed. Andreas Deutsch (Heidelberg: Universitätsverlag), pp. 265-80

Wieben, Corinne. 2010. '"As Men Do with Their Wives": Domestic Violence in Fourteenth-Century Lucca', *California Italian Studies*, 1: 1-13

Zmora, Hillay. 1998. *State and Nobility in Early Modern Germany: The Knightly Feud in Franconia, 1440-1567*, Cambridge Studies in Early Modern History (Cambridge: Cambridge University Press)

7

'schneident mir beid oren ab': The Comic Potential of Corporal Punishment in Sixteenth-century *Schwankbücher*

Sebastian Coxon
University College London

Compilations of short prose texts in the sixteenth century contain a relatively large number of anecdotes and stories to do with legal process.[1] Such material was in fact already a feature of collections of Latin *exempla* in the high and later Middle Ages. In terms of a programme of serious didacticism it is not hard to see why, with numerous stories of crime and punishment involving a fairly limited range of figures, scenarios and narrative outcomes to illustrate the wages of sin and wickedness, or the rationality of virtue, justice and wise governance. By the same token, the very clarity of the lines drawn in such texts, as well as the entrenched nature of the paradigm of crime and punishment in medieval Christian thought, made such material ripe for comic refunctionalization. These approaches are combined in Johannes Pauli's *Schimpf und Ernst*, an extremely large compilation of *exempla* and *Predigtmärlein* (some 693 in the first print of 1522), which contains numerous short comic anecdotes (denoted by the author-compiler as 'schimpff' [in jest]) as well as serious *exempla* (or 'ernst' [in earnest]) from a wide range of sources on any number of themes, including crime and punishment, judges and judgements (both good and bad), advocates (both honest and dishonest) and executions.[2] In many of these texts an unwavering sense of right and wrong is communicated, and the wicked meet the end they deserve; in others, however, the same themes are accorded a comic function and exercise a more obviously satirical function.[3]

---

[1] Critical awareness of this topic is growing; see Prinz and Rieger 2015.
[2] For a concise yet comprehensive interpretation of Pauli's collection, see von Ammon and Waltenberger (2010: 1-14).
[3] See 'ernst' no. 352, in which the narrator confidently asserts that even miscarriages of justice often turn out to be just: 'Also kumpt es offt, das einem ein rad vber ein bein gat nit vmb willen das man ein schuldiget, aber vm des willen das vergangen ist, gottes vrteil sein heimlich vnd verborgen.' [Thus it often happens that a wheel is taken to a man's leg not on account of what he is being accused of, but rather because of something else he has done in the past; God's judgements are shrouded in mystery.]; but see also 'schimpff' no. 591, where an executioner impresses with his ready wit: 'Es sprach einer zuo einem nachrichter: "Meister, ir haben zuo dem nesten den dieb redlich gehenckt." Der hencker zohe

In the *Schwankbücher* that followed in the wake of Pauli's *Schimpf und Ernst*, stories concerning comic goings-on in court come to represent the dominant text-type in this thematic field. In Michael Lindener's *Rastbüchlein* (1558), for example, story no. 20, in which a young woman's foolish revelation provokes hilarity in court ('Dauon yederman lachen ward' [Everyone laughed at this]), is followed in no. 21 by another instance of laughter in court ('Diser red die Herren alle lachten' [All the lords laughed at this speech]), this time at the wit of a young man; and this complementary pair of texts is followed by two further comic court cases in stories 22 and 23.

More often than not such texts concern the process of establishing guilt or innocence and attempts to either secure or pervert the course of justice. But what of the next step in the legal process? What scope is there in these collections for comic speech (*facete dictum*) or comic action (*facete factum*) in the context of corporal or even capital punishment? In terms of a cultural or literary history of pre-modern 'humour', the key point here is just how the issue of physical suffering is negotiated. Always assuming that we, as modern readers, are able to recognize pre-modern comic effects when we see them, the issue of pain (as one of the desired outcomes of severe physical chastisement) may serve as a touchstone for establishing the functional range of comedy in these texts.[4]

The *Schwankbücher* of the mid-sixteenth century are certainly not the only literary texts which are relevant for this question.[5] But they do constitute a rich body of material, published within a relatively short space of time and constituting a series of six or seven works that, strictly speaking, begins with Georg Wickram's *Rollwagenbüchlein* (first printed 1555) and ends with the first volume of Hans Wilhelm Kirchhof's *Wendunmuth* (1563). It should be noted, however, that Pauli's *Schimpf und Ernst*, which was reworked and reprinted numerous times in subsequent decades, was viewed as a *Schwankbuch avant la lettre* by later authors in this tradition: I will do the same here.[6] A large number of the narratives contained in these collections are grounded in the realities of sixteenth-century urban life, and not a few of them even seem to cater for a thirst for 'news' (Emmelius, forthcoming). However, any depiction of late medieval and early modern practices of punishment

---

sein huot ab vnd sprach: "Ia, her, ein dieb henck ich, gegen dem andern zühe ich den huot ab."' [A certain fellow said to an executioner: 'Master, you recently gave a thief a good and proper hanging!' The hangman doffed his cap and said: 'Indeed, lord, one thief I hang, to another I doff my cap.']

[4] For a way into the extremely large body of scholarship on this topic, see Kipf (2013).
[5] For judicial punishment as a point of reference in late medieval (verse-couplet) *Mären*, see Frohne (2008).
[6] For the significance of Pauli's *Schimpf und Ernst* in the development of the later 'Schwankbücher', see Kipf (2010b).

here is always likely to be subject to the comic requirements of the *Schwankbücher* themselves. These comic requirements are in fact the principal focus of this article, which aims to identify various ways in which the comic potential of physical punishment was realized in the form of short prose narrative in the course of the sixteenth century.

Wit

Text no. 579 of Johannes Pauli's *Schimpf und Ernst* is short and to the point:

> Vf ein mal was ein böser knab in einer stat, der ward offt gedömelt, vnd kam doch alwegen daruon, vnd sagt wa er bei den lüten was: 'Meine herren der stat dy wissen bei einem quintlin, wie schwer ich bin, sie haben mich wol als offt gewegen, vnd mich lenger gemacht, dan ich vor was; also haben sie mich gestreckt.'

> [There was once a wicked knave in a city who was often strung up with weights yet somehow always got away with it, and whenever he was in company he would say: 'My lords of the city, they know to the nearest ounce how heavy I am, they have weighed me so often and made me longer than I was before, [so often] have they stretched me in the same way.]⁷

The witticism in question is that of an incorrigible delinquent, whose crimes or misdemeanours remain unspecified, and who makes light of the punishment or torture of *dömeln* (a form of hanging) he has suffered on more than one occasion in the past. Any notion of pain and suffering is retained only in so far as it is denied by the speaker, who deliberately misconstrues the process of punitive hanging as an excessively elaborate method of ascertaining his bodyweight, before conceding that physically – if not morally – he is a changed man. Most notably, the joke is removed from the actual moment of punishment and is addressed to an unspecified and uninvolved 'audience' ('bei den lüten' [in company]); its effect is enhanced by the semblance of respectfulness shown by the delinquent ('Meine herren der stat' [my lords of the city]), which is then entirely undermined by his public refusal to admit his guilt or acknowledge the sense of the measures taken against him.

In its compact structure and emphasis on the spoken word (however awkward or inefficient the delivery of the actual point may be), this anecdote is in fact quite compatible with the Humanist *facetiae* collected and made famous in early sixteenth-century Germany by authors such as Heinrich Bebel (in Tübingen) and Adelphus Muling (in Strassburg).⁸ It thus comes as no surprise that text no. 579 is

---

[7] All translations are mine unless otherwise stated.
[8] It is extremely likely that Pauli would have been familiar with Muling's *Margarita facetiarum*; see Kipf (2010a: 294-338).

classified by Pauli as 'schimpff' rather than 'ernst', although given the overriding moral imperative of the collection as a whole, it is striking that nothing explicit is done by the author-narrator to mitigate the fact that the witty utterance belongs to 'ein böser knab' [a wicked knave]. A didactic frame for this text is implied solely by its immediate context, for this anecdote is both preceded and followed by *exempla* in which the wayward behaviour of sons is explicitly addressed: a son wastes the riches he inherits from his father (no. 578); a son refuses to accept the advice of his father (no. 580); a son is punished by his father for playing at dice (no. 581). Thus, although text no. 579 belongs to a larger section (564–630) which Pauli purports to leave free for others to organize – and interpret – as they see fit, a sequential reading of *Schimpf und Ernst* at this point suggests that the 'böser knab' [wicked knave] of no. 579 is another such 'sun' [son] or 'iung gesel' [young fellow], or at the very least, embodies the stubbornness of youth.[9] In this interpretation the wittiness of the speaker's utterance serves ultimately to make the folly of his behaviour all the more memorable.[10]

Foolish speech

As may have already become clear, the distinction between witty and foolish speech in texts of this type is not always obvious. Story no. 32 of the sixty-seven collected (and penned?) by Georg Wickram in his *Rollwagenbüchlein* (1555) is perhaps a case in point, in spite of the comparative wealth of narrative detail it contains. A petty thief, or a good-for-nothing wastrel ('Ein unnützer nasser vogel'), who has been caught many times but has always been able to talk himself out of trouble, finally commits one crime too many, is imprisoned and duly sentenced to be executed. On being informed of the day of his hanging 'ein tag oder drey darvor […] damit er sich koent darein schicken' [a day or three beforehand […] so that he could come to terms with his fate], he makes an impassioned last-ditch appeal, culminating in the declaration:

> Ich wirde die urteil nit annemen God gebe waß ir machen so wirde ichs nit thuon. Aber also wil ich im thuon darmit ir meine Herrn sehen das ich selbs nichts unbilligs begeren

---

[9] This part of the collection – the 'breadcrumbs' – is given the following heading: 'Etliche exempel kurtzweilige reden von mancherlei dingen, da keins zuo dem andern gehört, hat Frater Johannes Pauli hieher wöllen setzen für brösamlin, das sie nit verloren würden, mag iederman zuo articulen vnd titulen, wie es im gefelt.' [Numerous *exempla* and entertaining anecdotes about all sorts of things, not in the least related to one another, put here by Frater Johannes Pauli as breadcrumbs so that none go to waste; anyone may give them titles and arrange them as they please.]

[10] Elsewhere in Pauli's collection this strategy is used to satirical effect; see, for instance, the witty utterances placed in the mouths of a dishonest judge ('schimpff' no. 125) or a false advocate ('schimpff' no. 128).

will thuond eins und schneident mir beid oren ab unnd hawen mich mit ruoten auß und wil euch noch zehen gulden darzuo geben ist das nicht ein erbers und eerlichs erbieten?

[I shall not accept the verdict, whatever you do, by God! I shall not do it. But I shall do the following so that you, my lords, see that I am not making an unreasonable demand. Do this one thing and cut off both of my ears and thrash me with switches and I shall, in addition, give you ten guilders. Is that not an honourable and honest offer?]

Irrespective of one scholar's rather damning verdict of Wickram's collection – 'Die Moral ist nicht moralisch, und der Witz ist nicht witzig' [The moral is not moral, and the wit is not witty] (Kartschoke 1993: 82) – since the *Rollwagenbüchlein* was intended to be a *Schwankbuch*, it is legitimate to ask where the comic potential might lie in this particular scenario. Is it perhaps the delinquent's deviant folly of refusing to accept a just verdict and its compassionate (!) announcement to him? Or is there comic incongruity in a condemned man suggesting his own form of punishment and thereby displaying his own personal sense of justice? Or is it the content of the proposal itself, the extent to which the thief is prepared to suffer to live, a threefold punishment (physical, social, financial) which the fundamentally dishonourable and dishonest thief summarizes as 'ein erbers und eerlichs erbieten' [an honourable and honest offer]? This juxtaposition of honesty and dishonesty is certainly something which the narrator wishes to foreground. Indeed, not only does the same phrase of 'eerlichs erbieten' [an honest offer] appear as the story's catchphrase in the title – 'Von einem der ein eerlichs erbieten an die Herrn thet' [Concerning a man who made an honest offer to their lordships] –, the narrator repeatedly uses it in the text's conclusion, compounding the joke on the narrative level: 'Des erlichen erbietens muosten die Herren lachen / brachten es also wider hindersich an ir oberherrn / also wurden sie zuo radt unnd kamen seim eerlichen erbieten nach.' [Their lordships had to laugh at this honest offer; thus they took it back themselves to their overlords, discussed the matter and took him up on his honest offer.]

As far as the delinquent's severe corporal punishments of maiming and thrashing are concerned, these are explicitly referred to only in the direct speech of the thief, and serve primarily as points of incongruous contrast with the phrase 'ein erbers und eerlichs erbieten' [an honourable and honest offer]. The thief's offer to sacrifice both of his ears is drastic, yet it remains primarily a matter of comic hyperbole. Indeed, it is symptomatic of Wickram's restraint in this respect that although the laughing 'Herren' [lordships] eventually agree to comply with the condemned man's request, the punishment that follows is largely elided or displaced by the final reiteration of the story's main joke. Thus, the emphasis here is on comic speech, which may be read as involuntarily foolish or, depending on how clever we judge this 'nasser vogel' to be, as intentionally witty. Arguably, it does not really matter as Wickram directs the reader's interest towards the comic speech or 'joke' in its own right by virtue of the effect that it has on the judges, who are subsequently moved to take the highly irregular step of changing their initial verdict. In spite of the unconventional behaviour of the 'Herren' [lordships], law and order are seen to be maintained as afterwards the thief never returns to commit another crime ('also kam er nimmermer' [and so he never came back again]). That the lords laugh at the thief's (foolish?) proposal may just be a function of the stylization of social institutions and processes in *Schwank*-literature per se, where susceptibility to being amused is projected back into the narrative world itself; but it also appears to support the notion that the laughter of those in positions of authority is not detrimental in the slightest to social order and justice.[11]

Comic consequences

We can get a proper sense of Wickram's restraint by drawing on another prose *Schwank*-text for comparison, which appeared in print several decades before Wickram in a later edition of Pauli's *Schimpf und Ernst* (Strassburg 1533; no. 493), where comic capital is struck from the same form of corporal punishment.[12] A rogue travels to market in Frankfurt and asks a 'kremer' [pedlar] how much it would cost to buy a ribbon long enough to extend from one ear to the other in order to stop his 'baret' [cap] from being blown off by the wind. Just two 'Kreuzer' [pence], the merchant guesses, only to discover that his less than honest customer has just the one ear:

> Der kremer nam die bendel vnd zoch jm das baret ab, vnd will jm zuo dem andern or messen so sicht er das es ist ab geschnitten, vnnd spricht: 'Wo ist das ander or? Es ist doch nit da.' Der gesell oder abenteurer sprach: 'Es stot zuo Ertffurt an dem branger genagelt; mesz mir bisz dohin.'

> [The pedlar held his ribbon and took his cap off; and intending to measure to his other ear he sees that it has been cut off, and he says: 'Where is the other ear? It's just not

---

[11] For a more detailed analysis of the narrative motif of laughter in Wickram's collection as a whole, see Alessandrini (2014).

[12] Elsewhere in Pauli's *Schimpf und Ernst*, the punishment of cutting off a person's ears is used as a (comic) threat to terrify a gullible 'gast' [guest] ('schimpff' no. 364) and the famous fool Claus Narr (1533: no. 49); whilst in 'schimpff' no. 647 it is carried out as the last in a series of severe corporal punishments to an envious man ('das man im ein aug vsz steche' [he had an eye put out]), an avaricious man ('stach man beid augen vsz' [both of his eyes were put out]) and a proud man ('stach man beid augen vsz, vnd schnit im die oren darzuo ab' [both of his eyes were put out and his ears were sliced off as well]).

there!' The fellow or rogue said: 'It's nailed to the pillory post in Erfurt; measure all the way there for me!']

The rogue's ear is not sliced off in the 'here and now' of this narrative either. Nevertheless, his deception and its comic value for the reader both depend on the bodily reality of being mutilated. Furthermore, social norms and expectations go out of the window when the shameless delinquent himself explicitly draws attention to the grim fact that a part of his body is nailed up on a pillory-post elsewhere. Far from concealing his mark of shame, he tries to make a profit from it.

Once more the narrative account of the event at the heart of the *Schwank* provides the reader with some reassurance as to the aftermath: the pedlar refuses to pay up and the case comes before the 'burgenmeyster' [burgomaster] who encourages them (as sensible men and not 'eynfeltig kinder' [silly children]) to come to an agreement on their own so that he is not required to make an official adjudication. Just what the content of this agreement or compromise is remains unspecified;[13] the emphasis lies on the restored social harmony. One (conservative) reading of this conclusion would take comfort in the fact that in the end the honest pedlar does not lose his living as a result of a dishonest knave's ruse. Another reading would be to view the burgomaster's refusal to intervene officially as a tacit recognition of the cleverness of this ruse; the burgomaster does not simply find against the rogue on the basis that he is a convicted and maimed criminal.

Absurdity and obscenity

In and of itself the slicing off of an ear is not comic, not even in texts where this punishment or the very notion of it gives rise to comedy, as it was a recognized form of severe corporal punishment in the sixteenth century. However, it was possible for the process of corporal punishment itself to be comically distorted. This strategy is pushed to its limit in story no. 83 of Jakob Frey's *Gartengesellschaft* (first print 1556, containing 129 texts), which is one of around 25 tales Frey draws from Poggio Bracciolini's *Liber facetiarum* (first extant print 1470; *facetia* no. 205). This particular story is set against the historical backdrop of the antagonistic relations between the Genoese and the Greeks in the trade colony of Pera (Galata) 'bey Constantinopel' [near Constantinople]. Following an outbreak of violence between the two factions in which a number of Genoese are killed and wounded, the 'keyser von Griechen' [emperor of the Greeks] takes immediate action: 'der liess die seinen

---

[13] The text appears to suggest that the onus is placed on the 'kremer' [pedlar] to make the deal: 'Der burgenmeyster [...] schuoff mit dem kremer das er mit dem gesellen eyn friden macht' [The burgomaster arranged with the pedlar that he would make peace with the fellow].

fahen unnd inen zuo straff die bärt abscheren' [he had his men arrested and their beards shaved off as a punishment]. Incensed by this perceived insult to Genoese honour, the (Genoese) Governor of Pera encourages his men to attack and murder any Greeks they wish, only to arrest them at the behest of the Greek emperor, whom he appeases with a promise to punish the malefactors 'nach ihrem verdienst' [as they deserve]. All the necessary preparations are made for a series of public executions. But in a speech to the assembled crowds the governor announces his belief that 'alle gleich mässige händel auch mit gleichförmiger peen compensiert und verglichen sollen werden' [all equivalent crimes be compensated for and countered with equivalent punishment]. Thus, just as the Greek emperor had the beards of his men shaved, so he instructs his executioner to place their condemned stomach-down on a table 'und ihnen allen nach einander das haar im arßloch und umb die kerb sauber und glatt herausser abscheren' [and to all of them, one after the other, give the hair in their arseholes and around their cracks a clean and smooth shave], suggesting that the Greeks should feel free to take a closer look 'mitten in das gewölb' [right in their arse] to ensure that justice has been done.[14]

For all of its wealth of narrative detail – not all of which is welcome – this text is organized around the fundamental *Schwank*-narrative structure of provocation and retaliation, whereby the act of retribution is generally accorded the licence to be (even) more excessive.[15] In this case the historically attested (ancient) practice of punitive shaving is countered by an utterly absurd and obscene variant.[16] The comic effect of this structure is enhanced in two ways. First, the Genoese governor's directive comes as a surprise to the recipient as well, as the build-up to the critical scene is presented in the most serious and conventional terms: 'Es was ein grausam und ernstlichs wesen. Die gefangnen wurden daher gefürt; man truog inen die creutz vor, man tröstet sie und bettet ihnen vor.' [It was a terrible and serious business. The prisoners were brought out; crosses were carried before them; they were comforted and prayers were said for them.] Second, in spite of its absurdity and obscenity the punishment is actually carried out, much to the horror of the spectators who run away. This reaction could not be more different to the one envisaged by Frey on the part of his readers, who are encouraged by the narrator to take delight in the

---

[14] This 'joke' is of Frey's own making; the bonmot of the Genoese Governor in Poggio's *facetia* is somewhat different: 'asserens Genuenses barbam, non in facie, sed circa nates ferre' [declaring that the Genoese did not wear a beard in their face but rather by their buttocks].

[15] The most fundamental observations on *Schwank*-structures are (still) to be found in Bausinger (1967).

[16] That the punitive shaving of beards is historically verifiable for the Greeks is in fact implied by the narrator: 'unnd inen zuo straff die bärt abscheren, welches dazuomal ein grosse schand und straff bey ihnen war' [and to punish them by shaving their beards, which in those days was regarded by them as a terrible disgrace and punishment]; Frey takes this line directly from Poggio: 'quae mulcta apud eos ignominiosa habetur' [which in their country was regarded as terribly disgraceful].

scatalogical detail: not only is the source of the spectators' dismay explained quite gratuitously ('habend ihnen in ihre finsteren schwartzen kerben nit sehen mögen' [not wishing to look into their dark and black cracks]), the text is concluded simply with a crude and reductive summary of the events: 'Damit ist die abscherung der bärt mit der bescherung des haars im arßloch gegen einander verglichen worden' [Thus, the shaving-off of the beards was countered by the shaving of the hair in the arseholes].[17] The narrative context is no longer of interest, just the comic potential of the two punishments, as an 'alien' punishment of shaming is absurdly and obscenely parodied.

Comedy and capital punishment?

All the examples so far have been concerned with corporal punishments of varying forms of severity (and seriousness). It remains to be seen what difference, if any, it makes to the comic principles and structures we have identified when the ultimate physical sanction of execution is brought into play.[18] When it comes to capital punishment the *Schwankbücher* as a whole reveal a preference, if one can call it that, for hanging, the most common form of execution in German cities of the sixteenth century. This strictly curtails any action on the narrative level and the extent of any comic consequences, these effectively being restricted to the walk to the gallows and the ensuing proceedings on the platform of execution. The enforced passivity of the condemned also means that there is an almost exclusive concentration on *facete dictum* rather than *facete factum*. Two apparent exceptions are to be found in Pauli's *Schimpf und Ernst*, both of which deal with the relations between parents and their children: a young man bites his father's nose off just before he is hanged, with the words: 'hettestu mich gestrafft in der iugent, so wer ich nit zuo der schand kumen' [if you had [only] punished me in my youth, I would never have come to this disgraceful end] ('schimpff' no. 19); a young man fulfils his mother's prophecy by one day making an obscene gesture to her from the gallows: 'da er nun gehenckt ward da macht er die feigen an dem galgen, vnd sties den daumen durch die zwen finger' [when he was hanged he made the sign of the 'fig' from the gallows and stuck his thumb through two fingers] ('schimpff' no. 439). But in fact these two *exempla* (of very different origins) just go to show how dependent on the spoken word such scenarios otherwise are.[19]

---

[17] Poggio's text concludes with effectively the same line: 'Ita rasura et faciei et culi aequata maleficii poena est' [Thus, the shaving of face and arse were (considered) an equal punishment of crime].

[18] For an alternative reading of some of this material, see Althaus (2010).

[19] As Pauli himself makes clear 'schimpff' no. 19 is an ancient *exemplum* derived from Boethius ('von

The (imagined) gravity of imminent execution effectively raises the stakes and serves, on the one hand, to heighten the comic effect of the wit or foolish speech, which in these stories typically constitute the very last words of the condemned; there can in fact be nothing wittier or more foolish than the following utterances which are in every case (or so we are to understand) followed by death:

> Pauli, *Schimpf und Ernst*: as he is led to the gallows a condemned man (only) regrets leaving his red cap in prison ('schimpff' no. 27); a condemned man asks for the flour to be dusted off his last bite of bread as he has heard it is unhealthy ('schimpff' no. 28); a fox asks to be treated to a last sight of geese on the way to the gallows ('schimpff' no. 29).

> Frey, *Gartengesellschaft*: a condemned thief asks the priest (who is trying to console him) if he would not prefer to take his place in order to have the honour of dining in heaven that night; the thief, moreover, is happy to throw in 'zwen groschen zuo steur' [two pennies as a tip] as he has more pressing matters to attend to (no. 126).[20]

> Michael Lindener, *Katzipori* (1558): a man convicted of manslaughter (?) tells the priest (who is trying to console him) that he would prefer to die like a 'ein Ehrlicher frommer Landtsknecht' [an honest and good mercenary] rather than 'ein frommer Christ' [a good Christian], a comment which amuses the crowd of onlookers: 'Deß mochte das volck wol lachen' [At that the people had a good laugh] (no. 69).

> Kirchhof, *Wendunmuth* (I): a thief asks a priest to take his place (no. 298; same source as Frey, *Gartengesellschaft*, no. 126, ie. Bebel II, 42); a condemned blasphemer tells a crowd of young boys that there is no need to rush ahead as the spectacle (of his drowning) cannot start without him (no. 299; Bebel II,97); a condemned thief asks for a new scaffold to be erected as he does not want to hang next to another thief (no. 300); a

---

dem Boetius schreibt' [about which Boethius writes]), whereas 'schimpff' no. 439 is, purportedly, based on recent and historically verifiable events (in Milan): 'das hat bruder Bernhardinus de Busti gesehen, ee er ein barfuoser ward' [this was witnessed by Brother Bernhardinus de Busti before he became a Franciscan].

[20] Frey draws on one of Heinrich Bebel's *facetiae* (II, 42) for this story: 'Cum fur quidam ab patibulum duceretur, sacerdosque ei pro confirmatione et consolatione adiunctus (ut moris est) aeternam illi felicitatem, si ultro mortem pro emendatione peccatorum suorum subiret, polliceretur eumque apud superos cenaturum affirmaret, conversus fur ad sacerdotem dixit: '*Ist es also, lieber herr, so bit ich, ir wellen fur mich das nachtmal essen. Ich will euch zwen blaphart an dem mal schencken.*' Hoc est: 'Si ita est, bone pater, cenato tu ita pro me, et ego tibi in subsidium sumptuum duos Bohemos denarios (quos vocant) donabo.' [When a certain thief was being lead to the gibbet, the priest who was accompanying him (as is the custom) – to strengthen him in his faith and console him – promised him eternal happiness if he accepted death as a penance for his sins, and swore that he would be dining that evening at the table of the heavenly host, whereupon the thief turned to the priest and said: '*Ist es also, lieber herr, so bit ich, ir wellen fur mich das nachtmal essen; ich will euch zwen blaphart an dem mal schencken.*' That is: 'If that's the case, dear father, then dine in my place tonight and I will give you two (so-called) Bohemian pennies to cover the costs.']

condemned thief tells the gatekeeper 'an das Newenstetter thor' (in Kassel?) that there is no need to keep the gate open for him that night (no. 301).

However, the very seriousness of situations such as these also appears to demand that the utterances in question be framed by some kind of response or interpretation on the part of the respective author-narrator. Hence for Pauli there can be no better illustration of a sinful preoccupation with 'nerrischen dingen' [foolish things] (no. 27) at the end of one's life, or of people's concern with 'kurtzweil und fröd' [merriment and joy] rather than the fate of their souls even when on their deathbed (nos 28 and 29). Frey too (unlike Heinrich Bebel) cannot let the thief's wit stand in its own right and portrays the execution itself before taking it upon himself to counter the hanged man's *bonmot*: 'Das was dem pfarrherrn nit gelegen, ließ den hencker mit im fürfaren. Damit ward er verdienter straff nach gehenckt, got geb wer gast zuom nachtmal gewesen sey oder nit.' [That was not to the priest's liking; [he] let the hangman continue with him. Thus he was hanged as a fitting punishment. God only knows who was guest at the dinner that evening or not.] In Lindener's story the narrative is complicated by the fact that the manslaughter happened some fifteen years previously and the narrator is critical of the 'verraeter' [traitor] who betrays the soldier to the law; the crowd of spectators too are eventually moved to pity ('Vnnd hette ein yederman ein groß mitleyden' [And everyone felt great pity]), before space is then given to an account of the condemned man's final garbled prayers, a rare narrative privilege as it were. Finally, Kirchhof explicitly draws attention to the fact that the terror of imminent death is so great that men scarcely know where they are going or what they are saying: 'schier nit wissen, [...] was sie reden' (no. 299); thus, a remarkable discrepancy arises between the seriousness with which the condemned speak ('Er aber sagt ernsthafft [...] wer weiß, vileicht auß zuofelliger wanwitzigkeit' [But he spoke seriously [...] who knows, perhaps from some further insanity] (no. 301)) and the comic effect on the reader of their last words.

Conclusion

The German *Schwankbücher* of the mid-sixteenth century contain significant evidence concerning the comic potential of officially sanctioned corporal punishment. Indeed, it is possible to identify a number of comic principles and categories in this domain (wit and foolish speech; comic consequences; absurdity and obscenity) and to say, with no small degree of confidence, that in most if not all cases a considerable degree of restraint is exercised vis-à-vis the issue of pain and suffering. At the same time it cannot be denied that in terms of sheer numbers prose *Schwank*-texts detailing such corporal punishment are relatively few and far between. On the whole it would thus appear that this part of the broader processes of law and order was not one that was deemed especially suitable for comic treatment in the *Schwankbücher*, or rather: not one that commercially aware authors necessarily wanted to test the patience of their readers with. This conservative attitude is even more apparent in those stories dealing with execution, since the validity of the process, the justness of this severest punishment of all, is never explicitly questioned or satirized. The pre-modern comic imagination that we can detect in these texts is almost always preoccupied with the witty or foolish speech of the condemned – men, never women, it should be noted – and, not infrequently, its effect on those around them.[21] It is difficult to avoid the impression that for the producers and recipients of this literature there was something ethically dubious about dwelling for too long on physical torment and death in narratives or narrative sequences that were meant to provoke laughter. The evidence in its totality is not straightforward, however; not least because of the suggestion that on occasion in the entirely non-comic narratives that feature in the *Schwankbücher*, humour (of the basest kind) was required to make otherwise unpalatable details acceptable. Thus, in the exceptionally brutal 'history' used by Martin Montanus to bring his *Ander theil der Gartengesellschaft* (1560) to a conclusion, the protracted death of a Jewish fraudster (hanged alive between two dogs and left in the cold to suffocate to death) is summed up sarcastically by the narrator: 'Also hat der frumb jud sein leben schaelcklich geendet' [Thus the pious Jew ended his life like a wastrel] (no. 115). If anything this final text should act as a reminder that the study of laughter, comedy and humour, whether pre-modern or modern for that matter, is not always a pleasant one.

---

[21] One exception to this 'rule' is to be found in Kirchhof's *Wendunmuth* (I, 300), where the crowd is amused by the priest's choice of words when relaying the news that the thief is getting the new gallows he wished for: '"Sey getrost, lieber son, die bitt ist ja, und geht dir nach all deinem willen." Solchs wurden alle, die es höreten, lachen, vermeineten, daß, so es nach seinem willen gehen sölte, müßte er ledig, und etwa in einem wald weit darvon seyn.' ['Be of good cheer, dear son, the answer to your request is yes and everything shall be to your liking.' Everyone who heard this started to laugh, opining that if everything were indeed to be to his liking, he would be free and in some forest far away.]

Works cited

Primary Sources

Georg Wickram: Das Rollwagenbüchlein, ed. Hans-Gert Roloff, Georg Wickram: Sämtliche Werke, 7, Ausgaben deutscher Literatur des XV. bis XVIII. Jahrhunderts (Berlin: de Gruyter, 1973)

Heinrich Bebels Facetien: Drei Bücher, ed. Gustav Bebermeyer, Bibliothek des litterarischen Vereins in Stuttgart, 276 (Leipzig: Hiersemann, 1931)

Jakob Freys Gartengesellschaft (1556), ed. Johannes Bolte, Bibliothek des litterarischen Vereins in Stuttgart, 209 (Tübingen: Litterarischer Verein, 1896)

Johannes Pauli: Schimpf und Ernst, ed. Hermann Österley, Bibliothek des litterarischen Vereins in Stuttgart, 85 (Stuttgart: Litterarischer Verein, 1866)

Martin Montaus: Schwankbücher (1557-1566), ed. Johannes Bolte, Bibliothek des litterarischen Vereins in Stuttgart, 217 (Tübingen: Litterarischer Verein, 1899)

Michael Lindener. Schwankbücher: Rastbüchlein und Katzipori, ed. Kyra Heidemann, 2 vols, Arbeiten zur Mittleren Deutschen Literatur und Sprache, 20:1-2 (Bern: Lang, 1991)

Poggio Braccionlini: Facezie, ed. Stefano Pittaluga (Milan: Garzanti, 1995)

Wendunmuth von Hans Wilhelm Kirchhof, ed. Hermann Österley, Bibliothek des Litterarischen Vereins in Stuttgart, 95 (Tübingen: Litterarischer Verein, 1869)

Secondary Sources

Alessandrini, Jan-Luigi. 2014. 'Laughter and Narrative in Jörg Wickram's *Rollwagenbüchlein*'. Diss. University College London.

Althaus, Thomas. 2010. 'Auf dem Weg zum Galgen: Literarisierte Exekutionsberichte als ein Archetyp frühneuzeitlichen Erzählens', in *Fortunatus, Melusine, Genofeva: Internationale Erzählstoffe in der deutschen und ungarischen Literatur der Frühen Neuzeit*, ed. Dieter Breuer and Gábor Tüskés (Berlin: Lang), pp. 475-94

von Ammon, Frieder and Michael Waltenberger. 2010. 'Wimmeln und Wuchern: Pluralisierungs-Phänomene in Johannes Paulis *Schimpf und Ernst* und Valentin Schumanns *Nachtbüchlein*', in *Pluralisierungen: Konzepte zur Erfassung der Frühen Neuzeit*, ed. Jan-Dirk Müller, Wulf Oesterreicher and Friedrich Vollhardt, Pluralisierung und Autorität, 21 (Berlin: de Gruyter), pp. 1-30

Bausinger, Hermann. 1967. 'Bemerkungen zum Schwank und seinen Formtypen', *Fabula*, 9: 118-36

Emmelius, Caroline. Forthcoming. 'Verbrechen und Schwank: Überlegungen zum medialen und narrativen Status von Fallgeschichten in Schwanksammlungen des 16. Jahrhunderts'

Frohne, Bianca. 2008. 'Narren, Tiere und *grewliche Figuren*: Zur Inszenierung komischer Körperlichkeit im Kontext von Bloßstellung, Spott und Schande vom 13. bis zum 16. Jahrhundert', in *Glaubensstreit und Gelächter: Reformation und Lachkultur im Mittelalter und in der Frühen Neuzeit*, ed. Christoph Auffarth and Sonja Kerth, Religionen in der pluralen Welt, 6 (Berlin: Lit), pp. 19-54

Kartschoke, Dieter. 1993. 'Vom erzeugten zum erzählten Lachen: Die Auflösung der Pointenstruktur in Jörg Wickram's *Rollwagenbüchlein*', in *Kleinere Erzählformen des 15. und 16. Jahrhunderts*, ed. Walter Haug and Burghart Wachinger, Fortuna vitrea, 8 (Tübingen: Niemeyer), pp. 71-105

Kipf, J[ohannes] Klaus. 2010a. '*Cluoge geschichten*': Humanistische Fazetienliteratur im deutschen Sprachraum*, Literaturen und Künste der Vormoderne, 2 (Stuttgart: Hirzel)

—. 2010b. 'Auf dem Weg zum Schwankbuch. Die Bedeutung Frankfurter Drucke und Verleger fur die Ausbildung eines Buchtyps im 16. Jahrhundert', in *Frankfurt im Schnittpunkt der Diskurse: Strategien und Institutionen literarischer Kommunikation im späten Mittelalter und in der frühen Neuzeit*, ed. Robert Seidel and Regina Toepfer, Zeitsprünge, 14 (Frankfurt a. M.: Klostermann), pp. 195-220

—. 2013. 'Lachte das Mittelalter anders? Relative Alterität und kognitive Kontinuität komischer Strukturen in Schwankerzählungen des 13.-15. Jahrhunderts', in *Wie anders war das Mittelalter? Fragen an das Konzept der Alterität*, ed. Manuel Braun, Aventiuren, 9 (Göttingen: V&R unipress), pp. 233-63

Prinz, Katharina and Hannah Rieger. 2015. 'Tagungsbericht [Rechtsnovellen: Rhetorik, narrative Strukturen und kulturelle Semantiken des Rechts in Kurzerzählungen des späten Mittelalters und der Frühen Neuzeit]', *Zeitschrift für deutsche Philologie*, 134: 107-13

8

Penitential Punishment and Purgatory: A Drama of Purification through Pain

Racha Kirakosian
Harvard University

Although the Premonstratensian order is not specifically known for forms of mysticism that emphasize the body, it is within this order that we encounter a mystic whose spiritual path reads as a dramatic plot, staging pain as the pivotal force in an effective programme of penance. The mystical *Life* of Christina of Hane (1269–92?) allows us to study the relationship between internal penance and physically suffered penance in a way that considers the historical background of penitential practices and beliefs in their individual and collective natures.[1] The grand narrative that penance as a personal act of reconciliation evolved under the influence of Gratian's *Decretum*, forming part of a general tendency towards the internalization of religious acts and thoughts, seems attractive but needs refinement and adjustment. The shift towards the inner realm as space of judgement does not necessarily imply that the penitential did not need to be manifested outwardly any longer.[2] There is no doubt that internal acts such as personal penance and confession were increasingly favoured over bodily and hence exterior means (Baldwin 1998: 198-205), but such developments evolved over the course of centuries and can be traced back to the Carolingian period (Hamilton 2011). The thirteenth century, then, appears to be a time in which concepts and ideas that developed over a long period became codified, in some cases with the aim to regulate.[3] In the same

---

[1] The critical edition of the text cited in this article is Kirakosian (2017). The text was first edited by Mittermaier in two journal issues as 'Lebensbeschreibung der sel. Christina, gen. von Retters' (1965; 1966).
[2] For a very critical, yet constructive reading of the history of penance and its reflection in scholarship, see De Jong (2000; 2009).
[3] One may think of the prohibition of priestly involvement in trials by fire and water by the Fourth Lateran Council in 1215 as an example of one of the many outcomes of debates on penance, as shown by Mäkinen and Pihlajamäki (2004: 536-37, 40). Baldwin (1990: 191) concludes that 'Canon 18 of the Council attempted to put an end to the ordeal' while 'Canon 21 sought to encourage and formalize the technique of private penance'. Medieval scholars judged the ordeals to be 'both canonically unsound and theologically suspect' (McAuley 2006: 475). In legal theory, trials by fire and water were a means of protecting the innocent from an unjust sentence and punishment. Medieval formulae (*ordines*) show that the ritual the accused party had to undergo during an ordeal was also one of penitence and punishment.

century in which the movement towards a greater interiority entered the written discourse, the idea of purgatory developed a long-lasting impact on religious thought.[4] Purgatory as a topographical and mental space of punishment and purification offered the possibility of a prolonged process of penitence, extending the path to salvation beyond the actual death of the human body. Atonement in purgatory, though removed from the realm of the world, remained a corporeal form of purification. Yet internal remorse still played an important role. Both concepts – penance and purgatory – are arguably part of an increasingly theologically debated, and religiously practised, focus on the individual soul and the modality of suffering within an eschatological order. In thirteenth- and fourteenth-century bridal mysticism, penance and purgatory are recurrent themes. Female mystical accounts allowing women to express deliberations about and experiences with the divine often mirror and engage with contemporary, scholastic debates.[5] The tension resulting from the juxtaposition of internalized forms of penance and spirituality with outwardly manifested forms of punishment in purgatory (as referred to in visionary literature of the time) means that the relationship of internal penance to purgatory needs further exploration.[6]

The little studied thirteenth-century Premonstratensian mystic Christina von Hane offers a unique insight into the field of penitential practices and their link to purgatory. Her concrete penitential behaviour, most distinctively expressed in self-harm, paired with a strong presence of prayer for the souls in purgatory, allows us to study the relationship between penitence, penance, punishment, and purgatory. These four aspects – whether deliberately ordered thus or not – appear chronologically in the *Life* of Christina of Hane. Although this order does not imply a linear chain of actions it makes sense theologically for the *Life* to treat them in this order, especially when considering Abelard's threefold division of penance

---

Medieval formulae of ordeals reveal the omnipresence of a devil whose counterwork (namely his 'magical arts') is to prevent the sinner from confession and repentance. All relevant passages are listed and analysed in Kirakosian (2012: 273). With the quasi-abolition at the beginning of the 13th century, this public expression of penitence and purgation was officially dismissed in favour of more rational investigative methods; see McAuley (2006: 512).

[4] For earlier developments, stemming back to late Antiquity, see Brown (1997), who explores the relation between purgatory, amnesty, and penitence. For the relation of penitence to purgatory and the latter's scholastic foundation, see Le Goff (1981: 319-87).

[5] Newman (1995: 109) asserts that 'of all Catholic doctrines, none has been more deeply shaped by female piety than the notion of purgatory, which filled an overwhelming place in the visions, devotions, and works of charity undertaken by religious women'.

[6] The link between female spirituality and purgatory has already been addressed in research, just as female spirituality and its tensions between inner and outer world have also been mentioned. On women and purgatory see: Bynum (1987: 120-21); McNamara (1991: 213-18); Newman (1995: 109-36); Elliott (2004: 74-84); and for the ongoing debate about female spirituality and its relation to the inner (mind) and outer senses (body) of sanctity, see Elliott (2010: 32-34).

into 'penitentia', 'confessio', and 'satisfactio' (Baldwin 1998: 201-02). Penitence, penance, and punishment are – as this study shows – particularly interlinked, which is not surprising when we take into account how all three terms relate back to Latin *poena*, signifying indemnification and compensation as well as expiation, punishment (Poena is the goddess of punishment or vengeance), and hardship in the sense of torment and suffering. The double-layered meaning of an abstract sort of pain (*poena damni*) and material torment (*poena sensus*) can also be found in Dante's *Comedy*. Dante's work has been described as the 'greatest of all visions of the life to come' (Knox 2006: 33) and it is indeed an important source for the medieval understanding of pain and punishment in their relationship to reparation and salvation. Manuele Gragnolati explains that in Dante's 'otherworldly journey taking place in the eschatological time before the Last Judgement – that is, when the soul is separated from its body – pain constitutes a significant part of the soul's identity and experience' (Gragnolati 2007: 240).

The study of purgatory and its relationship to penitential self-punishment in the case of Christina of Hane helps us to understand the importance of pain for the process of purification. The concept of proxy pain is suggested here as a way to describe this relationship. The *Life* stands in the tradition of thirteenth-century bridal mystical accounts containing immaterial visions as well as corporeal concepts. Indeed, this tradition helps us date the anonymous work, which survives only in one sixteenth-century manuscript (the copyist is also unknown) but which was probably written and rewritten much earlier (Kirakosian 2014a: 189-91 and 2014b: 22). The *Life* begins in a structured and clear hagiographical tone but ends abruptly and is characterized by several shifts in style. Mapping between a close reading of the text on the one hand and sets of theological positions on penance on the other, we can see how the *Life* moves within those beliefs, but it becomes also apparent where it is different, especially when emphasizing bodily aspects of penance.[7] Christina's penitential plot connects her self-harm to her prayers for the souls in purgatory and creates a dramatic space in which the significance of purification through pain can evolve as part of a Christological salvation history.

Exposition: Penitence, or how true remorse is expressed
In the *Life*, Christina's repentant character is drawn very early on. She is still a child when she first shows sorrow and regret for her sins. The anonymous hagiographer even specifies that the sins were very trivial: Christina having lived in the convent since the age of six means, according to the hagiographer's rationale, that she could

---

[7] Bynum (1991: 222-38) underlines the body's importance for medieval female religious experience.

not have committed many sins. She still turns all her attention to how to go about confessing:

> Doch weche sie jre sunden gar groiße yn yrem hertze, want der gerecht ist eyn schuldicher syns selbs. Dar vmb gynge alle yre betrachtonge dar vff, wie sie yrem abt gentzelichen alle yre sunden bychten wultde, vff daz sie yre hertze altzo mail gelutert van allem gestůvppe der sunden.
> (Christina of Hane: 4)
>
> [But she rued her sins very strongly since he who is just feels guilty towards himself. Therefore she directed all her devotion to how to confess all her sins to her abbot so that her heart would for once be cleared from all the undergrowth of sin.][8]

The word used to explain Christina's feeling towards her own sins is 'wechen', derived from 'wê', the Middle High German interjection for the sensation of pain. As voiced by Christina, the verb does not simply express the pain experienced by her inner self. Instead, 'wechen' becomes an expression of lament, grievance, and remorse; we could translate the passage as: 'But in her heart (her inner self) she grieved about her sins heavily'. The original expression still maintains the connotation of physical pain. Christina's painful remorse is laudable according to the hagiographer's judgement, making clear that it was right to feel regretful towards oneself and hereby alluding to the psalmist's words in the Old Testament: 'Dixi, confitebor aduersum me iniusticiam meam Domino et tu remisisti inpietatem peccati mei' (Psalm 31:5).[9] The mystic's introspection, manifested by the contemplative character of her exercise ('betrachtonge'), leads to a state of personal guilt, and emphasizes her individual circumstances. Sins, in the *Life* described as 'dust' polluting the heart ('gestůvppe'), appear to be something wholly personal, which it is the sinner's responsibility to get rid of. The disposing of sins is described as an act of purification: 'lutern' (here 'gelutert') alludes to the material process of purifying gold.

As a consequence of her repentant behaviour, Christina comes to understand that she received absolution, although the intended confession to the abbot is never mentioned:

---

[8] Translations by Racha Kirakosian. A full English translation is currently in preparation.

[9] The whole passage reads: 'Delictum meum cognitum tibi feci, et injustitiam meam non abscondi. Dixi, confitebor' [I acknowledged my sin to you, and I did not cover my iniquity; I said, "I will confess my transgressions to the Lord," and you forgave the iniquity of my sin]. Gratian referred to this Psalm in his treatise on penance, *De pen*. D.1 c.4. This also links to Job 31:33: 'si abscondi quasi homo peccatum meum et celavi in sinu meo iniquitatem meam' [if I have concealed my transgressions as others do by hiding my iniquity in my heart]. All bible quotations are from the Vulgate and English translations from the English Standard Version unless stated otherwise.

Vff eyne tzijt wart sie hoiren eyn stymme eyns geistlichen ynsprechs, als vnser here zo yrer selen sprach: 'Kynt myns, dyße gesicht sy dyr eyn waire vrkuntde, daz dyr alle dyne sunden synt vergeben, die du noch ye gedayn haist.'
(Christina of Hane: 4)

[One time she heard a cleric's voice speaking as our lord said to her soul: 'My child, this saying shall be a true testimony to you that all the sins you have ever committed are forgiven.']

The *Life* does not specify whether or not oral confession took place; 'confession by mouth [...] belonged to the exterior forms of penance' (Baldwin 1998: 202). The close attention given to the absolution expressed by the divine voice instead emphasizes the outcome. The result is indirectly delivered through the voice of a cleric whose words of absolution, usually spoken after the confession, are not specified. Their allegorical meaning is deployed, and the temporal alignment of both the clerical and the divine voice refers once more to the personal, even private character of penitence, as the absolution is granted within the visionary experience (strictly speaking she has an audition). This kind of absolution is in line with Gratian's treatise on penitence, according to which mercy for an evil deed can be given without confession to the church and the judgment of a priest. As Gratian argues, 'Sunt enim qui dicunt, quemlibet criminis ueniam sine confessione ecclesiae et sacerdotali iudicio posse promereri' (*De pen.* D.1 d.a.c.1).[10] Confession then appears only as a demonstration of penance, and mercy has already been received (Gratian *De pen.* D.1 d.p.c. 37; Larson 2014: 58).

Although she is granted absolution, remorse and repentance persist in Christina's case: still a child, she has an outburst of remorse in a moment of loneliness and contemplation. The sight of running water in a stream makes her think of all the time that she spent 'uselessly' [vnnutzelich]: 'Da so hobe sie an zo schreye myt groißem jamer vnd claget gode myt heyßen threnen, daz sie yn nyt alle yre dage myt allem flyße gesucht haitte' [At this point she started to cry with heavy sorrow, lamenting to God with fervent tears that she had not searched him every day with full diligence] (Christina of Hane: 8). The sudden release of remorse, accompanied by fervent tears, creates a sense of deep regret, which again corresponds to Gratian's view on penitence. The focus on tears rather than words (Christina thinks, but does not speak) underlines the direct relationship between sinner and God as there is no articulated utterance that would allow her penitence to be shared with others. Gratian referred among others to Peter's tears after his denial of Christ in order to

---

[10] See also Larson (2014: 40). Gratian still did not mean to support the abolition of confession; see Larson (2014: 78).

highlight this speechless form of penitence (*De pen*, D.1. c.1; Larson 2014: 41). Theologians after Abelard agreed that interior penance ('penitentia', later referred to as 'contritio cordis'), 'was the most important element of penance' (Baldwin 1998: 201–02). Christina's outbreak is a personal act, which precedes a form of penitential behaviour that results in self-punishment.

Rising Action: Penance, or how often may one sin
Notwithstanding the blurry line between penitence and penance, the first is more generally used for regret whereas penance, often describing a sacramental act, implies a long-lasting cathartic effect on the sinner. While Atria Larson argues that according to medieval theology before Gratian, penance was a one-time affair that could not be repeated – otherwise it would not have been true penance the first time (Larson 2014: 102) – it must be once more highlighted that the privatization of confession and hence the repeated absolution of sins had begun long before Gratian's *Decretum*. The Hiberno-Scottish mission, gaining ground on the European continent as early as the seventh century and quickly finding liturgical acceptance, encouraged a daily practice of penance in which the secret nature of the confession and pardon of sin was established. The concept of the repeated sinner and the belief that true penance was possible more than once in a human's life is therefore older than Larson acknowledges (2014: 104-67). In the case studied here, after her absolution Christina falls back into a state where she needs to repent again. This is important to note when considering the *Life* and its didactic function within the monastic community. Christina served as a model for a pious life and as such her trajectory too is portrayed as an exemplary one. To regain the state of sin after having been granted absolution must be acceptable despite the model character of her spirituality repeatedly referred to by her hagiographer.

The model character is still maintained since Christina's developing temptation for sin is treated as a probation, conveying her saintly character rather than her own evil:

> Dyße swere lange anfechtonge verhenget vnser lyeber here vber sie nyt an sachen, want er woilt sie versuchen vnd beweren als den heilgen Tobiam, zo dem der engel sprache: 'So du gode woil befellest, so was noit, daz dich anfechtonge vnd vngemache beweret.' Auch ist geschreben yn dem boiche der wyßheit: 'Der here hait geproberet syne vßerwilten als daz golt yn dem oben des fuvrs.' Auch verhencket vnser here zo dem anderen mail dyeße groiße anfechtonge vber sie, dar vmb daz yre strytde eyn lere were allen den, die bekarunge vnd anfechtonge lydent.
> (Christina of Hane: 10)

[Our lovely lord charged her with this heavy temptation not as consequence of any specific deed but because he wanted to probe her just as Saint Tobias to whom the angel said: 'As you were pleasing to God it was necessary that you stood the test of temptation and hardship.' We also find written in the Book of Proverbs: 'The lord has probed his chosen ones like the gold in the furnace's fire.' Another time the lord charged her with a strong temptation so that her battle would be an example for all those that suffer from seductions and temptations.]

It is made explicit that there is no factual reason for Christina's temptations ('nyt an den sachen') but rather that they are a sign of her distinction. Her process of penance is consolidated with exegetic arguments. The comparison with the Book of Tobias works in a twofold way. Firstly, Sarah, Tobias's future daughter-in-law, is liberated from an evil spirit that had affected her sexuality: all seven men betrothed to her had died on their wedding night. The link to Christina's sexual temptations is that a female figure is innocently charged with an outward diabolic energy, which according to the rationale of a typological reading of the scripture can only be defeated by the right bridegroom, who in Christina's case turns out to be Christ.[11] Secondly, despite his noble and God-fearing character Tobias turns blind and is scorned by his friends. His misfortune is presented as exemplary probation: 'hanc autem temptationem ideo permisit Dominus evenire illi ut posteris daretur exemplum patientiae eius sicut et sancti Iob' [Now this trial the Lord therefore permitted to happen to him, that an example might be given to posterity of his patience, as also of holy Job] (Tobias 2:12).[12] Like Tobias, Christina's trial is not a punishment but a form of reward with a didactic outcome. The allusion to Proverbs 17:3 ('sicut igne probatur argentum et aurum camino ita corda probat Dominus' [The crucible is for silver, and the furnace is for gold, and the Lord tests hearts] underlines the didactic nature, which is reinforced by the hagiographer's comment that Christina's temptations are suffered for the sake of others. The *Life* follows a tight rationale that does not allow any room for doubt. Christina's decline towards sin is meticulously outlined as an opportunity for penance that is realized through pure self-examination and observance that serves as a model for others.

The *Life* explains this decline, referring to a period in which Christina had to leave the convent school for six months, as other novices would have done, because of the nunnery's alleged financial struggles. Historical documents confirm that from the year 1265 the convent of Hane had to constantly revise its numbers to a total of

---

[11] A similar treatment of female sexuality as morally condemnable is found in medieval legends of Mary Magdalene's conversion. Such a legend is transmitted alongside the *Life* of Christina of Hane. See Kirakosian (2014a: 393-98) for an analysis of the alignment of both texts in this regard.

[12] The English translation is from the Douay-Rheims Bible.

50, perhaps because of economic problems combined with an increasing influx of members.[13] Despite the emphasis on clarifying that there was no factual reason for Christina's probation, the time spent outside the convent walls is used to justify the bodily temptations that she suffers at her return. The hagiographer wants to certify that the monastic world, as opposed to the outside world, is secure and pure:

> Da dyße heilge jonffrauwe was gesant zo yren fruntden, alstu vor gehoirt haist, vnd voille eyn hailffe jare yn der werelt waz gewest vnd wieder vmb heymme quam yn yre cloister, da warff yr der vyant vor myt boißen gedancken die werelt vnd werntlichen sachen, die sie yn der werelt hatte gesehen vnd gehoirt. Vnd myt den gedancken goiße er yre ynne also starcken anfechtonge vnd bekarunge des fleiße, daz sy dick selber duchte, hette sy got nyt eygentlichen myt der hant syner barmhertzicheit vnd genaden vffenthaillen, iß were vnmogelichen gewest, das sie moicht die selbe erlieden hayn.
> (Christina of Hane: 10)

> [At the return to the convent after having spent six months in the world – this holy virgin had been sent to her family as you have heard before – the enemy assaulted her with evil worldly thoughts and worldly things which she had seen and heard in the world. And with such thoughts he poured into her such heavy temptations and desires of the flesh that she often thought to herself that it would have been impossible for her to withstand all this without God actually holding her with his merciful and gracious hand.]

The internal character of the temptations is highlighted: Christina's mind becomes infected with evil thoughts triggered by 'worldly images and words'. Borrowing an image from Neo-Platonism that conventionally appears with divine grace, doubts and temptation are 'poured' into her, hereby subverting the original implication of the imagery ('vnt myt den gedancken goiße er yre ynne'). Divine grace still comes into play but on a mental level. Christina thinks ('daz sy dick selber duchte') that she can only withstand the temptations with the help of God's grace and mercy. This fits the general conviction of her time that 'humanity is always dependent on God's help in human action(s)' as propagated, for example, by Hildegard of Bingen (Ruge 2014: 229).

Hildegard's twelfth-century *Liber vite meritorum* also relates penance to self-examination (Ruge 2014: 241). Her instructions for penitential behaviour help us to understand Christina's approach to self-chastisement as a consequence of her introspection. In one of the penitential catalogues Hildegard lists such measures:

---

[13] It is surprising though that the convent should have been poor considering the deeds of gifts during the thirteenth century; see Mittermaier (1960: 79). It seems likely, however, that the number of members went down and reached around 30 by 1289; see Krings (2009: 182).

Sed qui in seculo huic uitio insistunt, si suasionem huius diabolice artis neglexerint et si penas eiusdem uitii abhorruerint, carnem suam secundum qualitatem et tenorem eorundem peccatorum suorum ieiuniis affligant, in quibus etiam pretiosum potum deuitent, secundum rectum iudicium iudicium suorum.
(*Liber vite meritorum*: 1.88; 53–54, ll. 15202-07)

[Whoever follows such vices in this world, but then desires to put aside the whisperings of this diabolic art and shudders with horror before the punishments meted out to this vice, he should chastise his flesh, according to the type and degree of his transgressions, through fasting and avoiding expensive beverages, according to the judgement of his judge.]
(Ruge 2014: 240)

Chastisement of the flesh, fasting, and abstinence from expensive drinks would help to counter diabolical vices; all are penitential acts performed by Christina of Hane. It is important to note, however, that Hildegard of Bingen, unlike her teacher Jutta of Sponheim, was not in favour of severe ascetic exercises. In her correspondence, Hildegard warns of an 'incongrua abstinentia' [unsuitable abstinence] and emphasizes the importance of the wellbeing of the body. She repeatedly uses the word 'rationabilis' [rational], as in 'rationabilis abstinentia' [rational abstinence] (Felten 2001: 52-68). Hildegard's call to a mild form of asceticism includes hermitage (Ruge 2014: 241), which Christina practises in order to stop sin being provoked. Christina literally 'drives' away 'places and people and all things' that induce her to temptation.[14] Such people, places, and things could also refer to mental places, people, and things experienced during the time outside the convent: it is the power of (here visual) memory that retains an impact. Christina's ardent fear of 'God's anger' ('yn groißer vocht des gotlichen tzorns') and her eagerness to repent are not enough to turn away her 'unchaste' thoughts (Christina of Hane: 10). As such they are unrealized ('yn gedancken'), but she goes on to apply concrete penitential measures expressed in self-punishment. Although Christina's temptations are portrayed as proof of her sanctity, the *Life* continues by detailing a severe self-punitive seven-year-long programme that – despite its physical nature – takes on a form of 'secret penance'.[15] (Re)conceiving the relationship between penance and penitence in light of how remorse and self-observation is treated in the *Life*, it becomes apparent that penitence is an initiator for a longer process of penance that includes relapses and continuous efforts.

---

[14] Christina of Hane: 10: 'Dar vmb dryeffe sie van yre alle sunden vnd orsachen der sunden, daz ist alle stetde vnd lude vnd alle sachen, die yr moichten syn eyn orsache zo der bekarunge. Sye hyelte sich yn groißer hirtickeit, daz sie da myt des fleiße woilluste an yre moicht verließen.'
[15] For secret penance, sometimes referred to as 'private penance', see Meens (1998: 50-52).

Climax: Punishment, or how to cast away the devil

Christina's battle to overcome the flesh is portrayed as a fight against the cardinal sins, categorizing her effort within an institutional framework with a soteriological impact. Despite the assumed belief that theoretically all seven deadly sins lead equally to damnation, the space dedicated to renouncing lust (carnal *luxuria*) in the *Life* exceeds by far that of all the others. Christina undergoes various trials in defence of her chastity.[16] As the ancient idea of virginity as an important factor of sainthood still prevailed, this nun too is highly concerned with her sexuality.[17] That 'the genitals were judged to be the parts most severely afflicted with the spirit of revolt' (Elliott 2010: 14) – an Augustinian idea based on the assumed autonomous power of sexual organs – can be shown with Christina's targeted and self-inflicted harm.

Inspired by saints' legends, Christina sits unprotected on glowing coals, evoking images of trials by fire. Medieval ordeals that applied a form of glowing or burning object are particularly connected to stories of adulterous wives (Ziegler 2004: 6). Fire seems therefore unsurprising as an instrument to detect carnal lust; it also symbolizes the fire of temptation ('daz fŭvre der bekarunge'). In order to extinguish the 'abstract fire of the flesh' ('daz geistlichen fŭvre yrs fleiße'), Christina exposes her genital area to 'material fire' ('lyplichen fure') (Christina of Hane: 10). Exactly which saints' lives serve as model is not specified, but St Radegund is a possibility, since her application of fire to the body is similarly described; her male hagiographer Fortunatus explains: 'ut refrigeraret tam ferventem animum, incendere corpus deliberat' [to cool her fervent soul, she thought to burn her body] (Fortunatus, §26 (373); trans. McNamara, Halborg and Whately 1992: 81). In addition to Radegund, whose self-chastisement is a means principally to deny the flesh – possibly in order to prevent sin –, Christina's measures are a reaction to experiencing lust and are hence a form of penitential punishment and not solely ascetic exercises.

Christina outperforms the practice of glowing coal by introducing fire into her body, something that is judged by her hagiographer to be even more astonishing than what she had done before ('daz was noch erschrecklicher'):

> Zo eym anderen mail namme sie eyn burnende hoiltze vnd stieße daz selbe also gluedich yn yren lyffe, also daz daz lypliche fure das fure yrer bekarunge myt groißen

---

[16] This stands in the tradition of the early Christian discourse about chastity or *enkretia*, Greek for sexual renunciation, as a secure way to salvation. See Koltun-Fromm (2010: 110-11).

[17] Elliott (2010: 19–20) argues that the factor of virginity was revived in the twelfth and thirteenth centuries but earlier medieval legends and tales about virtuous women show that it has always remained an important aspect of female sanctity..

smertzen verleyst. Jch loben viel me die sach vnd die meynunge, yn der sie iß dede, dan ich die daytde loben. Dan iß was eyn vnuernoifftige kaistigonge.
(Christina of Hane: 10)

[At another time she took a burning piece of wood and prodded it glowing as it was into her body. In this way the physical fire extinguished with immense pain the fire of her desire. I praise the background and the motivation of her action rather than the actual deed because it was an irrational chastisement.]

The self-charged penetration of a burning woodblock into the 'body' with the result of severe pain, a pure physical sensation, is another way to put an end to Christina's 'fire of desire'. The hagiographer's critique of her self-chastisement alludes to ethical values, praising the intention while condemning the action as 'irrational'. Such a judgement gives us a glimpse of the hagiographer's implied readership. It reminds us of Hildegard of Bingen's attitude towards severe ascetic practices, and shows a pastoral concern for the wellbeing of a readership of nuns. The distinction between motivation ('menynunge') and action ('daytde') enables the hagiographer to simultaneously laud Christina's actions and warn against imitating her. According to the hagiographer, there is something shameful about Christina's handling of lust ('eyn deyle schemelichen zo schryben'), but we still find the detailed account of how she preserved 'the treasure of her chastity' ('wie sye den schaitze yrrer kußheit behylde vnbefleckte') (Christina of Hane: 10).[18] The effective way is to suffer pain: 'Aber wan der pynen des smertzes wart verleißen die bekarunge' [because of the pain's torment the temptations were expunged]. As long as the self-induced pain lasts, Christina's chastity seems safe. According to this principle, recurring lust requires the renewal of pain:

Dar vmb dede sie aber gar eyn grußelich swere dynge. Das was, si nam kalcke vnd essich, vnd macht dar vße eynen deiche vnd dede den aber yn yren lyffe, so sie aller ferste kontde. Wer kayn gesaigen, was groißen smetzen sie leyt?
(Christina of Hane: 10)

[For that reason she did a gruesomely severe thing, that was the following: she took chalk and vinegar and mixed it into one dough and infused this into her body as vigorously as she could. Who can even speak about the immense pain that she suffered?]

---

[18] The hesitation expressed on behalf of the hagiographer is a literary topos inherent to saints' lives that aims to intensify the effect of superhuman behaviour, see e.g. Fortunatus, §25 (372): 'Itaque post to labores, quas sibi poenas intulerit, et ipse qui voce refert perhorrescit.' [But I shudder to speak of the pain she inflicted on herself over and above all these labors; trans. McNamara, Halborg and Whately 1992: 81].

Wordless pain inflicted by a chalk-vinegar mixture introduced, again, into the 'body' does still not mean the end of her trial. Christina's lecherous listening [myt loiste] to a layperson's conversation about 'carnal and worldly things' leads to stopping her surveillance [huytde].[19] In great detail the reader gets to find out how the nun counters the new temptation, this time by infusing a urine and chalk mixture into her 'body' causing symptoms such as swollen body parts and genital bleeding. Previously unspecified, the part of the body that is maltreated is implicitly named when the symptoms are listed:

> Da myt verswallen der lyffe van den fußen an byß yn den gurtel, das keynne waiße van yre moicht komen. Daz wertte woil echt dage. Dar na gynge drye dage vnd dry nachten bloit van yr yn der stait, da daz waißer her komen sult.
> (Christina of Hane: 10)

[Because of this her body swelled so badly from the feet up to the hip that she could not pass water. This lasted for eight days. Then she bled for three days from the place where water is supposed to come from.]

'The place where the water should come from' is the urethral meatus, suggesting that Christina attacks her sexual organs. More specifically, one might think of the clitoris, which is anatomically close to the urethral meatus. The description of introducing material 'into the body', however, means that we deal with an orifice, most likely the vagina, as target of her self-inflicted punishment. Even though the *Life* is no medical treatise, its way of speaking about the genitals illuminates medieval understanding of the sexual organs. It is the general genital area that is concerned when Christina sits on glowing coals. While the urethral orifice would be a difficult one to penetrate, its indirect mentioning ('the place where the water comes from') means that there might have been some sort of knowledge about the clitoris as an erogenous zone. Whether the hagiographer was aware of the vagina's sensitivity to sexual stimulation or not, it must be taken into consideration as the actual orifice that Christina targets. Although the description is vague, we can reasonably deduce that the general genital area is meant, the vulva being a sort of

---

[19] 'Eyns mails da quam eyn man, den hoirt sy reden myt eyner frauwen van fleißelichen vnd werenclichen sachen, so sie myt loiste zo hoirt vnd vergaiß yrer huytde vnd sie gaiffe orsache zo der bekarunge' (Christina of Hane: 10). 'Huote' as a concept can be understood as a major female virtue from vernacular poetry of the time, thereby alluding to a literary discourse on ideal courtly femininity. The 'huote'-principle, described by Schweikle (1995: 129) as 'Sittencodex', has been discussed for various medieval German songs and epics such as Gottfried von Strassburg's *Tristan* (Huber 2013: 129-140), but no comprehensive study has yet been presented. Sayce (1967: xiv) defines the primary meaning of 'huote' as 'guard' or 'watch' in relation to 'merkaere'. It then refers to the activity of the 'merkaere' as 'the custodians of correct behaviour'.

aperture. This possibility is buttressed by the association of Christina's wound with Christ's side wound in the *Life*.

The torment inflicted by the threefold penetration (once woodblock, twice infusion) is aligned with the passion, with Christina having a vision in which Christ reveals to her his five wounds, 'each a man's hand wide' [eyns mans spanne], inviting her furthermore to explore them: 'Sieche heryn jn myne wonden. Synt sy nyt wyte genunge, dastu dynen vngemache yn myr verbergest?' [Look here into my wounds; are they not large enough for you to hide your suffering in me?] (Christina of Hane: 10). This kind of 'visual materialization', a term used by Caroline Walker Bynum for late medieval depictions of Christ's passion, evokes the image of mandorla-shaped wounds (Bynum 2011: 89-101 (99); Karras 2012: 67-68).[20] Combined with the indicated dimension of the wounds in the *Life* (a hand as a unit) and the possibility to look 'into' them, i.e. their depth, the proximity to Christina's own active wound (vulva) is striking. The sharing of similar wounds does not simply feminize Christ but converges him with Christina. Through her genital maltreatment Christina can penetrate the deity 'hiding her wound in his'. Jeffrey Hamburger suggests that 'nuns regarded [the opening in Christ's side] as an invitation to introspection, a literal looking inward' (Hamburger 1997: 219).[21] Christina's inspection of Christ's wounds is linked to her own wound so that her flesh becomes the trigger for self-oriented soul-searching.

Christina's punitive behaviour means that while defeating deadly sins she cultivates virtues: chastity against lust, patience against wrath, humility against pride, and so forth.[22] In her fight against sloth she buries her lower body from the hips downwards in snow and subsequently beats her frozen legs with a hard whip (Christina of Hane: 11). After the heat of the fire, she suffers the discomfort of cold and hunger, torturing her flesh 'in order to defeat it'.[23] The Augustinian paradigm of spirit over flesh influenced piety throughout the Middle Ages (Biernoff 2002: 26-31; Elliott 2010: 15). It is palpable in the self-punitive and flesh-defeating measures described in the *Life*. The sin of wrath too is countered with infliction of pain, such as sleeping in a bed laid out with nettles and standing bare-footed on the chapel

---

[20] Tammen (2006: 90) speaks of a 'quasi vulvale Präsenz'.
[21] See also Tammen (2006: 101-03) for a discussion about the visual depiction of Christ's side wound in medieval books as means of contact with the deity.
[22] Christina is punished twice by someone else, by her abbess ('mistress' for the convent of Hane) for her ardent practice of kneeling before the cross for too long (Christina of Hane: 7), and by the Virgin Mary who in a vision slaps her face for arrogance in exaggerating the practice of prayer (Christina of Hane: 28). In Christina's vision Mary voices the reproach: when kneeling, Christina's intentions were not totally innocent and she rather has herself trained in humbleness.
[23] Christina of Hane: 11: 'Myt soilicher hartticheit verdreyffe sie alle tracheit van yr, also daz yre lyffe altzo mail gehoirsam wart dem geist'.

floor paving stones. Keeping anger towards others to herself and avoiding slander against another nun, Christina of Hane bites her own tongue, forcing the blood to escape through nose and mouth.[24] Binding a rough and dirty cloth around her head at the time of divine office, Christina uses a visible sign of humility as part of her battle against pride. She takes on voluntary work in the kitchen and infirmary, and repeatedly falls unconscious as a consequence of the pain and weakness caused by severe fasting.

As the hagiographer ascribes successful outcomes to bodily chastisement and self-inflicted wounds, the mutilation of the genitals means that Christina loses any sexual characterization – were we to apply Ruth Mazo Karras' idea that 'chastity was a sexual identity' (Karras 2010: 63). Since chastity plays no further role in the *Life*, one might speak of a new asexual gender that brings the mystic close to the theoretically acclaimed androgynous state of a virgin who leads an angelic life.[25] Chastity of body, abolishing any sexual identity, comes along with chastity of soul, enabling the mystic to move beyond the flesh and enforce the spiritual virtues.

Although the described self-penitential behaviour has a character of privacy to it (hence secret penance), there remains an underlying educational programme to Christina's self-punishment, and it is linked to the ideal of the charitable and sacrificing asexual virgin as well as to the concept of purgatory:

> Sye hyelte sich yn groißer hirtickeit, daz sie da myt des fleiße woilluste an yre moicht verließen, want sie dan dem vyant, der sie myt flyße anfecht, durch den dage also stercklichen wieder stontde. So sye des nachtes slaiffen sultde gayn, so bracht er yr yme slaiffe vor boiße dreûme, boiße wullust vnd bekarunge. Aber daz sie yme auch dar vmb festelichen wiederstonde vnd vberwant, want sie yn der nacht erwachte, so stontde sie also swygenden vff van dem bette vnd gynge an eyn heymeliche stait vnd zoge sich vß vnd name drye starcker dysciplynen myt eym beyßem. Eyne dysciplyne name sie vor alle sunder. Die ander vor alle selen, die yn dem fegefûre synt. Die drytte vor alle gude lude, daz die got bestedigen wultde an rechter kußheit.
>
> (Christina of Hane: 10)

[She exercised most extreme asceticism in order to defeat the flesh's desire as she so was able to powerfully withstand the foe's incessant attacks during daytime. At bedtime he inflicted her in her sleep with evil dreams, evil lust, and seduction. But in order to steadfastly withstand and overcome him she stood up in silence, left the bed, and went to a secret place where she got undressed and lashed herself three

---

[24] This manoeuvre can be understood as a type of circumcision, according to medieval theology: as for the foreskin of men, the part considered dirty gets preventively removed (see Kirakosian 2017:147-50).
[25] The androgynous state of angel-like virgins was an early Church belief that had not entirely faded away by the thirteenth and fourteenth centuries; see Elliott (2013: 24).

times vigorously with a besom. She took one lash for all sinners, a second lash for all the souls in purgatory, and a third for all good people that God may keep them in righteous chastity.]

Self-flagellation as described here builds upon an ancient ascetic tradition, according to which the sensation of pain liberates one from the flesh. While Catherine Vincent understands flagellation as ultimately leading to the discipline of the soul (Vincent 2000: 613), Niklaus Largier argues that, for the late medieval phenomenon of flagellation in mystical contexts, the beating with a whip was less about pain and more about the ritual of immediacy between humans and God (Largier 2001: 29-36). Christina's case shows that self-flagellation and other forms of self-harm can be both an efficient way to defeat the flesh in order to overcome its potential sexuality, and a way to identify with Christ's passion, whilst the wounds become a 'physical gate' into the divine, as shown in the example of Christina's vision of Christ after the mutilation of her genitals. This sort of private penitential behaviour has more to do with corporeality than the idea of interiority and introspection would suggest in the first place. Corruptness is reparable in this personal form, which is not simply manifested in the physical but where the body itself becomes the medium of the introspection.

Models of saints and martyrs certainly influenced the *Life*, meaning that traditional aspects must be taken into account, too. Christina turns her self-flagellation into a threefold prayer, making the link between physical pain and its resulting gain straightforward: beating her own flesh as redemption for all sinners, for all souls in purgatory, and for righteous people to maintain their chastity shows that she functions as a paragon in the context of her supposed readership, the nuns of Hane (Kirakosian 2014a: 391-92). She not only cleanses herself while considering communal aspects by acting charitably, but with a private and individual programme of self-punishment she also appears as a helper of sinful, suffering, and struggling souls. While there is the sense that physical pain is ultimately suffered in order to learn a spiritual lesson, the corporeality remains an important aspect of Christina's piety. Once the battle against the cardinal sins is portrayed as successfully fought, the weakness of Christina's body ties her to the sickbed: she turns into a living martyr constantly redeeming souls in purgatory.

Falling Action: Purgatory, or how to do penance for others
Christina's personal, certainly self-inflicted 'trials by fire' foreshadow and mirror her service to the souls in purgatory. The purging effect of fire makes this element a metonymy for purgatory. The identification of purgation and of purgatory with fire

in particular rests on 1 Cor 3.13-15: 'uniuscuiusque opus manifestum erit dies enim declarabit quia in igne revelabitur et uniuscuiusque opus quale sit ignis probabit [...] ipse autem salvus erit sic tamen quasi per ignem' [each one's work will become manifest, for the day will disclose it, because it will be revealed by fire, and the fire will test what sort of work each one has done [...] though he himself will be saved, but only as through fire]. The traditional difference between purgatory and hell lay within the terms of punishment: in purgatory the punishment was temporary rather than eternal, allowing change in the individual soul, to which the Augustinian notion of 'purgatio' actually refers. While physical pain was experienced in purgatory as it was in hell, its effects on the soul were considered completely different. It is in Dante's *Inferno* that the effects of this essential difference become evident: 'Qui vive la pietà quand' è ben morta' [Here pity lives when it is quite dead] (*Inferno* 30:28; trans. Durling 1996: 305). The pilgrim's pity on the souls in hell has no significance. True compassion was only appropriate towards the living, which includes souls in purgatory because they can change. In hell, pain was mechanical, repetitive, and useless, allowing neither change nor self-knowledge; it was completely at one with the sin corrupting the soul into the afterlife and indicating its permanence and the loss of the *imago Dei*. In purgatory, the process of purgation, or what Gragnolati terms 'productive pain' (Gragnolati 2005: 135-38), rested precisely on the possibility of the soul learning through its experience: it suffers its punishment and pain willingly.[26] The first references to Christina's effect on purgatory happen in the context of mystical raptures, 'when her soul is inwardly received in a clear light' [Da wart jre sele ynwendich vmbfangen myt eyme clairen lyecht] (Christina of Hane: 30; see also chapter 23). Her path is portrayed as rounded and perfected so that the hagiographer anticipates her pleasing God, angels, saints, and the souls on earth and in purgatory (Christina of Hane: 30), a trope also known from Catherine of Siena's *Dialogue*.[27] The prolific release of thousands of souls from purgatory – a feature that she shares with the mystic Adelheid Langmann – mirrors Christina's own pure soul.[28] The claim that the souls would have otherwise suffered several hundred years (specified in one case as 350, in another as 500 years) reinforces and inflates the mystic's virtuous status that functions as counterbalance to the weight of sins: her singularity carries the significance of a multitude. This notion is alluded

---

[26] Gragnolati's concept is discussed by Walls (2012: 74-75); Tylus (2009: 266); Lombardi (2012: 30–31).
[27] Catherine of Siena: 33: 'The willing desire to suffer every pain and hardship even to the point of death for the salvation of souls is very pleasing to me.'
[28] Christina of Hane: 51; 56 (1,000 souls); 57 (3,000 souls and the soul of a brother of the order named Jacob); 70 (12,000 souls); 78 (5,000 souls, who would have otherwise stayed in purgatory for 500 years); 83 (2,000 souls).

to in an extended allegory right at the beginning of the *Life* where Christina is compared to the biblical figure Esther ('Sie ist woil die ander Hester') (Christina of Hane: 1). This typological explanation sets Christina as saviour of many in her capacity as heavenly queen.[29]

The idea of mechanical rules for atoning the sins of souls in purgatory, also found in Mechthild of Magdeburg's *Flowing Light of the Godhead* (Mechthild of Magdeburg: III, 17; 200-02), reminds us of Germanic legal repayment systems where a particular crime could entail certain monetary punishment in the form of an assessed fine ('wergild').[30] Lisi Oliver mentions the fact that 'the responsibility for payment would not rest solely upon the loser of the suit, but would be shared by his kingroup' (Oliver 2011: 46). Mayke de Jong argues that the early medieval 'tariffed' form of penance 'has been viewed as the direct forerunner of the "private" confession as prescribed by the Fourth Council of the Lateran but the development to internal forms of penance is not straightforward; rather 'public penance has always been in a state of decline' (De Jong 2000: 187). Reinforcing the link between Germanic law and purgatory, it is noteworthy that the payment of a fine was a collective responsibility. Even secret penance can be thought of as 'a kind of communal ritual' (Meens 1998: 50). A communal aspect is also inherent to the idea of purgatory where interceding prayers work as catalysts for the sins' expiation.[31]

For Hildegard of Bingen, the punitive purification by fire in the afterlife can be 'partially or completely mitigated through earthly repentance' (Ruge 2014: 238). Christina of Hane seems to take on this task for the sake of others; with her own repentant character and subsequent suffering, she acts in service of salvation. The living martyrdom can be seen as part of a form of somatic mysticism often associated with women: Elliott points out that 'much of the physical suffering attributed to these women was allegedly undertaken voluntarily to help individuals in purgatory' (Elliott 2010: 25). Christina is in a constant state of illness and fragility of the body. She not only physically embodies the passion of Christ: in connection with her achievements in releasing souls from purgatory her body is used as a constant sacrifice to what is portrayed as the glory of God, resonating the words of the liturgy 'give our bodies as a living sacrifice' (Romans 12:1).[32] She does not fight a

---

[29] Christina of Hane: 1: 'Dyß ist alles geistlich an dyeßer jonffrauwen ernuwet. Ach, wie ist sye vor den augen des ewigen konyncks also sere woille gefellich! O, wie hait er sie also wirdenclichen gecroynnet vor vns allen! O, wie dick hait er freden vnd genade alle dyeßem lantde durch sie gegeben, want er hait yn rechter vereynionge wyrtschaift myt yrer selen gemacht ewenclichen.'

[30] The etymology of the Latin *poena* derives from the Greek word for quitmoney, the fine paid by a delinquent to the party injured by him, or to his kinsmen.

[31] See Kirakosian (2014a: 384-85) on the function of purgatory in the early modern reception of Christina's *Life*.

[32] Bynum (1987: 418, n. 54) stresses 'the characteristically Christian idea that the bodily suffering of one

battle against the body; on the contrary her suffering turns into a sign of devotion and an outward manifestation of the inner intimacy that her soul shares with her bridegroom.

The physical suffering itself, however, is not an automatic mechanism to release souls from purgatory, since there is an active engagement in the form of prayer. Christina's pleading is repeatedly successful, which brings her close to a power that would normally be attributed approbated saints. Traditionally it is the Virgin Mary who is responsible for the relief of pain suffered in purgatory. Combined with the Marian features with which Christina is described – she is adorned with a crown and is described as the throne of God – she acquires the character of the judicial intercessor for the souls in purgatory normally ascribed to Mary (Schreiner 1994: 162). Indeed, the idea of purgatory is linked to the emergence of Marian devotion in the twelfth century (Thali 2003: 7). Mary as *co-redemptrix* was seen as in charge of purgatory (Schreiner 1994: 162; Büttner 1983: 89), 'an intercessor of great force who could determine the destiny of souls' (Rubin 2009: 224). The culture of penance encountered in the *Life* stands in this context, since 'Mary was attractive not only for her purity, but for the intimacy that linked her to the redemption by her son' (Rubin 2009: 131). The typological understanding of Mary being the bride of the Song of Songs takes us back to the bridal mystical text in which Christina of Hane advances to be bride, co-redeemer, and living martyr. In Dante's *Purgatorio* it is 'the holy woman [a general role] as medium and mediatrix [...] whose compassion takes her through the portals of hell and heaven that she may lead souls out of purgatory' (Newman 1995: 108).[33] The complexity of the idea of purgatory shows how interwoven pain and purification are and how they are linked to the cultures of devotion and penance. The pain suffered on Christina's behalf functions as a ransom for the souls in purgatory. It is preceded by her own purging pain on a private penitential level. Thus her own suffering in the light of her 'achievements' for the souls in purgatory can be described as proxy pain.

Conclusion: Purifying Pain

Achieving a perfect state means going through purification. This crucial premise is laid out right at the beginning of the *Life*. In one of Christina of Hane's very first visions, which she has when still a child, the Infant Jesus is playing in the sunbeam

---

person can be substituted for the suffering of another through prayer, purgatory, vicarious communion' and suggests 'that this idea should not be taken for granted as an implication of the Crucifixion. Rather, it should be explored as one of the most puzzling, characteristic, glorious, and horrifying features of Christianity.'

[33] The female figure Matelda is generally assumed to be identifiable with the mystic from Helfta Mechthild of Hackeborn, a contemporary of Christina of Hane.

that streams through the chapel window into the choir stalls, 'as if the child wanted to make himself a bed out of sun'. The hagiographer explains:

> Also gaiffe er yr zo verstayn, daz er alleyn wille rogen yn dem hertzen, daz da luter ist als die sonne. Nach der tzijd kerte sie alle yren flyße dar zo, wie sie yre hertze gelutert myt eyner vollenkomen lycht, alstu her na fyndest geschreben.
> (Christina of Hane: 3)
>
> [In this way he [the child Christ] made her understand that he only wanted to rest in that heart that is brighter than the sun. Hereafter she turned all her diligence to how to illuminate her heart with a perfect light as you will find written later on.]

Although Christina quickly succeeds in achieving this, it soon becomes clear that she needs to adorn her heart with virtues ('Iß moiße auch getzeirt syn myt hemelschen roißen, daz ist myt allen doegenden', Christina of Hane: 5). Here is where the devil comes into play. As antagonist, he has his own will and power over her thoughts – traits of the devil that remind us of those described in the medieval formulas for trial by water and fire. With the twelfth-century theologian Peter Chanter we can see how the ideas of a powerful devil and a divine miracle are linked to penance, since he argues that miracles and ordeals should be replaced by faith and good works (Chanter, *Verbum*, PL 205, 226D and 228B; Baldwin 1998: 208). The purging effect becomes the true miracle. The *Life* of Christina of Hane presents to us a mixed form of penance, one that is utterly private and internal, and that is combined with external penitential behaviour, aiming to cultivate a pure soul and the willingness for charitable works, including the service to souls in purgatory. The grand narrative of the internalized penitential practices, as opposed to early medieval more public and corporeal rituals, does not hold and needs further consideration.[34]

Private forms of penitence did not mean that purification was less external; one only needs to consider the physical pain that Christina suffers and the agony endured by the souls in purgatory – in other contemporary documents vividly described with thoroughly bodily attributes – to understand that externalized forms of penance were prevailing. Even the idea of paying someone else's debts is reiterated in the way the release of souls from purgatory works. What seems special, however, is the juxtaposition and often also the conflation of all these aspects –

---

[34] *Purgatio* as an equivocal term with a theological or legal notion takes us back to the ritual of ordeals seen as a form of purgation (Evans 2002: 140). The outward testimony of truth was one that was visible and corporeal and that functioned at the same time as purification from guilt. The alignment of the increasing unacceptability of such judgements with the emergence of purgatory raises the question as to whether these developments are linked to supposed shifts in the penitential tradition.

penitence, penance, punishment, purgatory – in the mystical text. As Christina's dramatic stages of penitence and punishment show, there is a direction from mind to body; this shift, however, is not simply explained by a pious practice preferred by women who found 'female flesh' to be 'an integral part of female person' (Bynum 1991: 238). Considering the internal/external question, the analysis of punishment and pain shows that the *Life* eludes either the 'dualistic view' (two separate entities) or the 'hylomorphic view' (inseparably united) of body and soul (Kirkpatrick 1996: 239; Gragnolati 2007: 239). As an account of a personal relationship between God and soul, yet with a claim to universal validation, the interior workings integrate exterior penitential forms, endorsing the potential tension between the two, rather than resolving it.

Works Cited

Primary Sources

Decretum magistri Gratiani, ed. by Emil Friedberg, Corpus Iuris Canonici, 1 (Leipzig: Tauchnitz, 1879; rpt. Graz: Akademische Druck- u. Verlagsanstalt, 1959)

Die Vita der Christina von Hane: Untersuchung und Edition, ed. Racha Kirakosian, Hermaea. Neue Folge, 144 (Berlin: De Gruyter, 2017): 283-346

Fortunatus, De Vita S. Radegundis, ed. by Bruno Krusch, MGH SS rer. Merov., 2 (Hannover: 1887)

Catherine of Siena, *The Dialogue*, trans. and introduction by Suzanne Noffke; preface by Giuliana Cavallini, Classics of Western Spirituality (New York: Paulist Press, 1980)

Dante Alighieri, *Commedia*, ed. and comm. Anna Maria Chiavacci Leonardi, vol. 1: *Inferno* (Milano: Mondadori, 1991)

—. The Divine Comedy of Dante Alighieri, vol I: *Inferno*, ed. and trans. Robert M. Durling; introduction and notes by Ronald L. Martinez and Robert M. Durling (New York: Oxford University Press, 1996)

Hildegard of Bingen, *Liber vite meritorum*, ed. Angela Carlevaris, Corpus Christianorum. Continuatio Mediaevalis, 90 (Turnhout: Brepols, 1995)

'Lebensbeschreibung der sel. Christina, gen. von Retters', ed. Mittermaier, Franz Paul, *Archiv für Mittelrheinische Kirchengeschichte*, 17 (1965): 226-51; 18 (1966): 203-38

Mechthild von Magdeburg, *Das fließende Licht der Gottheit*, ed. Gisela Vollmann-Profe (Berlin: Insel, 2000)

Secondary Sources

Baldwin, John W. 1998. 'From the Ordeal to Confession: In Search of Lay Religion in Early-Thirteenth-Century France', in *Handling Sin: Confession in the Middle Ages*, ed. Peter Biller and A. J. Minnis, York Studies in Medieval Theology, 2 (Woodbridge: York Medieval Press), pp. 191-209

Biernoff, Suzannah. 2002. *Sight and Embodiment in the Middle Ages*, New Middle Ages (Basingstoke: Palgrave Macmillan)

Büttner, Frank O. 1983. *Imitatio pietatis: Motive der christlichen Ikonographie als Modelle zur Verähnlichung* (Berlin: Mann)

Brown, Peter. 1997. 'Vers la naissance du purgatoire: Amnistie et pénitence dans le christianisme occidental de l'Antiquité tardive au Haut Moyen Âge', *Annales. Histoire, Sciences Sociales*, 52: 1247-61

Bynum, Caroline Walker. 1987. *Holy Feast and Holy Fast: The Religious Significance of Food to Medieval Women*, New Historicism, 1 (Berkeley: University of California Press)

—. 1991. *Fragmentation and Redemption: Essays on Gender and the Human Body in Medieval Religion* (New York: Zone Books)

—. 2011. *Christian Materiality: An Essay on Religion in Late Medieval Europe* (New York: Zone Books)

De Jong, Mayke. 2000. 'Transformations of Penance', in *Rituals of Power: From Late Antiquity to the Early Middle Ages*, ed. Frans Theuws and Janet L. Nelson, The Transformation of the Roman World, 8 (Leiden: Brill), pp. 185-224

—. 2009. *The Penitential State: Authority and Atonement in the Age of Louis the Pious, 814-840* (Cambridge: Cambridge University Press)

Elliott, Dyan. 2004. *Proving Woman: Female Spirituality and Inquisitional Culture in the Later Middle Ages* (Princeton: Princeton University Press)

—. 2010. 'Flesh and Spirit: The Female Body', in *Medieval Holy Women in the Christian Tradition c. 1100-c. 1500*, ed. Alastair Minnis and Rosalynn Voaden, Brepols Essays in European Culture, 1 (Turnhout: Brepols), pp. 13-46

—. 2013. 'Gender and the Christian Traditions', in *The Oxford Handbook of Women and Gender in Medieval Europe*, ed. Judith M. Bennett and Ruth Mazo Karras (Oxford: Oxford University Press), pp. 21-35

Evans, G. R. 2002. *Law and Theology in the Middle Ages* (London: Routledge)

Felten, Franz J. 2001. '"Noui esse volunt ... deserentes bene contritam uiam...": Hildegard von Bingen und Reformbewegungen im religiösen Leben ihrer Zeit', in *"Im Angesicht Gottes suche der Mensch sich selbst": Hildegard von Bingen (1098-1179)*, ed. Rainer Berndt, Erudiri sapientia, 2 (Berlin: Akademie), pp. 27-86

Gragnolati, Manuele. 2005. *Experiencing the Afterlife: Soul and Body in Dante and Medieval Culture*, The William and Katherine Devers Series in Dante Studies (Notre Dame: University of Notre Dame Press)

—. 2007. 'Gluttony and the Anthropology of Pain in Dante's "Inferno" and "Purgatorio"', in *History in the Comic Mode: Medieval Communities and the Matter of Person*, ed. Rachel Fulton and Bruce W. Holsinger (New York: Columbia University Press), pp. 238-50

Hamburger, Jeffrey F. 1997. *Nuns as Artists: The Visual Culture of a Medieval Convent* (Berkeley: University of California Press)

Hamilton, Sarah. 2001. *The Practice of Penance, 900-1050*, Royal Historical Society Studies in History New Series (London: Royal Historical Society)

Huber, Christoph. 2013. *Gottfried von Strassburg: Tristan*, Klassiker-Lektüren, 3, (Berlin: Erich Schmidt)

Karras, Ruth Mazo. 2012. *Sexuality in Medieval Europe: Doing unto Others*, 2nd ed. (London: Routledge)

Kirakosian, Racha. 2012. '"Hoc iudicium creavit omnipotens Deus": Über die Ritualität von Gottesurteilen', *Francia: Forschungen zur westeuropäischen Geschichte*, 39: 263-84

—. 2014a. 'Rhetorics of Sanctity: Christina of Hane in the Early Modern Period – with a Comparison to a Mary Magdalene Legend', *Oxford German Studies*, 43: 380-99

—. 2014b. 'Which is the Greatest – Love, Knowledge or Enjoyment of God? A Comparison between Christina of Hane and Meister Eckhart', *Medieval Mystical Theology*, 23: 20-33

—. 2017. See above under *Die Vita der Christina von Hane*

Kirkpatrick, Robin. 1994. 'Dante and the Body', in *Framing Medieval Bodies*, ed. Sarah Kay and Miri Rubin (Manchester: Manchester University Press), pp. 236-53

Knox, Bernard. 2006. 'Introduction', in *Homer, The Odyssey*, trans. Robert Fagles, introduction and notes by Bernard Knox (New York: Penguin Books), pp. 1-67

Koltun-Fromm, Naomi. 2010. *Hermeneutics of Holiness: Ancient Jewish and Christian Notions of Sexuality and Religious Community* (Oxford: Oxford University Press)

Krings, Bruno. 2009. 'Die Frauenklöster der Prämonstratenser in der Pfalz', *Jahrbuch für westdeutsche Landesgeschichte*, 35: 113-202

Largier, Niklaus. 2001. *Lob der Peitsche: eine Kulturgeschichte der Erregung* (Munich: Beck)

Larson, Atria A. 2014. *Master of Penance: Gratian and the Development of Penitential Thought and Law in the Twelfth Century*, Studies in Medieval and Early Modern Canon Law, 11 (Washington, D.C.: The Catholic University of America Press)

Le Goff, Jacques. 1981. *La Naissance du purgatoire* (Paris: Gallimard)

Lombardi, Elena. 2012. *Wings of the Doves: Love and Desire in Dante and Medieval Culture* (Montreal: McGill-Queen's University Press)

Mäkinen, Virpi, and Heikki Pihlajamäki. 2004. 'The Individualization of Crime in Medieval Canon Law', *Journal of the History of Ideas*, 65: 525-42

McAuley, Finbarr. 2006. 'Canon Law and the End of the Ordeal', *Oxford Journal of Legal Studies*, 26: 473-513

McNamara, Jo Ann. 1991. 'The Need to Give: Suffering and Female Sanctity in the Middle Ages', in *Images of Sainthood in Medieval Europe*, ed. Renate Blumenfeld-Kosinski and Timea Klara Szell (Ithaca: Cornell University Press), pp. 199-221

McNamara, Jo Ann, John E. Halborg and E. Gordon Whatley (ed. and trans.). 1992. *Sainted Women of the Dark Ages* (Durham, NC: Duke University Press)

Meens, Rob. 1998. 'Frequency and Nature of Early Medieval Penance', in *Handling Sin: Confession in the Middle Ages*, ed. Peter Biller and A. J. Minnis, York Studies in Medieval Theology, 2 (Woodbridge: York Medieval Press), pp. 35-61

Mittermaier, Franz Paul. 1960. 'Wo lebte die selige Christina, in Retters oder in Hane?', *Archiv für Mittelrheinische Kirchengeschichte*, 12: 75-97

Newman, Barbara. 1995. *From Virile Woman to WomanChrist: Studies in Medieval Religion and Literature*, Middle Ages Series (Philadelphia: University of Pennsylvania Press)

Oliver, Lisi. 2011. *The Body Legal in Barbarian Law*, Toronto Anglo-Saxon Series, 9 (Toronto: University of Toronto Press)

Rubin, Miri. 2009. *Mother of God: A History of the Virgin Mary* (New Haven: Yale University Press)

Ruge, Susanne. 2014. 'The Theology of Repentance: Observations on the "Liber Vite Meritorum"', in *A Companion to Hildegard of Bingen*, ed. Beverly Mayne Kienzle, Debra L. Stoudt, and George Ferzoco, Brill's Companions to the Christian Tradition, 45 (Leiden: Brill), pp. 221-48

Sayce, Olive. 1967. *Poets of the Minnesang* (Oxford: Clarendon Press)

Schreiner, Klaus. 1994. *Maria: Jungfrau, Mutter, Herrscherin* (Munich: C. Hanser)

Schweikle, Günther. 1995. *Minnesang*, 2nd edn, Sammlung Metzler, 244 (Stuttgart: Metzler)

Tammen, Silke. 2006. 'Blick und Wunde – Blick und Form: Zur Deutungsproblematik der Seitenwunde Christi in der spätmittelalterlichen Buchmalerei', *Bild und Körper im Mittelalter*, ed. Kristin Marek, Raphaèle Preisinger, Marius Rimmele and Katrin Kärcher (München: Wilhelm Fink), pp. 85-114

Thali, Johanna. 2003. *Beten, Schreiben, Lesen: Literarisches Leben und Marienspiritualität im Kloster Engelthal*, Bibliotheca Germanica, 42 (Tübingen: Francke)

Tylus, Jane. 2009. *Reclaiming Catherine of Siena: Literacy, Literature, and the Signs of Others* (Chicago: University of Chicago Press)

Vincent, Catherine. 2000. 'Discipline du corps et de l'esprit chez les Flagellants au Moyen Âge', *Revue Historique*, 302: 593-614

Walls, Jerry L. 2012. *Purgatory: The Logic of Total Transformation* (New York: Oxford University Press)

Ziegler, Vickie L. 2004. *Trial by Fire and Battle in Medieval German Literature*, Studies in German Literature, Linguistics, and Culture (Rochester, NY: Camden House)

9

Körpergebrauch, Kontrolle und Kontrollverlust in den Askeseschilderungen der *Vita* Elsbeths von Oye

Björn Klaus Buschbeck
Stanford University

Vertraut man der Definition der *Theologischen Realenzyklopädie*, dann beschreibt der Begriff ‚Buße' im Kern ein Konzept der Transformation, der Umkehr, der korrigierenden Selbstveränderung aus eigener Kraft und aus eigenem Willen heraus. Denn während, so heißt es dort, ‚Sünde [...] die [...] kontingente Verkehrung dessen ist, wie der Mensch leben und sein sollte, so ist Buße der Versuch, diesen Zustand der Verkehrung umzukehren' (Wißmann 1981: 431). Durch den Bußakt vollzieht sich auf diese Weise eine Wandlung, infolge derer der Büßende vom Zustand der Sündigkeit in den ursprünglicheren Status der Unschuld zurückversetzt wird oder sich diesem zumindest wieder annähert. Somit wird der ‚Bußhandlung die Kraft zugetraut, wenigstens tendenziell den durch Sünde geschaffenen Zustand zu *verbessern*, eine versuchsweise vollzogene Heilung einer der Heilung bedürftigen Situation herbeizuführen [und] damit das Geschehene, wenn auch nur in seinen Wirkungen, unschädlich oder ungeschehen zu machen' (ebd. 1981: 432).

Der (zumeist profanierten) Strafe dahingegen eignet einerseits die gleiche korrektive Funktion – als ‚*Negation der Negation* des Rechtes' (Schroth 2011: 2111) dient sie der Reparatur eines verletzten Rechtszustands und wird gleichzeitig auch ‚als etwas verstanden, das dem Täter die Möglichkeit zur Sühne geben soll' (Schroth 2011: 2108), ihn also seine Schuld aufheben lässt. Auf der anderen Seite jedoch unterscheiden sich Buße und Strafe in dem zentralen Punkt des sie jeweils ausführenden Subjekts: Im Gegensatz zur Strafe, die in aller Regel von einer übermächtigen, äußeren Instanz über den Bestraften verhängt wird, stellt die Buße eine Kulturpraxis dar, die der Büßende intrinsisch motiviert an sich selbst vollziehen muss.

Die folgend behandelten Passagen aus der *Vita* Elsbeths von Oye schildern im engsten Sinne weder Buße noch Strafe – denn eine konkrete Sünd- oder Schuldhaftigkeit, die einen umkehrhaften Ausgleich erfordert, spielt hier höchstens eine nebensächliche Rolle.[1] Dennoch erscheint es legitim, die in Elsbeths *Vita* beschriebene Frömmigkeitspraxis zumindest in die Nähe von Strafe und Buße zu rücken. Der Grund hierfür liegt in der transformativen Wirkabsicht dieser Praxis: Die Protagonistin kasteit sich zwar ohne die Ursache einer abzugeltenden Sündenlast, zielt damit allerdings gleich einer Büßerin auf eine Wandlung und Umkehr, die zwar keine Schuld, dennoch aber ihre als defizitär aufgefasste menschliche Natur und Identität zugunsten einer Annäherung an das Göttliche aufzuheben vermag. Zudem fungiert sie dabei zwar als Agentin dieses über den Gebrauch des eigenen Körpers vollführten Vorgangs, als dessen eigentlicher Urheber jedoch wird, wie unten genauer ausgeführt, ihr in der Vision geschautes göttliches Gegenüber benannt. Aus diesem Blickwinkel heraus überschneidet sich das, was in Elsbeths *Vita* geschildert wird, sowohl mit Buß- wie auch mit Bestrafungspraktiken – freilich in einer entscheidend abgewandelten Form: Elsbeths schmerzhafte Askese bedarf keines auslösenden Moments der Schuld oder Sünde und zielt demgemäß weniger auf einen korrektiven als vielmehr auf einen transgressiven Prozess der Selbstwandlung.

Zwischen Literatur und historischer Realität:
imitatio Christi im Gebrauch des eigenen Körpers

In erster Linie ist es wohl die extreme Körperlichkeit des dargestellten Leidens, welche sowohl die Faszinationskraft als auch das Verstörungspotential der *Vita* Elsbeths von Oye ausmacht. Der zu großen Teilen auf einen um 1340 entstandenen mutmaßlichen Autographen der Verfasserin zurückgehende Text aus dem Schwesternbuch des Züricher Dominikanerinnenklosters Oetenbach beschreibt eine schier endlose Reihe von Selbstfolterungen, denen die Protagonistin sich unterzieht: Sie schlägt sich über neun Jahre hinweg mit einer nadelgespickten Geißel, bindet sich mithilfe eines Dornengürtels ein mit spitzen Nägeln versehenes Kreuz in die Haut ihrer Hüfte sowie ein weiteres Kreuz auf den Rücken, leidet freiwillig unter nächtlicher Kälte, trägt ein verfaulendes Gewand und setzt sich dem darin nistenden parasitären Ungeziefer aus.

Gott, Jesus und einige Heilige, mit denen Elsbeth während ihrer Kasteiungen im Dialog steht, halten sie nicht von diesen Handlungen ab, im Gegenteil – eine für den modernen Leser grundsätzlich irritierend erscheinende Lust an ihrem Schmerz

---

[1] Im Folgenden wird im Fließtext unter Angabe von Kapitel und Zeile aus der Edition von Schneider-Lastin (2009) zitiert. Dieser Text stellt eine spätere Auswahl und Bearbeitung der bisher unedierten Offenbarungsschrift Elsbeths (Zürich, Zentralbibliothek, Codex Ms. Rh. 159) da, eignet sich aufgrund seines Status als zu Rezeption und Verständnis durch zeitgenössische Leser aufbereitete Fassung für die folgenden Untersuchungen jedoch bestens.

empfindend, fordert Gott immer neues Leid: ‚Als natürlichen es dir ist ze einer peine, als minniklichen ist es mir zu grundlosem herczenlüste' (I, 213–14). Ziel von Elsbeths Körpergebrauchs ist dabei weder Buße noch Unterdrückung sinnlichen Begehrens. Auf die Frage hin, ob ihre defizitäre Natur wirklich derart grausame Schmerzen notwendig mache, antwortet Gott ihr: ‚Es geschihet nit von keiner unordenunge deiner natur, es ist mein ewig ordenunge gesein, das du mir külest meinen prinnenden durst, den ich ewiglichen han gehabt nach der minne deines herczen' (I, 147–150). Elsbeths Askese wird statt als Bußübung als Mitleiden (*compassio*) und Nachahmen (*imitatio*) der Passion Christi dargestellt – auf göttlichen Befehl hin formt sie in der als Akt der Selbstvergöttlichung verstandenen Schmerzzufügung ihren Körper zum Christuskörper und gleicht damit auch sich selbst als Person dem Gottessohn an. Hierbei bleibt jedoch unklar, inwieweit sie selbst ihre Handlungen kontrolliert – der Antrieb und die Kraft für ihr Handeln werden bei (dem jedoch zunehmend mit ihr verschmelzenden) Gott verortet, der sie geradezu zur Selbstfolter zwingt, denn wenn Elsbeth ihre Askese unterbricht, entzieht er ihr seine Präsenz: Sie fällt daraufhin in Depressionen oder erkrankt.

Die Schilderung einer solchen Grausamkeit Gottes und der über die Härte des Klosteralltags weit hinausgehenden Asksesepraktiken brachten die germanistische Forschung schnell zu abwertenden Urteilen:[2] ‚Es ist eine ich-süchtige Leidensbereitschaft, ja Leidensbesessenheit, die geradezu pathologische Züge annimmt', konstatierte beispielsweise Peter Ochsenbein und rief nach ‚der Deutung des Anthropologen oder Psychoanalytikers' (1986: 437). Die (wenn auch spärlich gesäten) jüngeren literaturwissenschaftlichen Arbeiten zu Elsbeth haben sich von dieser Sichtweise verabschiedet: So arbeitete bereits 1995 David F. Tinsley die Sonderstellung von Elsbeths Offenbarungsschriften im Vergleich mit dem unter anderen in der *Vita* Heinrich Seuses dargestellten spirituellen Dreistufenweg heraus und verortete Elsbeths Kasteiungspraxis im Kontext der mittelalterlichen Auseinandersetzung mit den *Vitaspatrum*; im Jahr 2000 betrachtete Monika Gsell den Text in Hinblick auf seine Rezeptionsangebote und seine Darstellung spezifisch weiblicher Subjektivität. Zudem analysierte Burkhard Hasebrink ihn 2008 in Hinblick auf performative Konstruktionen sakraler Identität, Gregor Wünsche setzte sich 2009 in der einzigen neueren Monographie zu Elsbeth mit der kulturellen Semantik ihrer Schmerzschilderung sowie deren theologischen Implikationen auseinander und arbeitete, wie auch Johanna Kershaw (2011), zur Johannes-Rezeption Elsbeths.[3]

---

[2] Angenendt (1997: 564) stellt zu mittelalterlichen Heiligenviten im Allgemeinen fest: ‚Bewundernd stellen sie Leib- und Weltfeindlichkeit heraus, und so durchzieht die mittelalterliche Askese ein rigoristischer, nicht selten auch roher und zuweilen zerstörerischer Zug'.

[3] Neben Wünsches Dissertation existiert noch eine ältere textgeschichtliche Monographie von Hanel

Der vorliegende Aufsatz möchte nun eine Thematik in den Fokus rücken, die in all den genannten Forschungen, auf die im Folgenden dankbar zurückgegriffen werden wird, zwar angeschnitten wurde, jedoch niemals wirklich im Zentrum stand – gemeint ist der Körper der Protagonistin, seine Rolle für ihr mystisches Erleben sowie die Mechanismen seines Gebrauchs. Welche Funktion erfüllt in der Gotteserfahrung des Text-Ichs nicht nur der empfundene Schmerz, sondern auch und vor allem der ganz konkrete, diesen Schmerz empfangende Körper? Welche Folgen birgt diese Form radikalen Selbstgebrauchs in der Askese für die Spiritualität der Protagonistin – gewinnt sie durch die Erfahrung göttlicher Präsenz im selbstinduzierten physischen Leid die Kontrolle über ihr religiöses Erleben oder verliert sie im Gegenteil dieselbige?

Dieses Fragen werfen ein Problem auf: Zunächst gilt zu klären, über welchen Gegenstand überhaupt gesprochen wird, wenn vom Körper Elsbeths von Oye die Rede ist, und der Hybridcharakter des Texts macht eine Antwort darauf schwierig. Auf der einen Seite handelt es sich bei der *Vita* Elsbeths um einen sprachlich elaborierten und durchgeformten literarischen Text, der beinahe leitmotivartig immer wieder auf bestimmte Metaphernkomplexe zurückkommt: Siegelungen und Spiegelungen, Blut und Knochenmark werden wiederholt als sprachliche Bilder herangezogen, um die religiösen Erfahrungen des Text-Ichs zu verdeutlichen. Elsbeths Askeseschilderungen stellen keine bloße Berichterstattung dar – der Schmerz der Protagonistin wird dem Leser im Wechselspiel von erzählenden, dialogischen und ausdeutenden Passagen sprachlich vor Augen geführt. In diesem Sinne ist der Text zu lesen ‚als Konstrukt einer unbeständigen religiösen Identität, die sich im literarischen Prozess einer Iterativität zu konstituieren sucht, der Erzählung und Kommentierung gleichermaßen umfasst' (Hasebrink 2008: 260). Literarizität und der kommunikative Aspekt der *Vita* stehen somit in den folgenden Betrachtungen im Vordergrund – biographische Schlussfolgerungen über die historische Person Elsbeth von Oye und Spekulationen über den Wahrheitsgehalt des Textes werden im gleichen Atemzug unterlassen. Körperlichkeit und Körpergebrauch des Text-Ichs werden in diesem Sinne als sprachlich entworfen und im Medium der Literatur vermittelt angesehen.

Nun bedeutete jedoch eine Absolutsetzung dieses literarischen Charakters, die historische Realität der geschilderten Kasteiungspraktiken und den Faktualitätsanspruch des Texts zu ignorieren. Elsbeths *Vita* verlangt, als Biographie einer realen Person gelesen zu werden – die Einleitung eines anonymen mittelalterlichen Kompilators lässt daran keinen Zweifel: Die geschilderten Akte

---

(1958), die für die folgenden Betrachtungen jedoch genau wie einige editionswissenschaftliche Beiträge jedoch nur am Rande interessiert.

göttlicher Gnade seien deshalb so eindrücklich und erbaulich, ‚so viel sie got neŵlicher und gegenẃürtiklicher von unserm geistlichen geswisteret gewürcket hat' (Vorrede, 26-27). Der Wahrheitsanspruch des Textes zeigt sich als konstitutiv für seine Wirkabsicht, und tatsächlich zeigt ein Blick auf andere zeitgenössische Texte, dass Praktiken körperlicher Askese in der zeitgenössischen monastischen Kultur der Mendikantenorden einen realen Stellenwert besessen zu haben scheinen und die *Vita* Elsbeths somit in all ihrer Exzessivität ohne weiteres als faktualer Text wahrgenommen werden konnte.

An dieser Stelle sei, um Elsbeth anhand einiger Beispiele in einen historischen Rahmen einzuordnen, auf die *Vita* der Gutta Mestin aus dem Schwesternbuch des Dominikanerinnenklosters St. Katharinenthal bei Dießenhofen verwiesen, die neben anderen Asksepraktiken wie auch Elsbeths *Vita* eine Kasteiung mit einem von Ungeziefer bewohnten härenen Gewand erwähnt (*Katharinenthaler Schwesternbuch*: 154-59; bes. 156, 54-56), sowie auf die Mitte des 14. Jahrhunderts verfasste *Gnadenvita* der Adelheid Langmann aus dem Kloster Engelthal bei Nürnberg, in der Gott von Adelheid zusätzlich zum Gebet blutige Selbstpeitschungen fordert: ‚du solt nemen drei disciplin, itliche mit drein Misere und mit einer hecheln, dasz ez bluete, und solt weinen sueze zeher' [37]. Die vielleicht bekanntesten mittelalterlichen Schilderungen extremer körperlicher Kasteiung entstammen jedoch der *Vita* Heinrich Seuses, die in auffallender Ähnlichkeit mit Elsbeth von Selbstgeißelungen und Nagelkreuzen, von Schlafentzug und den Protagonisten plagendem Ungeziefer berichtet (15-53). Nun stellen auch all diese Texte literarisch überformte Schilderungen dar, zeugen aber in jedem Fall von einem hohen zeitgenössischen Interesse an Extremformen des religiösen Körpergebrauchs.

Die beschriebenen Praktiken blieben jedoch nicht unkritisiert. Seuses *Vita* zum Beispiel ist eher als eine beispielhafte Anweisung zum stufenweisen Hintersichlassen körperlicher Kasteiungen zugunsten innerer Versenkung und klerikaler Theorie zu verstehen denn als Aufforderung zu extremer Askese – seiner geistlichen Tochter Elsbeth Stagel rät er ausdrücklich davon ab, die eigenen früheren Übungen oder die Lebensführung der Anachoreten nachzuahmen: ‚Du solt nút an sehen ze ervolgen der alten veter strenkheit noh die herten uebunge dines geischlichen vaters' (107). Stattdessen solle seine Schülerin in geduldigem inneren Ertragen die Nähe Gottes suchen. Bei Elsbeth von Oye fehlt eine solche spirituelle Progression auf der *via triplica* hin zu einer unblutigen Askese vollständig. Ihr Weg führt nicht von der Körperpraxis über inneres Leid in die Gottesschau durch Theorie; sie bleibt bei der körperlichen Erfahrung göttlicher Präsenz im selbstzugefügten Schmerz, was zwar als unerträglich peinvoll, jedoch nicht als defizitär in Hinblick auf das Erreichen einer *unio mystica* angesehen wird (Tinsley 1995: 12-29).

Seuse ist nicht die einzige zur Mäßigung mahnende Stimme. Bereits Mechthild von Magdeburg warnt in in ihrem um 1250 verfassten *Fließenden Licht der Gottheit* vor ‚grúlichen, unmenschlichen arbeiten' (II, 1) und deutet diese als Ausdruck mangelnder Demut – eine aufschlussreiche Interpretation körperlicher Askese, auf die in Bezug auf Elsbeth noch zurückzukommen ist – und auch Meister Eckhart äußert sich mehrfach kritisch zu extremen Kasteiungspraktiken. In der Predigt 60 schreibt er: ‚Vastennes und betennes und aller kestigunge enahtet noch enbedarf got zemâle niht' [638]. Im Kontrast hierzu verlangt Gott bei Elsbeth ganz ausdrücklich das Leid der Protagonistin als Bedingung ihrer Anverwandlung an ihn: ‚Las mich nun trinken dein kreucz, es wird hiernach durch dich fliessende das mer meiner gotheit' (VI, 18–19).

Wie diese Beispiele zeigen, befindet sich Elsbeths *Vita* in einem Spannungsfeld zwischen literarischer Erzählung auf der einen und Beitrag zum kontrovers geführten zeitgenössischen Diskurs über eine historisch-reale Praxis auf der anderen Seite. Gleichzeitig Narrativ und Zeitdokument darstellend ermöglicht sie einen Einblick in eine an die historische Realität rückgebundene, literarisch vermittelte Diskussion von Körpererfahrung und Körpergebrauch. Im Folgenden gilt es nun zuerst, die genaue Rolle des Körpers in diesem Text zu analysieren, um anschließend die Mechanismen seines Gebrauchs ins Blickfeld zu rücken.

Der Kontrollgewinn der Asketin:
Körper, religiöses Erleben, Autorität und Identität

Zentraler Austragungsort von Elsbeths religiöser Praxis ist der eigene Körper, der intradiegetisch vollständig wirklich ist – im Gegensatz zum Beispiel zum *Fließenden Licht* Mechthilds, das durchaus auch körperliche Empfindungen von Lust und Schmerz schildert, um mithilfe dieser sprachlichen Bilder einen unsagbaren Seelenzustand auszudrücken,[4] ‚gibt es [bei Elsbeth] keinen metaphorischen Körper, in dem die Seele ihren Weg zu Gott gehen könnte, sie hat nur ihren realen Körper, und dieser ist es, den sie zum Medium ihrer Gotteserfahrung macht' (Haug 2003: 489).

Entscheidend ist die hier von Haug angesprochene Funktion als Medium, die

---

[4] So schreibt Mechthild über den Weg der Seele zu Gott in sehr körperlichen Metaphern: ‚Si wirt an dem crútze so vaste negelt mit dem hammer der starken minnelofte, das sie alle creaturen nit moegent wider gerueffen. [...] Ir licham wirt getoetet in der lebendigen minne, wenne ihr geist wirt gehoehet über alle menschliche sinne' (III, 10). Diese Sprachbilder sind jedoch allegorisch zu verstehen und nicht im Sinne einer tatsächlichen Körperpraxis. Eine solche Metaphorik, die innere Empfindungen mithilfe körperlicher Metaphern darstellt, ist durchaus typisch für das Spätmittelalter; dazu vgl. Assmann (1993).

Elsbeths Körpers erfüllt. Ihr göttlicher Dialogpartner stellt diese heraus, indem er auf die Frage, wie der Mensch die Schmerzen Christi begreifen könne, antwortet: ‚Den pein kan nimant geworten dann der allein, der ein würker ist der peine' (V, 32–33). Elsbeth praktiziert demzufolge ihre Kasteiung vor dem Hintergrund eines spezifischen Erkenntnisinteresses: Ziel ist, das Leiden Christi begreifen, indem sie es an sich selbst reinszeniert. Mittel zu diesem Begreifen ist ihr Körper, über dessen Empfindungsfähigkeit der Schmerz Christi erfahrbar und eine Angleichung an den Gekreuzigten somit möglich gemacht wird. Als Medium verstanden, liefert der Körper auf diese Weise kraft seiner Sinnlichkeit religiöse Erkenntnis an das Text-Ich.

Doch es bleibt nicht bei dieser Rolle des Erkenntnisvehikels: Die Protagonistin erfährt nicht nur mithilfe ihres Körpers, sie benutzt auch gezielt seine Empfindsamkeit und seine Verfügungsgewalt über sich selbst, um ihn überhaupt auf diese Weise als Medium instrumentalisieren zu können. So wird in der Selbstfolter Elsbeths Körper gleichzeitig zum Objekt, dem Schmerz zugefügt und das benutzt wird, wie auch im Akt dieser Schmerzzufügung und im Benutzen zum Subjekt: ‚In her excess, the mystic becomes at once both torturer and victim' (Finke 1993: 42). Zwischen Gebrauchendem und Gebrauchtem existiert damit kein Unterschied mehr. Bynum (1995: 12) führt aus: ‚Bodies are both objects and subjects of desire.' Gleiches lässt sich im Falle Elsbeths über ihren Körper und den Schmerz der Askese sagen.

Dieses Ineinander von Gebrauchen, Erleiden und Verstehen, welches erst durch ein extremes Kontrollieren des eigenen Körpers in Form der Selbstverletzung funktionieren kann, kann als Akt der Selbstermächtigung gefasst werden.[5] Elsbeth vermittelt sich mithilfe ihres auf sich selbst einwirkenden Körpers religiöses Wissen und Gotteserkenntnis, und zwar jenseits des theologischen Diskurses, von dessen Teilnahme sie als Frau weitgehend ausgeschlossen ist. Die körperliche Askese der Protagonistin tritt hierbei als Alternative zu theoretischer Betätigung auf: ‚Kanstu nit sprechen von mir, so kanstu mich aber leiden. Wer mich leiden mag in der pitterkeit seiner sele, das fleuset allein von der magenkraft meiner gotheit' (XV, 30-33). An die Stelle klerikaler Theorie tritt so die direkte Erfahrbarkeit göttlicher Präsenz im selbstzugefügten Schmerz – das Text-Ich gewinnt im Körpergebrauch die Kontrolle über seine eigene Religiosität.

Vor diesem Hintergrund verwundert es kaum, wenn die Askese als Möglichkeit dargestellt wird, die in der innerlichen Kontemplation unerfüllbaren Ideale

---

[5] Dieses ermächtigende Moment beschreibt u.a. Finke (1993). Eine detailliertere Analyse findet sich bei Caroline Walker Bynum (1992: 191). Die Autorin folgert hier: ‚women had to stress the experience of Christ and manifest it outwardly in their flesh, because they did not have clerical office as an authorization for speaking'.

der *vita religiosa* zu verwirklichen. Auf die Klage Elsbeths hin, sie könne nicht permanent aus Mitleid heraus das Leiden Christi beweinen, antwortet Gott ihr auf ihre Kasteiungspraxis hinweisend: ‚Plutig treher sind mir gar minniklich' (X, 28-29). Die Veräußerlichung des Leidens wird hier als Ausweg aus dem Dilemma von religiösem Anspruch und Wirklichkeit begriffen, denn während das Text-Ich über sein Gefühlsleben keine umfassende Kontrolle besitzt, kann es seinem Körper jederzeit willentlich christförmige Schmerzen zufügen und ist durch diese Externalisierung der *compassio* fähig, sein religiöses Erleben gezielt zu steuern. In ihrem Körpergebrauch schließt Elsbeth auf diese Weise die Lücke zwischen dem theoretischen Ideal der *imitatio Christi* und ihrer religiösen Praxis.

Nun ermächtigt Elsbeth sich jedoch nicht nur zur bloßen Erfahrung, sondern beansprucht darüber hinausgehend, über Gott und die eigene Gotteserkenntnis sprechen zu dürfen. Ihr Körpergebrauch verleiht ihr religiöse Autorität, wobei ein mehrfach wiederholter Schreibbefehl Gottes ihre Aussagen legitimiert: ‚Das ist mein günlich, das erkant werde, was mein minnekraft würcket an meinen usserwelten' (I, 71-73). Der Status des Auserwählt-Seins, der in der Askese seinen Ausdruck und Beweis hat, berechtigt das Text-Ich zur Teilnahme am religiösen Diskurs.

Wovon Elsbeth berichten soll, ist ihre durch die Askese hervorgerufene Annäherung an die Natur Christi. Der Prozess der Kasteiung, der Elsbeth zum Sprechen berechtigt, ist damit als aktiv betriebene Selbstheiligung zu verstehen, durch welche die Identität der Protagonistin sich immer stärker verändert: Je mehr sie sich in der Selbstfolter ergeht, desto stärker übernimmt sie die Position des Gottessohns – der physische Schmerz ist hier ‚nicht nur Stimulus von Affekt und Imagination, sondern ein Supplement, das den realen Schmerz und die bildhafte Gleichheit des Leidens zur Grundlage der imaginierten Einheit mit dem Gekreuzigten macht' (Largier 2001: 52-53). Für das Text-Ich jedoch ist diese Einheit nicht Imagination, sondern körperlich spürbare Wirklichkeit. Gott verspricht Elsbeth: ‚Als mein götliche nature gemenschet ward in der person meines sunes, also wird dein menschliche nature vergottet in dem peinlichen sere deines creuczes' (I, 55-57). Somit ist die Askese der Protagonistin nicht nur Aneignungsgeste in Richtung des eigenen Körpers und religiösen Empfindens sowie Selbstverleihung religiöser Autorität, sondern auch und in erster Linie ein aktives Umformen der eigenen Identitätsposition hin zur Gleichartigkeit mit Christus, wobei diese Selbstheiligung ihren Ausdruck wie ihre Ursache in der unerträglich peinvollen Manipulation des eigenen Körpers findet. Um Christus zu erfahren, muss Elsbeth seinen Schmerz nachleiden, und indem sie dabei gezielt ihren Körper dem Christuskörper angleicht, gleicht sie auch sich als Person Christus an.

Dies setzt sich fort bis in ein Stadium, an dem der Schmerz der Protagonistin nicht nur dem Schmerz Christi gleicht, sondern eben dieser Schmerz ist. Jesus erklärt dem Text-Ich die Natur christformigen Leidens wie folgt: ‚Es hat nit allein ein mitblüen mit mir ausser des vatters herczen, mer es ist ein frucht und ein blust meines bluttes' (I, 95-97). Aus der Gleichheit wird somit Nachfolge – Elsbeth transformiert in der Askese mindestens temporär ihre personale Identität vollends und wird gänzlich zum Ebenbild Christi.

Aufschlussreich zum Verständnis dieses Vorgangs sind zwei sprachliche Bilder, über die das Text-Ich die Wandlung seiner Natur ausdrückt. Zum ersten beschreiben die Protagonistin und ihre göttlichen Gesprächspartner die geschilderten Körperpraktiken mehrfach als ein Eindrücken von Siegeln. An einer Stelle fragt Gott: ‚Weder ist dir minniklicher, mein rwe in dir oder dein rwe in mir? Als du dein kreucz gesigelt hast auf dein Herz, also hab ich mich versigelt in den tieffen grunt deiner sele' (X, 18-21). Hier ist entscheidend, dass das Siegel nicht nur Metapher ist, sondern sich konkret auf das Marterinstrument Elsbeths bezieht, das sich in ihre Haut bohrt ‚als ein ingesigel in ein wachs' (I, 28). Wenn Elsbeth ihr Nagelkreuz in ihren Körper eindrückt, drückt auch Gott sich in sie ein und verschmilzt mit ihr. Zwischen Gott und der Protagonistin ist ‚kein ewig mittel' (IV, 38); im Schmerzerlebnis werden sie gleich.

Diese Selbstvergöttlichung funktioniert über eine ‚körperliche Vergegenwärtigung des Leidens Christi' (Hasebrink 2008: 265) – Elsbeths Verletzungen gleichen den Wunden Christi, welche dieser gegenüber der Protagonistin ebenfalls als Siegelungen darstellt: ‚Als das ingesigel dem wachss eindrücket sein forme, also hat der minne kraft, mit der ich den menschen geminnet han, eingetrücket sein pilde in mein hende und mein füsse' (XXVI, 14-16). Die Wunden Christi sind Zeichen seiner göttlichen Liebe, die sich an seinem menschlichen Körper manifestieren – und die Verletzungen Elsbeths besitzen den selben Zeichencharakter, sind jedoch auch gleichzeitig Ursache der Heiligkeit, die sie abbilden. Dabei ist die Folter des eigenen Körpers, das heißt das Zufügen dieser Zeichen, ein von der Protagonistin aktiv betriebener Prozess, der einerseits über ihre menschliche Natur erfahren wird, deren Identität andererseits aber auch in Richtung des Göttlichen transzendiert: ‚Es ist natürlich, das es dir unleidlich ist, aber übernatürlichen, das du es leidest' (I, 40-41), spricht Gott. Indem somit das Text-Ich die Wunden Christi wie ein Siegelzeichen in den eigenen Körper drückt, kennzeichnet es sich selbst als heilig und gewinnt so die Kontrolle über die eigene Identität. Da sich diese über das Empfinden und die Beschaffenheit des Körpers zu konstituieren scheint, wird das Verfügen über den eigenen Körper für die Protagonistin gleichbedeutend mit einer Verfügung über die eigene Identitätsposition.

Eine Steigerung erfährt dieser Gedanke des Zeichnens und Umformens in einem weiteren sprachlichen Bild, das sich gehäuft im Text findet: Immer wieder beschreiben Elsbeth und ihre göttlichen Dialogpartner die Askesepraxis als einen Austausch von Blut und Mark. Das Blut, das die Protagonistin bei ihrem Körpergebrauch vergießt, wird ‚auf der Ebene des Textes meist ganz dezidiert substanziell verstanden' (Wünsche 2009: 140), es bedeutet die menschliche Natur respektive die profane Identität Elsbeths. Sprachliche Bilder des Verlusts von Blut und Mark werden als allgemeines Gleichnis für die schmerzhaften Akte benutzt, die das Text-Ich an sich vollzieht: ‚Ich könde der peinlichen not kein geleicheit geben, denn ob ein lebende slange sich geslossen hette umb meinen leib und von mir süg mein innerstes marck' (I, 41-43). Das Bild der saugenden Schlange weckt hier gewalttätige Assoziationen, die sich auch in der Schilderung der Freude Gottes über den Schmerz Elsbeths fortsetzen, der sich am vergossenen Blut labt, nach dem ihm ‚ewiklichen hat getürstet' (I, 6). Es scheint oft, als bedürften die Gesprächspartner des Text-Ich seiner Schmerzen – Christus sagt, seine Wunden würden ‚getrenket werden von den innersten inadern deiner sele' (XI, 24-25), und Maria teilt mit: ‚Dein blutig essende kreucz ist mir alle zeit heilende das blüende ser meines müterlichen herczen' (I, 35-36). McNamara konstatiert an ähnlichen Beispielen aus der Frauenmystik eine Gebensethik des Leidens, die auch bei Elsbeth festgestellt werden kann. Die Protagonistin gibt für die Leidensgabe Christi ein ‚reciprocal gift' ihrer eigenen Schmerzen (McNamara 1993: 217).

Doch es bleibt nicht beim Verlust des so Weggegebenen, denn gleichzeitig mit dem Ausfließen oder gewalttätigen Aussaugen von Blut und Mark findet ein Einfließen göttlicher Natur statt. Der Körpergebrauch Elsbeths wird so als ein performativ funktionierender Identitätswechsel inszeniert: Im Tausch für ihre menschliche Natur, die Elsbeth sich im Blutverlust der Selbstfolter austreibt, vermittelt sie sich eine neue, sakrale Identitätsposition, die auf einem körperlichen Verstehen und Nachempfinden der Schmerzen Christi fußt. Ein Gott zugeschriebener Satz aus dem Text macht den Gegenseitigkeitscharakter dieses Weggebens und Annehmens überdeutlich: ‚Las mich nun trinken dein kreucz, es wird hiernach durch dich fliessende das mer meiner gotheit' (VI, 18-19).

Elsbeths Körpergebrauch ist also, um zusammenzufassen, als ein Akt der Kontrollübernahme und Selbstermächtigung in mehrerlei Hinsicht zu verstehen: Die Protagonistin verfügt frei über ihren eigenen Körper und benutzt ihn als Medium der religiösen Erkenntnis im Rahmen einer *imitatio Christi*. Zudem autorisiert sie sich selbst als Diskursteilnehmerin, indem sie in der als Selbstheilung verstandenen Körperpraxis ihre Identitätsposition verformt. Dass letzterer Akt neben dem über die Kontrollausübung am eigenen Körper forcierten Erreichen des Heiligen auch den Verlust der eigenen Personalität und damit die Übergabe des Selbst an etwas Fremdes impliziert, wird genau wie die Grenzen der Körperlichkeit, auf die die Protagonistin stößt, im nächsten Kapitel thematisiert.

Die Grenzen des Erträglichen, der Zwang zum Schmerz und die Unkontrollierbarkeit sakraler Identität

Gleichzeitig zu den nun beschriebenen Akten der Selbstermächtigung stößt das Text-Ich auf Resultate ihres Körpergebrauchs, welche sich ihrem Zugriff entziehen und das emanzipierende Moment des Kontrollgewinns in der Askese umschlagen lassen in Passivität, Unterwerfung und Abhängigkeit.

Dieser Doppelcharakter der Körperpraxis Elsbeths findet seinen Ausgangspunkt, wenn die Protagonistin mit den Grenzen ihrer körperlichen Erfahrungsfähigkeit konfrontiert ist. Sie erreicht wiederholt den Zustand, in dem ein weiteres Aushalten des selbstzugefügten Schmerzes ihr unmöglich wird und damit zwangsweise ein Unterbrechen der Kasteiung erfolgt: ‚Etwen ward ich getwungen, so ich mein gewand und mein kreucze von mir gelegte und es von unrw nit mer erleiden mochte an dem herczen' (I, 98-99). Im so gestalteten Versagen in seiner Rolle als Objekt verliert der Körper auch seine mediale Funktion – der Vermittler und Erzeuger religiöser Erkenntnis erweist sich als nur begrenzt belastbar.

Bynum (1995: 5) stellt bei einer Analyse des englischen Begriffs *body* fest, dass dieser sowohl auf ‚limit or placement' als auch auf das Gegenteil, auf ‚lack of limits', referieren kann – beide Facetten dieses Körperbegriffs sind bei Elsbeth realisiert: Ihr Körpergebrauch sprengt auf der einen Seite kraft seines Produzierens sinnlicher Erfahrung die fix erscheinenden Grenzen personaler Identität, gesellschaftlicher Verortung und religiösen Empfindens, zeigt sich andererseits jedoch auch auf prekär-unbefriedigende Weise als auf eine physische Struktur zurückgreifend, deren Belastbarkeit limitiert ist. Ihr Körper ist der Protagonistin in gleicher Weise Freiraum und Gefängnis, Möglichkeit und Beschränkung. Durch seine Potentialität ermächtigt er zum Erkenntnisgewinn, im Realisieren dieses Potentials aber wirft er die Gebrauchende zurück auf die defizitäre Seite der eigenen Körperlichkeit, welche sich der Kontrolle der Protagonistin entzieht.

Neben diese Schranken der Empfindsamkeit des eigenen Körpers tritt zudem Zwang zum sich übersteigernden Erfahren von Schmerz. Man könnte fragen, weshalb die Protagonistin ihre Askese nicht in einem so moderatem Maß betreibt, dass die oben gezeigten Grenzen unproblematisch erscheinen – die Antwort hierauf findet sich, wenn betrachtet wird, was passiert, wenn sie ihre Selbstfolter unterbricht: ‚Darnach uber etwan lang hat ich von mir gelegt mein kreucz, doch nit einen ganczen tag. Zuhant wart mir gar we an dem leibe. Ich viel auch in hertikeit und wart gar verfinstert in mir selber' (I, 202–05). Ein zeitweiliges Beenden der Askese stellt sich nicht als Erlösung dar, vielmehr wird der unerträgliche selbstzugefügte Schmerz ersetzt durch ein noch unerträglicheres, inneres wie äußeres Leid. Elsbeth verfällt in eine Art Depression, die sich auch körperlich manifestiert. Sie erfährt dies als Verlust der in der Askese erlangten göttlichen Präsenz: ‚Darnach kürczlichen zuckte mir got, was ich inwendig het' (I, 50). Das nach Wegfall des Körperschmerzes erfahrene Fehlen der Resonanzbeziehung zu Gott führt schließlich zur erneuten Aufnahme der Askesepraxis. So wird die Selbstfolter, deren ermächtigenden Charakter oben herausgestellt wurde, gleichermaßen zum Zwang: Das Text-Ich muss sich in der körperlichen Askese ergehen, um den ungleich größeren Verlustschmerz zu verhindern. In eine Form der Abhängigkeit verfallend, ist Elsbeth genötigt, sich immer größeren Schmerz zuzufügen, um der göttlichen Präsenz, die sie innerlich nicht entbehren kann, gewahr zu bleiben. Mit diesem addiktiven Zug im eigenen Körpergebrauch verliert die Protagonistin die Kontrolle über die eigene religiöse Praxis, welche sie durch ihn erst erlangte.

Burkhard Hasebrink stellt bezüglich des im Manuskript Z überlieferten Texts fest, dass zumindest in den von Elsbeth empfangenen Offenbarungen ‚[g]eistiger und körperlicher Vollzug des Leidens [...] ineinander überzugehen' [2008: 265] scheinen. Diese Verschwimmen von körperlicher und seelischer Pein ist ebenfalls charakteristisch für die *Vita*, wobei die beiden Formen des Schmerzes dort gleichzeitig in einer Wechsel- und Abhängigkeitsbeziehung stehen: Äußerer Schmerz stellt sich als Mittel dar, dem inneren zu entgehen. Gott fordert vom Text-Ich ständiges Leid, unter Androhung, seine Gegenwart ansonsten zu entziehen. ‚Wa nun sunliche geleicheit?' (I, 206), fragt er auf die Klage der Protagonistin über das Fehlen göttlicher Zuwendung außerhalb der Kasteiung hin – mit dem Resultat, dass diese ihre Selbstfolter wieder aufnimmt. Den Askeseschmerz, das heißt das ‚Einfallstor für die göttlichen Offenbarungen' (Wünsche 2010: 182), ununterbrochen aufrechtzuerhalten ist dem Körper der Protagonistin jedoch wie gezeigt unmöglich – und dies führt ins Dilemma: Elsbeth ist gefangen zwischen dem göttlichen Zwang und eigenen Willen zur Askese und der Grenze des Erträglichen, die zu überwinden ihr unmöglich erscheint.

Wie nun geht Elsbeth mit ihrer Unfähigkeit um, das Maß an Schmerz, zu dem sie gezwungen ist, zu erleiden? An einer Stelle gibt sie ganz konkret die Kontrolle über ihren Körper ab, indem sie sich selbst fesselt und so dazu zwingt, das sie plagende Ungeziefer zu ertragen, welches nicht von ihrem Körper zu entfernen ihr sonst unmöglich ist. In einer Imitation der Fesselung Christi beim Gang zum Kreuz bindet sie sich die Hände, so ‚das ich mir selben deheinen schirm möchte gegeben, ob mich mein natur darzu wolte han getwungen' (I, 89–90). Die aktive Handlung der Asketin führt so in eine Passivität, in der ihre Subjektrolle ausgeschaltet wird, um das Unerträgliche ertragen zu können. Kontrollabgabe über den eigenen Körper und sein Erleben scheint notwendig, um die Obergrenze des in der Selbstzufügung erreichbaren Schmerzmaßes zu überschreiten und damit eine anhaltende Nähebeziehung zum Heiligen zu garantieren. Elsbeth hat sich so zum Spielball des physischen Schmerzes zu machen, dessen Verfügung sie sich selbst verunmöglicht.

Zwei der Momente, über die Elsbeth in ihrer Askese Kontrolle ausübt – ihr Körper selbst und das über diesen vermittelte religiöse Erfahren – entziehen sich somit ihrem Zugriff im gleichen Atemzug auch wieder. Ähnliches gilt auch für die Identität des Text-Ichs, deren Umformung im letzten Kapitel beschrieben wurde. Die Annahme einer neuen, sakralen Identität unter Aufgabe der alten, personalen bedeutet neben einer Erhöhung des Selbst auch seine Veräußerung und Vernichtung. Verbildlicht in den oben angesprochenen Metaphern des Austauschs körperlicher Substanz, des ‚Hin- und Herfließens des Bluts aus ihren Wunden in die Wunden Christi und umgekehrt' (Haug 2003: 490), stellt sich die vom Text-Ich betriebene Identitätsverformung als eine Weggabe des Eigenen und eine Annahme des Fremden dar. Elsbeth verkörpert Christus im ganz wörtlichen Sinne, indem sie ihren Körper zu seinem macht – was von ihr selbst nach dem Ersetzen der eigenen Substanz durch die des Gottessohns noch bleibt, ist fraglich.

Der Text zumindest stellt sehr klar fest, ‚das es nit ir werck waß' (VII, 1). Es ist das bei Gott verortete Fremde in der Protagonistin, welches sie dazu bringt, immer neue Schmerzen auf sich zu nehmen, und das sie in der Askese auch immer erneut in sich einfließen lässt. Der so für die Askese verantwortlich gemachte Gott spricht zu ihr: ‚Nit von der kraft deines fleischen noch plutes würckest du diß werck, mere mit dem vergötteten blut meines sunes' (VII, 11-12). Die Christusnatur, die Elsbeth durch ihre Selbstfolter erlangt, ermöglicht diese auch und drängt zu neuem Schmerz. Über die eigene Identität besitzt Elsbeth Verfügungsgewalt und kann sie transformieren, dass Ziel dieser Transformation jedoch, die Natur Christi, ist fix und entzieht sich ihrem Zugriff. Das Umformen der eigenen Identität, das zuvor geschildert wurde, bleibt dabei Selbstverfügung und damit Selbstkontrolle – nur wird das Selbst dabei hin zu etwas Anderem geformt, das sich jedem Zugriff entzieht und die Protagonistin dazu zwingt, sich ihm konform zu verhalten, das heißt in diesem Fall, sich immer neue christförmige Schmerzen zuzufügen. Wenn das Fremde, dass sich Elsbeth in ihren Körper drückt, die Stelle des Eigenen übernimmt, schlägt der Selbstgebrauch um in Selbstaufgabe.

Offensichtlich wird dieses Prinzip in der Metaphorik von Spiegeln und Spiegelungen, die im Text wiederholt aufgegriffen wird. In der Verformung der Askese wird das Text-Ich zu einem ‚widerglestenden bilde' (VIII, 6-7), zur Spiegelung des Gottessohnes. Die Wahrnehmung seiner selbst als Spiegelbild von etwas anderem impliziert ein gewisses Moment der Fremdkontrolle: Der Spiegel ist ein an sich leerer Gegenstand, der nicht bestimmen kann, was in ihm erscheint. Wenn Gott Elsbeth erklärt, er erzeuge im Grund ihrer Seele einen ‚spiegelichen widerplick in daz lautter pilde meiner drivaltikeit' (XVI, 22-23), dann erscheint die Protagonistin vollständig passiv und zurückgeworfen auf die Rolle eines leeren, für das Eindringen des Fremden offenen Raums, der identisch wird mit dem, was in ihm präsent, aber nicht substanziell vorhanden ist.[6] Gleichzeitig jedoch nimmt sie selbst auch die Betrachtung Christi als Spiegel für sich wahr: ‚Ich pin etwenn in betrachtunge gestanden [...], und ist mir gar dick, als der in einen lauttern spigel blicket, so ich betrachte die peine unsers herren, und daz ist davon, daz es got lang in mir geübt hett' (XI, 9-12). Die durch göttlichen Willen und göttliche Substanz in ihr ausgelöste Anverwandlung an Christus in der Askese ermöglicht es Elsbeth, den Gottessohn als Spiegel und sich selbst als Gespiegeltes zu betrachten, also das Gleiche wahrzunehmen, was die göttlichen Gesprächspartner in ihr sehen. Ermöglicht durch die in der *imitatio* des Körpergebrauchs erlangte Gleichheit mit Christi verschwimmt die Unterscheidung von eigentlichem Gegenstand und Abbild.[7] Damit ist Elsbeth beides: aktiv und passiv, kontrolliert und kontrollierend, Eigenes und Fremdes. Die von der Protagonistin über ihre Körperpraxis aktiv angenommene Identität verwischt und transzendiert die Grenze zwischen ihrem Ich und dem Anderen: Sie, das heißt die Protagonistin in ihrer transformierten Identitätsposition, ist auf der einen Seite ganz das Produkt ihrer Handlungen, entzieht sich auf der anderen jedoch gleichermaßen wieder ihrer eigenen Verfügung. Zwar kann sie sich selbst umformen, darüber aber, wie die Christusfigur, zu der sie sich macht, beschaffen ist, besitzt sie keine Kontrolle.

Während zuvor herausgestellt wurde, wie Elsbeth sich durch ihren Körpergebrauch ermächtigt und die Kontrolle über ihren Körper, ihre religiöse Praxis, ihr Sprechen und die eigene Identität erlangt, zeigen die nun angeführten Textstellen, wie der gleiche Körpergebrauch diese Kontrolle auch untergräbt. Da ihr Körper, solange er seine Rolle als Subjekt wahrnimmt, nur begrenzt leidensfähig ist, muss er die Kontrolle über sich aufgeben, um sich ganz passiv dem Schmerz vollständig überlassen zu können, wodurch auch die religiöse Erfahrungswelt der

---

[6] Hasebrink (2000) diskutiert einen ähnlichen Gebrauch der Spiegelmetapher für Mechthild von Magdeburg.

[7] Wünsche (2009: 100-09) führt diese Metaphorik der Identität des Gespiegelten mit dem Spiegelnden zurück auf die zeitgenössische Johannesfrömmigkeit, für die auch Hamburger (2002: 132) feststellt: ‚John is Christomorphic insofar as he reflects without spot or flaw the glory of God'. Zum Einfluss der Johannesfigur auf Elsbeth vgl. Wünsche (2010) und Kershaw (2011).

Protagonistin nicht mehr in ihrer Gewalt ist. Bedingt wird dies durch einen Zwang zur Askese, der addiktive Züge annimmt. Dieser Zwang scheint auch aus einem Kontrollverlust über die Identität zu resultieren, die Elsbeth annimmt, indem sie ihren Körper umformt und sich über die Erfahrungen dieser Umformung Christus angleicht, denn die Identität des Gottessohnes verlangt immer neues Leiden – indem das Text-Ich sich selbstkontrollierend in Richtung des Heiligen transformiert, setzt es sich auch den unkontrollierbaren Zwängen zu steter Schmerzerfahrung aus, die mit seiner Christformigkeit einhergehen. Was am Ende von diesem Umschlag in die Fremdbestimmtheit unangetastet bleibt, ist die religiöse Autorität, die sich die Protagonistin verleiht – doch wer hier spricht, Elsbeth oder ein von Elsbeth entfremdetes vergöttlichtes Ich, lässt die *Vita* offen.

Das Ineinander von Kontrolle und Kontrollverlust

Der Körpergebrauch Elsbeths von Oye scheint sich singulären Zuschreibungen zu entziehen: Er stellt weder bloß einen Akt des Kontrollgewinns dar, mithilfe dessen die Protagonistin Macht über sich und ihre Erfahrungswelt ausübt, noch ist er reduzierbar auf das Moment des Kontrollverlusts und der pathologischen Selbstzerstörung, das die frühere Forschung oftmals hervorstrich. Auch heben sich die beiden gezeigten Aspekte der Askese Elsbeths nicht gegenseitig auf oder sind getrennt voneinander betrachtbar – vielmehr scheint es, als wäre das gezeigte Ineinander von sich steigernder Verfügung und zunehmender Unverfügbarkeit seiner selbst ein untrennbar zusammengehöriges Resultat der über den Körper des Text-Ichs vollzogenen Umformung von Identität und Erleben. Fast im Sinne einer *negatio negationis* transzendiert die Körperpraxis Elsbeths damit Vorstellungen von Selbstkontrolle und Unkontrollierbarkeit: Sie ist sowohl Ermächtigung und Machtlosigkeit, Kontrolle und Kontrollverlust, jedoch gleichzeitig auch keines der beiden Antonyme für sich allein genommen.

Entscheidend aber ist, dass es sich bei dieser Übersteigerungs- und Überwindungsfigur scheinbarer Gegensätze nicht um ein theoretisches Modell der *unio mystica* handelt, sondern um eine sehr praktische, bis ins Extrem sinnlich vollzogene Handlung der Protagonistin: Über das Bekannte hinausgehende religiöse Erkenntnis wird von Elsbeth nicht im gelehrt-theologischen Nachdenken gesucht, sondern in der Leidens- und Erfahrungsfähigkeit des eigenen Körpers. Sie schließt die Theorie-Praxis-Lücke christlicher Religiosität, indem sie ihren Körper zum Medium und Austragungsort des religiösen Geschehens macht.

Dies ist kein so einzigartiges Phänomen wie auf den ersten Blick scheinen mag. Schaub zum Beispiel zeigt in einer Arbeit zur Beziehung von Philosophie und Grausamkeit an einer Reihe von Beispielen auf, wie das Auftreten der

Theorie als ‚gewaltfreie Wahrheitsproduzentin' (Schaub 2009: 14-15) mit dem Wahrheitsfindungsanspruch denkbar gewaltförmiger Praktiken wie der Folter kontrastiert. Elsbeths *Vita* ließe sich in eine solche Gegenüberstellung konkurrierender Modelle von Wahrheitsproduktion nahtlos auf der Seite einer maximal drastischen Praxis einfügen, wobei der Text in seiner Darstellung von Kontrolle und Kontrollverlust den spezifischen Charakter einer solchen Methode des Erkenntnisgewinns in all seiner Ambiguität aufzeigt.

Doch es ist nicht in erster Linie die Praxisorientierung Elsbeths, die ihrer *Vita* ihr Verstörungspotential verleiht, sondern die Tatsache, dass die Protagonistin jene Praxis ohne jede Rücksicht am eigenen Körper vollzieht. Lentes nun stellt fest, dass christlich-religiöse Praktiken ab dem 15. Jahrhundert einem weitgehenden ‚Transformationsprozess von Außen nach Innen' (Lentes 1999: 54) unterzogen sind – Formen körperlicher Askese, wie sie in Elsbeths Vita beschrieben sind, fließen nur vereinzelt und abgeschwächt in die religiöse Kultur der Neuzeit ein. Rituelle Flagellation zum Beispiel spielte bis ins 17. Jahrhundert innerhalb der katholischen Kirche schubweise eine größere Rolle und wird vereinzelt bis in die Gegenwart praktiziert,[8] jedoch in im Vergleich sehr milder und eher zeichenhaft zu verstehender Form.

Ist die Aufwertung körperlicher Erfahrung zum primären Erkenntnismedium, wie sie in Elsbeths Text vollzogen ist, also ein rein historisches, auf das Spätmittelalter beschränktes Phänomen? Richtig ist sicherlich, dass religiöse Praktiken auf der Schwelle zur Neuzeit einen Verinnerlichungsprozess vollziehen, der schon in der *via triplica* Seuses angelegt ist – und dennoch scheint, als würden der Askese Elsbeths durchaus ähnliche Mechanismen des Körpergebrauchs bis ins Heute hinein in anderen Gesellschaftsbereichen und Texten eine Rolle spielen. Narrative und Inszenierungen von über den Körper vermittelten und erfahrenen Selbsttransformationen finden sich zuhauf und in unterschiedlichsten Diskursfeldern: In Medizin und Geschlechterforschung, Theater und *performance art*, Literatur und politischen Debatte werden Phänomäne der oft über den Körper ausgetragenen Selbst- und Identitätsumformung kontrovers thematisiert.

Es liegt nicht in der Absicht dieser Arbeit, gegenwärtige Narrative und Kulturphänomene mit der doch sehr speziellen Askeseschilderung Elsbeths gleichzusetzen oder diese sogar als Archetyp einer Erzählung von Körpergebrauch, Kontrolle und Kontrollverlust darzustellen. Dazu ist der historische Kontext der spätmittelalterlichen religiösen Kultur, in welcher sich dieser Text entwickeln konnte,

---

[8] Zur Geschichte dieser Praxis vgl. z.B. Largier (2001: 144-51). In der Gegenwart ereignen sich religiöse Selbstpeitschungen beispielsweise als Begleiterscheinung der Fastenumzüge im christlichen Mittelmeerraum, die häufig auch Prozessionen maskierter Flagellanten beinhalten.

viel zu entscheidend für seinen gesamten Charakter und kann dementsprechend nicht zugunsten einer Pauschalisierung abgetan werden. Aber trotz alledem: Die bei Elsbeth geschilderten mittelalterlichen Praktiken radikalen Körpergebrauchs mitsamt all ihren aufgezeigten Konsequenzen scheinen ein gewisses Nachleben und eine frappierende Aktualität zu besitzen, die zum weiteren Nachdenken über eine Kulturgeschichte solcher Praktiken einlädt.

Zitierte Literatur

Primärliteratur

Die Offenbarungen der Adelheid Langmann, Klosterfrau zu Engelthal, hg. von Philipp Strauch, Quellen und Forschungen zur Sprach- und Kulturgeschichte der germanischen Völker, 26 (Straßburg: Karl J. Trübner, 1878)

Das ‚St. Katharinentaler Schwesternbuch'. Untersuchung – Edition – Kommentar, hg. von Ruth Meyer, Münchener Texte und Untersuchungen zur deutschen Literatur des Mittelalters, 104 (Tübingen: Niemeyer, 1995)

Meister Eckhart, 'Predigt 60: In omnibus requiem quaesivi', in *Deutsche Werke*, I: Predigten 1-65, Texte und Übersetzungen von Josef Quint, hg. und kommentiert von Niklaus Largier, Deutscher Klassiker Verlag im Taschenbuch, 24 (Frankfurt a. M.: Deutscher Klassiker Verlag), S. 636-43

[Elsbeth von Oye:] Wolfram Schneider-Lastin, 'Leben und Offenbarungen der Elsbeth von Oye. Textkritische Edition aus dem Ötenbacher Schwesternbuch', in *Kulturtopographie des deutschsprachigen Südwestens im späteren Mittelalter. Studien und Texte*, hg. von Barbara Fleith und René Wetzel, Kulturtopographie des alemannischen Raums, 1 (Berlin/New York: De Gruyter, 2009), S. 395-467

Mechthild von Magdeburg, *‚Das fließende Licht der Gottheit'. Eine Auswahl. Mittelhochdeutsch – Neuhochdeutsch*, hg. von Gisela Vollmann-Profe, Reclam Universal-Bibliothek 18557 (Stuttgart: Reclam, 2008)

Heinrich Seuse, *Deutsche Schriften*, im Auftrag der Württembergischen Kommission für Landesgeschichte hg. v. Karl Bihlmeyer (Stuttgart: Kohlhammer, 1907)

Sekundärliteratur

Angenendt, Arnold. 1997. *Geschichte der Religiosität im Mittelalter* (Darmstadt: Wissenschaftliche Buchgesellschaft)

Assmann, Jan. 1993. *Die Erfindung des inneren Menschen. Studien zur religiösen Anthropologie* (Gütersloh: Mohn)

Bynum, Caroline Walker. 1995. 'Why All the Fuss about the Body? A Medievalist's Perspective', *Critical Inquiry*, 22: 1-33

—. 1992. 'The Female Body and Religious Practice in the Later Middle Ages', in Dies.: *Fragmentation and Redemption. Essays on Gender and the Human Body in Medieval Religion* (New York: Zone Books), S. 181-238

Finke, Laurie A. 1993. 'Mystical Bodies and the Dialogics of Vision', in *Maps of Flesh and Light. The Religious Experience of Medieval Women Mystics*, hg. von Ulrike Wiethaus (Syracuse, NY: Syracuse University Press), S. 28-44

Gsell, Monika. 2000. 'Das fließende Blut der ‚Offenbarungen' Elsbeths von Oye', in *Deutsche Mystik im abendländischen Zusammenhang. Neu erschlossene Texte, neue methodische Ansätze, neue theoretische Konzepte. Kolloquium Kloster Fischingen 1998*, hg. von Walter Haug und Wolfram Schneider-Lastin (Tübingen: Niemeyer), S. 455-82

Haenel, Klaus. 1958. *Textgeschichtliche Untersuchungen zum sogenannten ‚Puchlein des Lebens und der Offenbarung Swester Elsbethen von Oye'* (Göttingen: Univ. Diss.)

Hamburger, Jeffrey F. 2002. *St. John the Divine. The Deified Evangelist in Medieval Art and Theology* (Berkeley: University of California Press)

Hasebrink, Burkhard. 2008. 'Elsbeth von Oye, ‚Vita' (um 1340)', in *Literarische Performativität. Lektüren vormoderner Texte*, hg. von Cornelia Herberichs und Christian Kiening, Medienwandel, Medienwechsel, Medienwissen, 3 (Zürich: Chronos), S. 259-80

—. 2000. 'Spiegel und Spiegelung im *Fließenden Licht der Gottheit*', in *Deutsche Mystik im abendländischen Zusammenhang. Neu erschlossene Texte, neue methodische Ansätze, neue theoretische Konzepte. Kolloquium Kloster Fischingen 1998*, hg. von Walter Haug und Wolfram Schneider-Lastin (Tübingen: Niemeyer), S. 157-74

Haug, Walter. 2003. 'Innerlichkeit, Körperlichkeit und Sprache in der spätmittelalterlichen Frauenmystik', in Ders.: *Die Wahrheit der Fiktion. Studien zur weltlichen und geistlichen Literatur des Spätmittelalters und der frühen Neuzeit* (Tübingen: Niemeyer), S. 480-92

Kershaw, Johanna. 2011. '*Der Vater anplicket dich also in der glas miner sel*: John and the transfer of mystic union in the *Puchlein des lebens und der Offenbarung swester Elsbethen von Oye* of Elsbeth von Oye', in *Vermitteln – Übersetzen – Begegnen. Transferphänomene im europäischen Mittelalter und in der frühen Neuzeit. Interdisziplinäre Annäherungen*, hg. von Balázs J. Nemes und Achim Rabus, Nova Mediaevalia, 8 (Göttingen: V&R unipress), S. 19-32

Largier, Niklaus. 2001. *Lob der Peitsche. Eine Kulturgeschichte der Erregung* (München: Beck)

Lentes, Thomas. 1999. 'Andacht und Gebärde. Das religiöse Ausdrucksverhalten', in *Kulturelle Reformation. Sinnformationen im Umbruch 1400-1600*, hg. von Bernhard Jussen und Craig Koslofsky, Veröffentlichungen des Max-Planck-Instituts für Geschichte, 145 (Göttingen: Vandenhoeck und Ruprecht), S. 29-67

McNamara, Jo Ann. 1993. 'The Need to Give: Suffering and Female Sanctity in the Middle Ages', in *Maps of Flesh and Light. The Religious Experience of Medieval Women Mystics*, hg. von Ulrike Wiethaus (Syracuse, NY: Syracuse University Press), S. 199-221

Ochsenbein, Peter. 1986. 'Die Offenbarungen Elsbeths von Oye als Dokument leidensfixierter Mystik', in *Abendländische Mystik im Mittelalter. Symposion Kloster Engelberg 1984*, hg. von Kurt Ruh, Germanistische Symposien, Berichtsbände, 7 (Stuttgart: Metzler), S. 423-42

O'Reilly, Sally. 2009. *The Body in Contemporary Art* (London: Thames & Hudson)

Schaub, Mirjam. 2009. 'Grausamkeit und Metaphysik. Zur Logik der Überschreitung in der abendländischen Philosophie und Kultur', in *Grausamkeit und Metaphysik. Figuren der Überschreitung in der abendländischen Kultur*, hg. von Mirjam Schaub (Bielefeld: transcript), S. 11-31

Schroth, Ulrich. 2011. 'Strafe/Bestrafung', in: *Neues Handbuch philosophischer Grundbegriffe*, begründet von Hermann Krings, Hans Michael Baumgartner und Christoph Wild, neu hg. von Petra Kolmer und Armin G. Wildfeuer, III (Freiburg/München: Verlag Karl Alber), S. 2108-22

Tinsley, David F. 1995. 'The Spirituality of Suffering in the Revelations of Elsbeth von Oye', *Mystics Quarterly*, 21: 121-47.

Wißmann, Hans. 1981. 'Buße I: Religionsgeschichtlich', in *Theologische Realenzyklopädie*, hg. von Gerhard Krause und Gerhard Müller, VII (Berlin/New York: De Gruyter), S. 430-33

Wünsche, Gregor. 2010. '*Imitatio Ioannis* oder Elsbeths Apokalypse – Die "Offenbarungen" Elsbeths von Oye im Kontext der dominikanischen Johannesfrömmigkeit im 14. Jahrhundert', in: *Schmerz in der Literatur des Mittelalters und der Frühen Neuzeit*, hg. von Hans-Jochen Schiewer, Stefan Seeber und Markus Stock, Transatlantische Studien zu Mittelalter und Früher Neuzeit, 4 (Göttingen: V&R unipress), S. 167-87

—. 2009. *Präsenz des Unerträglichen. Kulturelle Semantik des Schmerzes in den "Offenbarungen" Elsbeths von Oye* (Freiburg im Breisgau: Univ. Diss.)

10

Strafen und Leiden im Martyrium: Überlegungen zu Konrads von Würzburg *Pantaleon*

Katharina Mertens-Fleury
Universität Zürich

Zentrale Ansätze, den Begriff der Strafe zu definieren, basieren auf der Annahme, dass ein Übel geschehen ist, das geahndet werden muss. Sie konzentrieren sich auf Fragen der Beurteilung eines Vergehens unter Einbeziehung der Intention des Täters und der Wirkung der Strafe, welche erzieherische oder abschreckende Funktionen erlangen kann. Kern dieser Begrifflichkeit ist daher einerseits eine Strafhermeneutik, welche das Vergehen vor einem normativen Hintergrund beurteilt und dazu ein zeitspezifisches Rechts- und Herrschaftssystem als Maßstab zugrunde legt (Hühn 1998; Hartung 1998). Zudem ist an diese Definitionen auch das Verständnis eines Wandels gebunden, da ein geschehenes Übel durch ein anderes (die Strafe) beseitigt und der Bestrafte dadurch von seiner Schuld befreit werden soll, aber auch eine innere Umkehr erwartet wird – letzterer Aspekt tritt je nach Epoche mehr oder weniger in den Vordergrund. Mittels der Strafe soll somit ein geschehenes Unrecht aufgewogen und abgegolten werden, wodurch der Affekt der Rache einer institutionalisierten Strafe weicht. Dazu orientiert sich die Bemessung der Wiedergutmachung am verursachten Schaden (Hartung 1998: 218).[1] Letztere Vorstellung vertritt Augustinus, der in seiner Strafdefinition römische Rechtsvorstellungen über die angemessene Beurteilung des Strafmaßes mit dem christlichen Wertehorizont verbindet. Nach seiner Auffassung hebt letztlich ein *malum* ein anderes auf.[2] Die Strafe führt auf diese Weise zu einer Abgeltung und Tilgung der Schuld, vollzieht also einen Wandel, indem der Verurteilte seine Schuld ablegen kann, sodass sich der Status des Bestraften ändert (Hartung 1998: 219). Sie prägt daher die Mitglieder einer Gesellschaft, denn die Macht des Strafenden beeinflusst nicht nur die Normvorstellungen, sondern

---

[1] Das trifft bereits für das römische Recht zu.
[2] Siehe dort den Verweis auf Aurelius Augustinus (PL 42: 169). Diese Auffassung entspricht dem ursprünglichen lateinischen Begriff der *poena*, welche ‚das Loskaufgeld' zum Verzicht auf Rache bedeutet.

kann je nach Straftat am Körper des Gestraften Spuren hinterlassen, oder ihn gar sukzessive vernichten (Foucault 1978: 34; 37).[3]

Die Straflogiken der Umkehr, des Wandels und der Deutung eines Verstoßes gegen Normen und deren Ahndung finden sich in der christlichen Vormoderne besonders im Martyrium (griech. μαρτύριον), dem ‚Glaubenszeugnis‘ (Drews / Schlie 2011: 9; Schöttler 2009: 1523; Hörner 2003: 327). Märtyrer sterben – im allgemeinen Sinn – für ihren Glauben, aus Gründen der Religion oder einer anderen Ideologie (Mitchell 2012: 1).[4] Ihr Tod basiert auf einem grundlegenden Normkonflikt zwischen den Gläubigen und ihrem Umfeld. In der Epoche der Spätantike kollidiert das Christentum mit der römischen, polytheistischen Staatsreligion. Entsprechend erfolgt die Be- und Verurteilung der Christen auf der Basis der römischen Normen, der Rechtsprechung und der Strafpraktiken (Gerlitz 1992: 197–202).[5] Die Christen verwerfen ihrerseits die pagane Vielgötterei und perspektivieren die Strafe auf ihre Weise. Im Martyrium wird die Strafe also doppelt relevant, weil sie aus zwei normativen Sichtweisen dargestellt wird, welche den Sachverhalt ganz anders beurteilen: Aus der Sicht der Bestraften und Verfolgten erscheint sie als Opfer der Unschuldigen, als Selbsthingabe des Märtyrers, bzw. als ‚die Hinnahme von Bestrafung für das Bekenntnis des christlichen Glaubens‘ in der Nachfolge Christi (Slusser 1992: 207; Fuhrmann: 2012; Henze 1997; Scheuer 1997),[6] sodass ‚die Todesstrafe [...] zum Sieg von Gerechtigkeit und Wahrheit‘ wird (Bergjan / Näf 2014: 27). Die Strafe wendet sich als Teil eines Heilsgeschehens in Lohn (Bachorski / Klinger 1999: 102-03).

Das erzählte Martyrium, wie es in den mittelalterlichen Martyriumslegenden präsent ist, akzentuiert diese Perspektivenvielfalt, sodass die Forschung in der Analyse bisher verschiedene Akzente gesetzt hat. Sie fasst die Martyriumserzählungen in ihrer Funktion als Vorbilder der Lebensführung oder als Medien der Vermittlung von Transzendenz auf, sie wertet sie im Hinblick auf körperliche Gewalt und

---

[3] Die darin beschriebenen Grausamkeiten des Strafsystems der Neuzeit stimmen in Vielem mit den Foltermethoden der Martyriumsschilderungen überein, die sich auf Foucault (1977) beziehen (Bachorski / Klinger 1999: 102-21). Der Foucaultsche Begriff der Strafe verdeutlicht die Verklammerungen zwischen Macht und Körper des Gepeinigten. Die Macht prägt sich öffentlich dem Körper des Gefolterten ein, deformiert, zerstückelt und zerstört ihn. Foucault belegt dies u. a. auch daran, dass Gestrafte die Mutilierung seines Körpers vom Gestraften immer wieder betrachten und somit zur Kenntnis nehmen (Foucault 1977: 34; 37).
[4] Mitchell (2012) bietet ein breites Spektrum an Beispielen für Martyrien verschiedener Epochen und Kontexte. Ich beschränke mich im Folgenden aufgrund meines mittelalterlichen Fokus auf die Spezifik christlicher Martyrien der Spätantike, welche in mittelalterlichen Legenden wiedererzählt werden.
[5] Gerlitz (1992) bietet einen konzisen Überblick über den Begriff.
[6] Es entsteht Henze (1997) zufolge in den ersten frühchristlichen Jahrhunderten ein Spektrum von Märtyrertexten, u.a. auch Briefliteratur und Apologetik.

Sprachgewalt aus (Koch 2008: 17).[7] Die Strafe und die mit ihr verbundenen Normkonflikte standen bisher im Hintergrund der Untersuchungen, weshalb diese auf der Grundlage der bestehenden Fragestellungen im Folgenden im Mittelpunkt stehen wird.

Märtyrerberichte präsentieren einen auf den ersten Blick juristisch geprägten Normenkonflikt. Schon seit den frühen Märtyrerakten finden die römischen Rechtsnormen bei der Ausgestaltung der Texte Berücksichtigung; sie beziehen hingegen ihre Funktion und Perspektive aus dem christlichen Kontext, welcher über die Sinngebung des Geschehens letztlich verfügt, sie sichern die Erinnerung und legitimieren Orte und Praktiken der Memoria (vgl. Bergjan / Näf 2014). Das geschilderte chiastische Verhältnis der Deutungen (römischen und christlichen) ändert sich auch in den späteren, mittelalterlichen Überlieferungen nicht. Zahlreiche Heiligenlegenden blicken auf die Christenverfolgungen der vorkonstantinischen Epoche zurück, handeln von Normbrüchen, Verurteilungen und Todesstrafen.[8] Im Martyrium vollziehen sich Prozesse der Be- und Verurteilung durch die politische Obrigkeit, doch wird die Strafe in bedeutenden Punkten umgedeutet: Der Märtyrer erfährt die Ausgestaltung zu einer komplexen Figur, schuldig vor dem weltlichen Gesetz, unschuldig, ja erhöht vor dem Hintergrund des christlichen Glaubens. Die weltliche Strafe gilt als erstrebenswerte Nachfolge Christi, orientiert sich an Jesu Passion, dem Umbruchsmoment der christlichen Heilsgeschichte, in der die Schuld der Menschheit durch das Opfer des Unschuldigen gesühnt und getilgt wurde (Slusser 1992: 208-09; Köpf 1997: 722-64). Das Martyrium führt deshalb den Gemarterten zum Lohn, die Strafe macht ihn mächtig, krönt ihn und schenkt ihm das ewige Leben (Bergjan / Näf 2014: 27). Aus der Demütigung der Strafe erwächst so die Erhöhung (Lucke 2014: 338).[9] Das Lebensopfer wird im Martyrium zur ‚leibhaftigen Waffe' umgewendet (Weigel 2007: 13). Die Umdeutung setzt voraus, dass das Leiden der Märtyrer als ein Leiden in der Nachfolge Christi bzw. für Gott impliziert bzw. als Rechtfertigung, Lohn oder auch Heiligung gewürdigt wird (Slusser 1992: 209). Die Strafe des Märtyrers ermöglicht somit den verbalen und physischen Ausweis des christlichen Glaubens. Das Martyrium steht in der Nachfolge Christi, wird daher als ein Moment perspektiviert, in dem das jeweilige

---

[7] Koch (2008) greift in ihrem Beitrag auf Judith Butler zurück, welche Sprechakte mit Akten körperlicher Gewalt differenziert. Siehe zur Funktion der *aedificatio* Schulmeister (1971); Jolles (1974); Rosenfeld (1982), zur Vermittlung von Transzendenz Strohschneider (2000; 2002), zur Körperlichkeit des Martyriums Bachorski / Klinger (1999; 2002); Kiening (2004).

[8] Feistner (1995) ist für die Beurteilung der Morphologie der Heiligen- und damit auch Märtyrerlegenden zentral.

[9] Siehe zum Begriff der ‚Heiligung' in literaturwissenschaftlichem Kontext von Heiligenlegenden Peter Strohschneider (2002b). Ich verwende im Folgenden ‚Sanktion' als Faktum und darauf basierend auch den Begriff der ‚Sanktionierung', um eine konkrete Ausführung zu bezeichnen.

Opfer in seinem Leiden die Passion Christi und damit den zentralen Wendepunkt der Heilsgeschichte partiell, analog nachvollzieht. Daraus lässt sich weiter schließen, dass auch das Martyrium mehrere Umbrüche nach sich zieht: Urteil und Strafe werden durch die christliche Deutung pervertiert, das Geschehen wandelt den Märtyrer vom Opfer zum Heiligen, befördert ihn von einer quälenden, paganen Welt voller Anfechtungen in die ewige Seligkeit, bekehrt die Anwesenden wie die Leser/ Hörer zum Christentum, führt zur liturgischen Memoria und herausgehobenen Heiligenverehrung, an die wiederum die Legende erinnert und welcher sie dient (vgl. auch Bachorski / Klinger 1999: 102-03). Um die poetische Komplexität der Strafe herauszuarbeiten, werde ich in einem ersten Schritt die Begriffsbestimmung vertiefen und in einem zweiten mittelalterliche deutschsprachige Überlieferungen einer Märtyrerlegende heranziehen (Bachorski / Klingner 2000: 309-33). Im Fokus steht die Legende des Pantaleon, weil sie die Partikularität aufweist, eine ganze Reihe von Strafen zu präsentieren, die verschieden gedeutet werden, wodurch dieser Problemkomplex besonders breit entfaltet wird und für eine differenziertere Analyse zur Verfügung steht.

Für die vorliegende Untersuchung möchte ich aufgrund der Doppeldeutigkeit den Begriff der ‚Sanktion' verwenden, da er positiv wie negativ gewendet und sowohl als Lohn wie als Strafe verstanden werden kann. Sie umreißt somit verschiedene Deutungsperspektiven, weil mit ihr die zwei Seiten der Bewertung des Geschehens wie die Wendung dieses Strafhandelns bezeichnet werden. Die ‚Sanktion' fungiert als Mittel/Instrument der sozialen Kontrolle und der Machtdurchsetzung und dient der Erhaltung einer gesellschaftlichen Ordnung, welche die Konformität Abweichender bewirken soll (Lucke 2014). Sie gründet in normativen Wertsystemen, die durchgesetzt werden sollen, zudem bezeichnet sie eine Möglichkeit ihrer Bewertung, da sie auch die ‚Billigung und Bestätigung' von überindividuell gültigen Normen umfasst (Lucke 2014: 338). Insofern, als sich mit der ‚Sanktion' Vergeltung wie Lohn verbinden, zielt die Verwendung des Begriffs im Folgenden darauf ab, ihn im Zusammenhang mit dem Martyrium zu verwenden, da es ebenfalls polysem angelegt ist, Schwäche in Stärke, Tod in Leben, Schmerz in Freude, Niederlage in Sieg gewendet werden können (Kraß 2008: 166). Die Strafe wie deren Deutung wird in den Erzählungen tradiert, erinnert und funktionalisiert (Till 2003: 1306).[10] Das Ziel der Untersuchung besteht darin,

---

[10] Die überlieferten Heiligenlegenden stellen sich mit ihren Inhalten, aber auch mit ihren dazu verwendeten argumentativen Strategien in den Kontext einer Rhetorik, welche Effekte beabsichtigt, insbesondere zielen sie auf „‚Überredung' bzw. ‚Überzeugung' (*persuasio*) eines Publikums.' (Till 2003: 1306). Sie ist insofern agonal konzipiert, als sie verschiedene Standpunkte impliziert und einen Standpunktwechsel mit allen rhetorischen Mitteln herbeiführen soll.

die Poetik literarischer Martyriumsdarstellungen zu fokussieren und einerseits den mit der Strafe verbundenen Normkonkurrenz zu untersuchen und andererseits deren hermeneutischen Potentiale und Wirkungen näher zu betrachten. Ich frage insbesondere nach den Strategien der Umsetzung dieser Prozesse, nach den Wendungen, Umbrüchen, Umdeutungen (Kraß 2008) und rhetorischen Persuasionsstrategien, welche die agonale Situation zwischen Christen und Heiden spiegeln (Knape 2003: 875; 889).[11] In der folgenden Textanalyse steht dieser Zugang im Vordergrund.

Die obigen Thesen möchte ich am Beispiel der Pantaleonlegende – einem Arztheiligen und einem der vierzehn Nothelfer – vertiefen, weil in dieser Erzählung die Semantiken von Pathologie und Heilung, von Zerstörung und Schöpferkraft in den Vordergrund, welche eine spirituelle Nuance annehmen (Neukirchen 2008: 102). Pantaleon weiss deshalb zu heilen, weil er die Kraft des christlichen Gottes durch seine Gebete erwirbt und vermittelt. Vor diesem Hintergrund gewinnen in dieser Erzählung Muster der *conversio*, des Umbruchs und Wandels an Bedeutungsgehalt. Die Legende des Pantaleon ist im Mittelalter im deutschsprachigen Raum in mehreren Fassungen überliefert (Stridde 2011: 1175-1177; Williams-Krapp 1986: 447 und 1989: 290).[12] Im Fokus der vorliegenden Analyse steht jene Konrads von Würzburg (=KvW),[13] welche die Taten des Heiligen am ausführlichsten schildert. Konrads Version entstand um 1380/90, ist aber erst rund 100 Jahre später unikal im Wiener Codex Vidobonensis 2884 überliefert (Neukirchen 2008: 84). Diese Erzählung ist mit 2158 Versen die ausführlichste mittelalterliche Pantaleonlegende des deutschsprachigen Raums (Neukirchen 2008: 84). Daneben sollen als Ausblick auch die kürzeren Pantaleonerzählungen der spätmittelalterlichen Legendensammlungen Berücksichtigung finden, nämlich aus dem *Märterbuch* (=Mb; Ende 13./Anfang 14. Jh.), aus der *Elsässischen Legenda Aurea* (1. Hälfte 14. Jh.),[14] die mit 34 Hss. aus der Zeit von ca. 1350 bis ca. 1475

---

[11] ‚Jeder Form von Persuasion haftet eben etwas Agonales an, das sich aus dem Wettbewerb um das richtige Ziel ergibt' (siehe dazu Knape 2003: 889). Das Ziel des Orators (oder genereller desjenigen, der strategisch kommuniziert) ist also immer die Persuasion seiner Adressaten; diese zeigt sich in einem ‚Wechsel bei Urteilen, Einschätzung und Haltungen' (Knape 2003: 875).
[12] Siehe auch Jackson (1972; 1983).
[13] Im Folgenden verwende ich die Textausgabe von Neukirchen (2008).
[14] Siehe dazu insbesondere Williams-Krapp (1986: 35). Er bezeichnet sie als das bedeutendste Legendar des deutschen Südwestens; es ‚zählt zu den frömmigkeitsgeschichtlich wichtigsten Prosadenkmälern' des vierzehnten Jahrhunderts. Sie ist mit 36 Hss. aus der Zeit ca. 1350 bis ca. 1475 überliefert; zwei Texte (Nr. 36, 67) seit Anton Sorg (1481/82) in 13 Druckauflagen von *Der Heiligen Leben* inseriert. Älteste und einzig komplette Hss. mit Winterteil (Advent bis 10000 Märtyrer) und Sommerteil (Johannes Baptista bis Kirchweih) sind München, cgm 6, von 1362 (mit hervorragenden Miniaturen eines unbekannten Heinricus) und Heidelberg, cpg 144, v. J. 1419, beide aus Straßburg und illustriert.

überliefert wurde und aus *Der Heiligen Leben* (=HL; Ende 14./Anfang 15. Jh.). Während das *Märterbuch* und *Der Heiligen Leben* von Konrads *Pantaleon* stärker abweichen und einen anderen Traditionsstrang bieten, steht die *Elsässer Legenda Aurea* Konrads Text inhaltlich von der Abfolge der Episoden bis hin zum Wortlaut bedeutend näher. Der punktuelle Rückgriff auf die Vergleichstexte ermöglicht es also, Nuancen in der Bedeutung der Strafen und deren Durchführung in die Analyse einzubeziehen. Mit der Frage nach der Sanktion stehen im Folgenden Normen, Werte und Machtgefüge, deren Umsetzung und Folgen im Zentrum. Die Textanalyse nimmt deswegen folgenden Weg: Sie fokussiert in Bezug auf das Strafgeschehen (1.) die konkurrierenden Normen, die im Text entfaltet werden, (2.) die Mehrdeutigkeit der Sanktionen, (3.) das Wechselspiel von Sprechen und Handeln sowie (4.) die Aus- und Nachwirkungen der Sanktionen.[15]

Konkurrierende Normen: Gott und die Götzen
Die Erzählung bringt den Konflikt schon zu Beginn durch eine Gegenüberstellung der verschiedenen Positionen auf den Punkt: Der römische Kaiser Maximianus verfolgt die Christen aufgrund ihres Glaubens, verteidigt die durch ihn repräsentierte polytheistische Staatsreligion, welche das Opfer für seine Götter vorschreibt. Seine kaiserliche Macht ist weithin sichtbar (KvW: 76-77) und er konsolidiert diese durch Christenverfolgungen (KvW: 70-79). Die Christen leben aus Angst vor dem Herrscher im Verborgenen, hausen in Verstecken im Wald (KvW: 83). Und so verbirgt auch der Priester Ermolaus seinen Glauben (KvW: 146-247, vgl. KvW: 164). Erst Pantaleon, Schüler des Ermolaus, lässt das Christentum durch Taten und Wunder an den Tag treten: Er rettet einen Knaben vor einer Natter, sodass sein Handeln zu einem ‚zeichen offenbere' (KvW: 354) wird. Das Gelingen bewegt Pantaleon zur Taufe und suggeriert zugleich die befreienden Eigenschaften des Christentums. Das zweite Wunder besteht in der Heilung eines Blinden, der von diesem Wunder ‚vurkunde geben kan' (KvW: 922).[16] Die Verkündigung des Christentums wird in dieser Episode mit der Blindenheilung verquickt. Dem Geheilten, der durch das Wirken der heidnischen Ärzte auch sein letztes Augenlicht sowie sein Hab und Gut verlor, eröffnet sich durch den christlichen Arzt eine neue Sicht und er berichtet öffentlich von diesem Heilsgeschehen. Es dient überdies der Überzeugung vom christlichen Glauben und führt zu Bekehrung des Vaters von Pantaleon. Auch er lässt sich taufen, schlägt seine Götzenstatuen entzwei und entfernt sie aus seinem Haus (KvW: 676-91). Pantaleon fährt fort, Blinde, Krumme

---
[15] Zu den sprachlichen Formen der Gewalt in der Märtyrerlegende vgl. Koch (2008).
[16] Und dieser ehemals Blinde, der Zeuge der Macht Christi ist, wird umgehend vom Kaiser umgehend geköpft (KvW: 920-22), sodass mit ihm auch der materielle Beweis der Heilkraft Christi beseitigt wird.

und Lahme in Christi Namen zu heilen, mit dem Potential weiterer Bekehrungen (KvW: 745-46).

Der Wettstreit zwischen der Heilkraft der Götzen (Asklepios und Hippokrates)[17] und der des christlichen Gottes wird am Kaiserhof – wie schon in den vorangehenden Szenen – auf dem Gebiet ärztlicher Kunst und damit auf der Ebene des Verfalls bzw. der Erneuerung des menschlichen Körpers ausgetragen: Die Heilung der Kranken wird zum Gottesbeweis, da sie von Gott als höchstem Arzt zeugt (vgl. KvW: 222), und die jene des Lahmen am Hof des Kaisers erweist Christus endgültig und offiziell als überlegen (KvW: 988). In dieser Konstellation dient sie aber nicht der Bekehrung, sondern der Darstellung der agonalen Situation, der konfligierenden Normen: In Konrads Legende reagiert der Kaiser auf Pantaleons Glaubensbekenntnis mit Strafen; er ordnet eine hohe Anzahl von Peinigungen an. Pantaleon wird über feuergefüllten Glasgefässen geröstet, in ein Bad aus heißem Blei getaucht, an einen schweren Stein gebunden im Meer versenkt, im Zirkus den Tieren vorgeworfen, dann eingekerkert, um danach gerädert zu werden. Die Szenen erlangen bei Konrad repetitiven Charakter, da die Leiden für Pantaleon stets milde zu ertragen sind (das heiße Blei erscheint ihm z.B. wie Honigmet und Meientau [KvW: 1313, 1343]), der Geplagte diese furchtlos erträgt, dann aber Gott doch um Hilfe bittet.[18] Letzterer steht ihm in Gestalt des Priesters und Lehrers Ermolaus bei.[19] Am Schluss erleidet der Märtyrer nur deswegen den Tod durch das Schwert, weil er zuvor eigens darum bittet.[20]

Die Sanktionen zielen auf die Vernichtung Pantaleons (wie des Christentums) ab, was nicht gelingt. Der Heilige erscheint dadurch schon während der Foltern stets als Sieger, als unantastbar, weil von Gott bewahrt, behütet und gerettet,

---

[17] An dieser Stelle wird klar, dass die medizinische Praxis ausschließlich auf dem Gebet beruht und die ‚Götter' eher inkonsequent sowohl mythologische (Äskulap) wie historische Personen bezeichnen (Hippokrates von Kos, 460-370 v.Chr.). Letzterer repräsentiert das Verfahren einer evidenzbasierten Medizin, seine Nachwirkungen reichen mit der Viersäftelehre in die mittelalterliche Heilpraxis hinein. Die ‚Götter' zeichnen sich durch den Mangel an Wirksamkeit aus. Hier findet sich folglich eine Abwertung der Naturwissenschaft zugunsten einer Aufwertung der Theologie.

[18] Diese Stelle erscheint allerdings ambivalent, weil das Blei zum einen angenehm, zum anderen aufgrund der Hitze dann doch bedrohlich wirkt (vgl. auch v. 1339). Es scheint hier deswegen eine gewisse Spannung auf.

[19] Das Motiv des Beistands ist auch in anderen Legenden verbreitet (Bachorski / Klinger 1999: 121). Als Beistand fungieren beispielsweise ein Engel, Jesus oder der Heilige Geist.

[20] Die Tendenz der Nivellierung der Qualen besteht allgemein in der mittelalterlichen Märtyrerdarstellung. Der Analyse von Schirrmeister (2000: 144-47) zufolge tritt die Ausmalung der Leiden und Schmerzen in der mittelalterlichen Hagiographie und bildenden Kunst zurück. Das arbeiten auch Bachorski / Klinger (1999: 118) heraus, die ebenfalls die *Legenda Aurea* zum Bezugspunkt wählen: ‚Alle Martern und Qualen, jeder Anschlag und die gesamte Vernichtungswut prallen an den Heiligen ab'. Sie halten fest, dass meist der Tod durch das Schwert am Ende der Martern steht (vgl. Bachorski / Klinger 1999: 123, Anm. 50).

sodass die Verfolger und ihre Strafen der Lächerlichkeit preisgegeben werden. Das *Märterbuch* und der *Der Heiligen Leben* setzen demgegenüber auf eine besondere Drastik der Foltern: Der Kaiser lässt Pantaleons Körper zerstören, das Fleisch abschälen bis auf die Knochen und ihn dann mit Fackeln fast ganz verkohlen, um ihn anschließend im Kerker (ver-)hungern zu lassen und dann ebenfalls ins Meer zu werfen und wilden Tieren vorzuführen. Aus Zorn über die Unzerstörbarkeit des Heiligen lässt Maximianus den Widerständigen zuletzt geißeln. Der höhere Grad der Zerstörung des Körpers trägt in diesen Versionen dazu bei, die besonders große Schöpfer- und Heilkraft Gottes zu verdeutlichen und die bestehenden Kontraste zu verstärken. Denn auch in den Versionen der Legendensammlungen erlangt Pantaleon seine Unversehrtheit zurück. Das *Märterbuch* und *Der Heiligen Leben* zeichnen hier sogar noch stärkere Kontraste, was auch das Ende der Strafen affiziert: Von Zorn entbrannt spaltet ein Ritter zuletzt Pantaleons Haupt. Der Märtyrer bittet Gott jetzt um ein Ende der Peinigungen, damit er erlöst werde, in sein Reich eingehe und zu ewigen Freuden gelange. Auf diese Weise werden Konkurrenzen deutlich, welche die destruktiven Normen und Werte des römischen Imperators, seinen Zorn und seine Zerstörungswut der tugendhaften Geduld des Heiligen sowie der Heil- und Lebenskraft des christlichen Gottes gegenüberstellen. Zusammenfassend haben die Sanktionen in Bezug auf die Normen gemeinsam, dass sie die agonalen Verhältnisse an der Figur des Pantaleon abbilden – und sie sind daher von jenen Heilungswundern zu unterscheiden, welche der Bekehrung und Überzeugung dienen. Diese Distinktionen werden im zweiten Teil der Erzählung jedoch unterlaufen, weil aus dem Normenkonflikt Wunder erwachsen, welche zur Bekehrung führen. Die Normen von Heiden und Christen bleiben während der Erzählung dichotomisch verfasst, sodass sich mit dem Christentum in diesem Kontext das (ewige) Leben verbindet, wohingegen die römische, wahrnehmungsunfähige Götterwelt (vgl. KvW: 880-85) nur aus starren und vor allem zerstörbaren, toten und todbringenden Statuen besteht (KvW: 1826). Während der Einfluss der Römer die Christenheit bedroht und den Körper des Heiligen zu destruieren sucht, zeigt Gott seine Lebendigkeit, rettet den Märtyrer und lässt seinen Tod nur auf ausdrücklichen Wunsch zu. Der Kampf zwischen römischer Staatsreligion und Christentum wird letztlich am Körper Pantaleons ausgetragen. Das *Märterbuch* und *Der Heiligen Leben* gehen an dieser Stelle noch einen Schritt weiter, da hier Kontraste vertieft werden. Das *Märterbuch* bezeichnet den Kaiser sogar explizit als ‚tiufels mann' (Mb: 13617), welcher Pantaleon, dem christlichen Heiligen, Heiler und Geheilten als Gegner gegenübergestellt wird.

Ein- und Mehrdeutigkeit

Martyrien bergen wie bereits ausgeführt hermeneutische Dimensionen. In Konrads *Pantaleon* zeigt sich die doppelte Auslegungsperspektive besonders dort, wo im Dialog zwischen Kaiser und Christen ein Erdbeben – Effekt des Gebets zum christlichen Gott – als Zorn der Götter erklärt wird (KvW: 1810).[21] Die ‚Strafe' erweist sich dadurch als deutungs- und perspektivenabhängig, wobei sich die Positionen der verschiedenen Akteure abzeichnen. Die verschiedenen Sichtweisen ergeben sich insbesondere aus dem Gespräch. Der Kaiser peinigt und tötet die drei Freunde und Lehrer Pantaleons (KvW: 1860–867), weil der junge Arzt den römischen Göttern nicht opfern will. Dann belügt der Kaiser Pantaleon, er habe die drei auf eine Reise in fremde Länder geschickt (KvW: 1937; 1952). Der Christ enthüllt die Lüge des Kaisers und begegnet ihr mit seiner Perspektive: Er legt die ‚Reise' der drei Freunde – ihr Martyrium – als Übergang in die himmlische Herrlichkeit, als Krönung im Himmel aus und er erklärt, dass auch er diesen ‚Weg' gehen werde.[22] Die Polysemie der Ereignisse entgeht dem Kaiser, wodurch sich seine Erkenntnisfähigkeit als eingeschränkt erweist und Analogien zu seiner wahrnehmungsunfähigen, starren, toten Götterwelt aufscheinen (vgl. dazu KvW: 880-85). Klar geht in den Dialogen aus der Wortwahl hervor, dass das Christentum die Perspektive der Römer sprengt. So bezeichnet der Kaiser etwa das Reden und Handeln der Christen auch als überflüssig und unnütz (‚vpeclich' [KvW: 1790; 1836]), es liegt unerreichbar jenseits seines Wertehorizonts. Die Mehrdeutigkeit ergänzt daher die dichotomischen Verhältnisse dadurch, dass sie die Wahrnehmungsfähigkeiten der Akteure differenziert.

An der Figur des Pantaleon zeichnen sich ebenfalls mehrere Perspektiven ab: Sein Wunsch besteht darin, Arzt zu werden und er wendet sich von der heidnischen Medizin ab, weil einzig das Christentum Heilkraft bietet. Nach seiner Bekehrung dienen seine Heilungswunder dem Beweis der Kraft Gottes und damit der öffentlichen Verkündigung des Christentums im feindlichen Milieu. Die Heilungswunder können als Steigerung gelesen werden, denn Pantaleons Glaubensbekenntnis vollzieht sich erst zaghaft im engeren Umkreis, dann am Kaiserhof und zuletzt im öffentlich zur Schau gestellten Martyrium. Auch in der intradiegetischen Funktion der Wunder ist eine Stufung wahrnehmbar, denn zunächst befreit Pantaleon einen Knaben aus dem Würgegriff einer Natter, um den Beweis für Gottes Hilfsbereitschaft zu erhalten und sich selbst zu bekehren.

---

[21] Schirrmeister (2000: 149) beobachtet in der Entwicklung der mittelalterlichen Martyriumsdarstellungen allgemein ‚eine Tendenz zur Vieldeutigkeit'. Konrad funktionalisiert diese allerdings nur innerhalb der Erzählung.
[22] Zum Motiv der Krönung im Himmel siehe Wild (2007: 71).

Die Heilung des Blinden weist eine Analogie zu den Heilungswundern Christi auf, sodass Pantaleon hier bereits ansatzweise zu einem Nachfolger Christi stilisiert wird.[23] Pantaleon verhilft in der Folge auch anderen Lahmen, Krummen und Blinden zur vollkommenen Genesung. Seine Form der Nachfolge gipfelt im Martyrium, der Passionsnachfolge bis in den Tod. Die Ähnlichkeiten mit Christus treten auch im Leiden und im Moment der Hinrichtung durch das Schwert in den Vordergrund. Pantaleon willigt in den Tod ein und wirft sich kreuzesförmig demütig nieder (KvW: 2083). Die partielle körperliche Angleichung an Christus trägt die innere Haltung nach außen; sie deutet den Wandel der Person und deren künftige Apotheose an, welche durch Gottes Stimme am Schluss bekräftigt und auch durch den Erzähler verkündet wird. Das christliche Handeln wie auch die passiv erduldete Sanktion ist somit per se mehrdeutig, weil auf etwas anderes ausgerichtet: Gott. Das Handeln des Kaisers ist in der Erzählung hingegen linear und ‚eindeutig', bezieht sich auf die Erhaltung der auf dem Polytheismus– in der Erzählung durch die Götzenstatuen repräsentiert – basierenden Macht und ist auch daher weniger perspektivenreich.

Die Wunder und das Handeln Pantaleons sind zugleich als Reaktion auf die Handlungen des Kaisers angelegt, sie erscheinen als Antwort auf die römische Gewalt, richten sich gegen die römische Staatsreligion und ihre Normen und konkretisieren das Wirken Christi in der Welt. Diese Konfrontation spitzt sich im zweiten Teil der Erzählung zu, als der Kaiser Pantaleon zu sich ruft. Der Heiler bekennt vor dem Kaiser explizit seinen Glauben und wendet sich gegen die alten Götter, die er als machtlos bezeichnet (vgl. KvW: 985-89).

Die Sanktionen künden zudem von einem ‚anderen' Wirken und einer anderen Wahrheit: Gott bewahrt Pantaleons Unversehrtheit, die Folter will sich dem Märtyrer nicht dauerhaft ‚einschreiben', ihn markieren und jene Spuren der Vernichtung hinterlassen, die vom Kaiser beabsichtigt sind.[24] Die Sanktionen werden damit stets durch Gott ins Gute gewendet. Das *Märterbuch* und *Der Heiligen Leben* erzählen die Peinigungen anders, forcieren die bereits erwähnte Drastik der Foltern: Als dem geduldig leidenden Pantaleon Haut und Fleisch abgezogen werden und er durch Einwirkung der Fackeln nahezu verkohlt, sorgt Gott dafür, dass die Hände der Peiniger verdorren, und er pflegt selbst den Gemarterten, sodass er vollkommen gesundet, ‚als ober nie wunt wer worden' (HL: 309, 10). Die Schöpferkraft kommt

---

[23] Siehe z.B. Io 9, 3 und Mc 8, 22-26. Vgl. später auch seinen Tod, bei dem er sich kreuzesförmig niederlegt.
[24] Vergleichbare Beobachtungen machen Bachorski / Klinger (1999: 125): ‚Mit aller Gewalt wird die Sprache der Macht auf den Körper geschrieben, der jedoch gerade in diesem gewalttätigen Zugriff nicht nur seine Integrität bewahrt, sondern eine neue transzendent anmutende Qualität bekommt, in der das selige Leben nach dem Tode im himmlischen Paradies aufscheint'. Vgl. auch Bachorski / Klinger 2002.

am Schluss vom *Märterbuch* und *Der Heiligen Leben* auch dort zum tragen, wo am dürren Baum, an dem Pantaleon schließlich hingerichtet wird, vom Märtyrerblut süße und reiche Früchte sprießen. Lilien und Rosen wachsen zwischen seinen Wurzeln.[25] Die Eigenschaften Gottes als alles überragender Schöpfer und Heiler gelangen dadurch in den Vordergrund. Konrads von Würzburg *Pantaleon* und die *Elsässische Legenda Aurea* erzählen hier anders, erwähnen an dieser Stelle keinen dürren, sondern einen kräftigen, grünenden Baum. Er trägt nach der Hinrichtung Pantaleons explizit neue Früchte im Überfluss (KvW: 2105-06), da das als Milch fließende Blut des Märtyrers seine Wurzeln begießt. Die Aussage erhält hier aber eine andere Nuance, da die Ereignisse sich immer wieder auf eine weitere Bedeutungsebene hin öffnen: Die Fruchtbarkeit ist hier lesbar als eine Anspielung auf die Fruchtbarkeit des Christentums, das in der Folge prosperiert. So drängen die Menschen aufgrund des Baumwunders in Scharen an diesen Ort, um es zu sehen und die Heiligkeit des Märtyrers anzuerkennen (KvW: 2113-17). Die sichtbare Heil- und Schöpferkraft Gottes wird auf diese Weise mit der Entstehung und Verbreitung des Christentums parallelisiert. In allen Erzählungen wird die Polysemie zu einem Charakteristikum der Christen und des Christentums. So scheint hinter den Phänomenen der Welt für sie immer noch eine andere, heilsträchtige und für den Blick des Unwissenden und Ungläubigen verborgene Wirklichkeit auf.

Sprechen und Handeln
Wie steht es im Vergleich dazu mit der verbalen Verkündigung des Glaubens und der Machtdurchsetzung durch Überzeugung (Lucke 2014: 338)? Deutlich wurde, dass die Sanktionen es ermöglichen, sichtbare Zeichen Gottes in der Welt zu setzen und die Kraftverhältnisse offenzulegen. Sie verhelfen dem Christentums mittels des physischen Ausweises von Heil und Heiligung zu einer neuen Öffentlichkeit (Till 2003: 1306). Pantaleon – so lässt sich festhalten – setzt durch seine Wunder und sein Leiden Prozesse der Verkündigung des Christentums in Gang. In Konrads *Pantaleon* entfaltet sich jedoch auch der Dialog zwischen dem Kaiser und Pantaleon. So ergeben sich die Foltern aus dem Glaubensbekenntnis Pantaleons und dem Streitgespräch zwischen dem Kaiser und Pantaleon, das durch Argumente keine Lösung erzielt (vgl. KvW: 1194-95).

Präsent ist vor allem die Praktik des Gebets, da dieses seit Beginn der *conversio* Pantaleons für die Heilungen entscheidend ist. Auch die Rettung des wiederholt Gepeinigten basiert auf dem Gebet zu Gott. Es ermöglicht die Entfaltung der

---

[25] Damit zeugt noch sein Tod von einem Wunder in der Welt, welches metonymisch auf seine Wundertaten als Nothelfer verweist. Siehe zur Typologie mirakulöser Nachwirkungen Bachorski / Klinger (1999: 124-25).

Wunder und Heilungen, ist dann als Antwort auf das Übel, ja als Gegengewalt der Christen ausnahmslos wirksam. Pantaleon bittet zuletzt, Christus möge seinen reuigen Schergen die Sünden vergeben, sie zur Umkehr bewegen und all jene, die seine Leiden ehren, dazu bringen, sich von den Sünden abzuwenden, und er möge allen barmherzig sein, die ihn aufgrund seines Martyriums anrufen. Durch die vorgeführten Wiederholungen dieser Praxis der Anrufung Gottes ‚schleift' sich ein Vorgang ein, der sich in Prolog und Epilog wiederholt: Sie heben den Nutzen des Gebets zu Gott und den Heiligen hervor und propagieren damit auch dessen Praxis.

Am Ende finden Pantaleons Anrufungen eine göttliche Antwort: Gottes Stimme verkündet, dass Pantaleon das Erbetene auch erhalten solle. Alle Kranken und Schwachen, Notleidenden und Armen, die Pantaleon darum anrufen, sollen seinen Trost und seine Hilfe bekommen (KvW: 2043-46). Pantaleon werde die Krone des Martyriums erhalten und in Gottes Reich eingehen. Der Übertritt in das Jenseits, die Erhöhung Pantaleons (vgl. KvW: 2052-55, vgl. auch 1707) sowie die künftige Nothelferfunktion entziehen sich der Wiedergabe. Sie sind Glaubenssache, können daher nicht gezeigt und bewiesen, sondern nur gesagt werden. Kurz vor Pantaleons Tod vollendet die ‚reine' (KvW: 2073) und für alle hörbare (‚gemeine' [KvW: 2074]) Stimme Gottes die Prozesse der Erzählung. Gott verleiht dem Heiligen in seiner Rede den Status eines im Himmel Gekrönten – so wie der römische Kaiser in der Welt eine Krone trägt, und doch ohne den christlichen Glauben hilflos ist. Die dichotomisch angelegten Relationen kehren sich also deutlich um: Der zu Beginn noch mächtige Kaiser wird entmachtet, sodass letztlich Pantaleon zum Richter und Verfolger (‚durehtere' [KvW: 2066]) der ‚tiuvel' (KvW: 2067) und selbst zum Strafenden des Bösen wird. Sein gottgegebener Status ist Pantaleon auf ewig garantiert, Maximianus hingegen hat seine Stellung lediglich auf Zeit und ohne letztgültige Autorität inne; sein Wort, mit dem er Sanktionen anordnet und die Christen ins Verderben führen will, erweist sich vollends als kraftlos.

Nachwirkungen

Die Sanktionen erweisen sich als Auslöser für eine Welle von Ereignissen: Das Christentum prosperiert dank der Sanktionen des Kaisers und Pantaleons Wirken immer mehr, das Negative wendet sich ins Positive, aus der Destruktion erwachsen ewiger Lohn, Leben, Unversehrtheit, Hoffnung. Die Sanktionen, welche Pantaleon zur Huldigung der Götter oder in die Vernichtung drängen sollen, strafen die böswilligen Zuschauer, welche statt Pantaleon in großer Zahl (‚Fvnf hvndert man' [KvW: 1638]) vom sich selbständig machenden Folterrad zermalmt werden.

Insofern bewirken die Sanktionen anderes als intendiert. Auch die Hinrichtung Pantaleons ist diesen Logiken geschuldet, da diese neues Leben hervorbringt.

Die Sanktionen führen letztlich zur Umdeutung des menschlichen Leidens, zur Heiligung des Märtyrers, der die Krönung im Reich Gottes erwirbt und damit wiederum in Opposition zum Kaiser gestellt wird und in Analogie zu Christus. Und so wandelt die Sanktion letztlich nicht nur die Märtyrer und die Versehrten, sondern auch die Umstehenden, die Zuschauer, da sie zur *conversio* anregt (KvW: 1486-92, 1116–20). Sogar die Schächer lassen sich zuletzt taufen (KvW: 2128). Die Anweisung, den Körper Pantaleon mit dem Holz des Baums zu verbrennen und alle Anzeichen des Heiligen zu vernichten, führen die Schergen schon nicht mehr aus – sie sind längst Teil des prosperierenden Christentums, haben sich bekehrt und lassen sich mit dem Taufwasser reinigen. Damit wird implizit deutlich, dass die römische, als tot bezeichnete Religion sich überlebt hat, da das Christentum immer mehr Anhänger findet.

Die Erzählung zielt – laut Prolog – darauf ab, das Christentum durch die Leiden und Wunder des Pantaleon offenbar werden zu lassen (KvW: 53-54). Das gilt auch für die Zeit der Abfassung: Der Autor definiert das Handeln des Heiligen in seiner Vorrede als vorbildlich und damit nachahmenswert (,bilde' [KvW: 24]), die Erzählung als gutes Beispiel, als ,Bischaft ze reinen tugenden' (KvW: 6), woraus sich ableiten lässt, dass der Rezipient Pantaleons Tugenden nachahmen und damit das Vorbild in neuem Kontext aktualisieren soll (KvW: 1-25).[26] Konrad regt zudem an, Pantaleon in seiner Funktion als Nothelfer anzurufen, da der Heilige den treuen Christen dann Trost und Hilfe zukommen lasse und das Leid vertreibe (vgl. KvW: 2154–58). Das korrespondiert mit dem Ausgang der Erzählung: Die Rede Gottes versichert den Menschen das Heil des Märtyrers im Jenseits (KvW: 2056-72). Die Märtyrerlegende verfügt somit in der Rahmung über rhetorische Strategien, welche die Rezipienten von der Wahrheit und der Wirksamkeit christlicher Nachfolge und Anrufung überzeugen sollen (Knape 2003: 874). Diese erzählten Prozesse und die Publikumsanreden werden somit zum Teil einer Persuasionsstrategie, die verbal auf einen ,Wechsel von einem mentalen Zustand in einen anderen' abzielen, und die persuasive Handlung zielt darauf ab, einen Bewusstseinszustand der Ungewissheit oder des Zweifels in die Gewissheit zu überführen.

Die Sanktionen initiieren folglich die Erniedrigung des Kaisers durch das Christentum, die letztlich auch durch die Zerstörung seiner Götzen an den Tag

---

[26] Bachorski / Klinger (1999: 103) (mit Verweis auf Jolles [1974: 30; 35; 36]) zufolge lässt sich als ein generelles Postulat der Märtyrerlegenden festhalten. Es ergibt sich daraus eine Logik Verkettung, da die Passion Jesu und das Postulat der Nachfolge Christi den Märtyrer zur *imitatio* drängt und auch der Rezipient zur *imitatio* Christi und des Märtyrers aufgerufen ist.

tritt (KvW: 1816-43). Konrad gestaltet in seiner ausführlichen Erzählung die Machtlosigkeit des Kaisers besonders breit aus. Die Anordnungen des Imperators tragen nicht weit. In seiner Einflusslosigkeit steigert sich sein Zorn, wenn die Foltern scheitern, sodass er tobt und nach neuen Maßnahmen sucht. Die Sanktionen erscheinen mehr und mehr als Rachehandlungen des Kaisers, wodurch er sich in einem Bereich außerhalb der Regeln der Rechtsprechung und jenseits ihrer Norm und Ratio bewegt. Der Verlauf der Handlung zeigt jedoch, dass Maximianus selbst in dieser Rage über das Leben der Christen wie des Protagonisten keinesfalls verfügt. Die weltlichen Sanktionen fallen vielmehr auf ihren Urheber zurück, weil er im Rahmen der eigenen beschränkten Handlungsmaximen und zugleich in der Maßlosigkeit der Affekte gefangen ist. Der Zorn des Kaisers zeugt von seiner Hilflosigkeit, welche noch akzentuiert wird, als ein Erdbeben die Götzenfiguren des Kaisers zerstören und dadurch entwerten kann (KvW: 1816-43).

Die Sanktionen ziehen auf unvorhergesehene Weise weitere Kreise, denn sie führen zur Missionierung des Volkes und zu weiteren Martyrien. So lässt der Kaiser 1000 Bekehrte töten (KvW: 1501). Die Strafen und Verfolgungen dehnen die Heiligkeit damit auf jene Menschen aus, welche die Wunder wahrnehmen. Insofern führen sie intradiegetisch zu einer *imitatio* wie sie im Rahmentext propagiert wird und bieten dem Rezipienten ein Vorbild. Der gewandelte Märtyrer kann als Vorbild für einen Sinneswandel, für eine *conversio* dienen (Knape 2003: 874-77). Konrads Text führt damit eine Rhetorik der Persuasion durch Zeichen und Worte vor: Durch die Sanktionen und die Wunder bekehrt sich in der Erzählung das Volk, sodass die Vorgänge als Vorbild – ein Negativbeispiel wird mit dem Kaiser gleich mitgeliefert – für eine Glaubenskonsolidierung der Rezipienten gelten dürfen. Der solche Ideale verbreitende Text leitet die Notleidenden dazu an, es Pantaleon in der Nachfolge Christi je auf ihre Weise nachzutun, ihr Leiden zu deuten und ihn und Gott im Gebet um Hilfe zu bitten. Der Text partizipiert – weil er auch als Vermittler fungiert und persuasive Funktionen übernimmt – partiell an den Eigenschaften des Heiligen. Der Protagonist, wie die Legende, welche von dem Vorbild und Beispiel christlicher Tugend berichten, werden zu siegreichen Verkündern des Christentums. Sie zeugen von der Fülle der Macht der Nachfolge Christi.

Fazit
Sanktionen dienen der Durchsetzung von Normen, welche von ihren Kontexten abhängig sind. Märtyrererzählungen blicken auf die zeitlich weit zurückliegende Situation der Christenverfolgungen zurück, in der die Normen des Christentums dem römischen Rechts- und Glaubenssystem gegenüberstehen. In der untersuchten Pantaleonlegende werden dabei paradoxale Machtgefüge deutlich. Maximianus

besitzt die Befehlsgewalt, Sanktionen zu verfügen, um weltliche Normen nach römischem Recht durchzusetzen. Er agiert im Namen der Götter, deren Kult er durchsetzen will. Als Strafgewalt sind die Sanktionen des Kaisers jedoch affektgeleitet, funktions- und zwecklos, gliedern den Märtyrer keineswegs in das Gefüge des römischen Rechtssystems ein, sondern stoßen damit gegenteilige Effekte an. Maximianus' Sanktionen fallen letztlich auf ihn zurück. Er fährt trotz aller Wunder – welche bereits viele Menschen bekehrt haben – fort, die christliche Religion gewaltsam zu bekämpfen. Zwar dezimiert Maximianus die Christen durch Verfolgungen und Hinrichtungen, doch ihr Blut wird zur Schöpfer- und Erlöserkraft des Christentums. So ermöglicht die Folter die Konformität des Märtyrers mit Christus und regt andere dazu an, dem Märtyrer und damit auch Christus nachzufolgen. Die Sanktionen münden somit in einen christlichen Sieg über die Peiniger, den Durchbruch der Transzendenz in der Immanenz: Gott hinterlässt durch die Sanktionen des Kaisers seine sichtbaren Spuren in der Welt. Aus der Destruktion der Sanktion erwächst letztlich die *aedificatio*.

Der sanktionierte Körper des Märtyrers wird letztlich zum ‚Schlachtfeld' zwischen Gott und seinen Widersachern. Die Straf- und Marterszenen haben gemeinsam, dass sie die Wirkungen der normativen Systeme an der Figur des Märtyrers, hier Pantaleons, abbilden. Das deformierte ‚System' des römischen Reichs schlägt sich in der Entstellung und Zerstörung der Körper christlicher Märtyrer nieder, welche durch Gott aufgehoben werden. Beobachtbar ist, dass sich dies auf den ‚Corpus Christi' auswirkt, d.h. die Schar der Christen: Sie wird unaufhaltsam größer. Die Destruktion der Strafe löst einen konstruktiven Prozess aus. Den in der Welt Mächtigen entgleitet dadurch ihre Macht, sie erreichen ihre Ziele nicht. Das ‚unterdrückte', versteckte Christentum bricht sich gerade durch die Sanktionen unaufhaltsam, durch Gott mächtig und ‚revolutionär' seinen Weg und wird aus der Sicht des Erzählers retrospektiv als immer wieder neu durchgesetzte Norm geschildert. Es wird sichtbar.

Vergleicht man Konrads *Pantaleon* mit den Versionen der Sammlungen des *Märterbuchs* oder *Der Heiligen Leben*, so wird deutlich, dass in ersterer die Erzählung der Sanktionen durch Monologe und Dialoge, d.h. vor allem Pantaleons Gebete und Reden zu Gott und dessen Antworten (handelnd oder in direkter Rede), ergänzt und erweitert werden. Das Wort, das Gebet, erhält dadurch einen höheren Stellenwert. So wird dem Leid und der Gewalt in den Wunderheilungen und Folterszenen das sehr viel einflussreichere Gebet entgegengesetzt und Gott angerufen, Gebrechen zu heilen und Leben zu schenken. Er muss am Schluss sogar gebeten werden, den Tod überhaupt zuzulassen, die Kraft der Regeneration zu unterbrechen. Pantaleon entgegnet der Unbill der Welt – der würgenden Natter und den unfähigen Ärzten sowie den Sanktionen des Kaisers Maximianus – das Wort des Gebets und die Machtfülle des christlichen Gottes als überlegene und setzt seine Normen durch. Prolog und Epilog konturieren Pantaleon überdies als Fürbitter, als Bote zu Gott, als Vertreiber des Unglücks. Aus der Kette der Ereignisse der Erzählung und der Argumentationsstrategien ergibt sich, dass sich das Wort als letzte kraftvolle Antwort auf jegliche Sanktionen und Unglücksfälle erweist. Die Erzählung des Martyriums, welche letztlich darin mündet, die Hörer zu ermuntern, sich in der Not im Gebet an Pantaleon zu wenden, wird selbst Teil dieser Strategien. Analog zur Figur des Pantaleon kann man dem Text letztlich auch die Funktion zusprechen, als Mittler zwischen den Menschen und Gott zu fungieren. Er wird zu einer Anleitung, Tugenden nachzuahmen und Hilfe bei Gott und dem Heiligen zu finden. Dadurch, dass die Pantaleonlegende retrospektiv aus der Sicht der Zeit einer institutionalisierten und konsolidierten Christenheit erzählt, wird dessen endgültiger Sieg vorausgesetzt. Vor diesem Hintergrund lassen sich die Sanktionen als Initialpunkt für Prozesse der Verkündigung und Vermittlung christlicher Normen auffassen, die sich bis in die Gegenwart des Pro- und Epilogs als siegreich und gültig erweisen.

Zitierte Literatur

Primärliteratur

Aurelius Augustinus, *Contra adimantum Manichaei discipulum*. Hg. von Jacques Paul Migne, Patrologia Latina, 42 (Paris: Migne, 1841), S. 169

Der Heiligen Leben. Hg. von Margit Brand, 2 Bde, Texte und Textgeschichte, 44; 51 (Tübingen: Niemeyer, 1996-2004)

Konrad von Würzburg, *Pantaleon*. Hg., übersetzt und mit Anmerkungen versehen von Thomas Neukirchen, Texte des späten Mittelalters und der frühen Neuzeit, 45 (Berlin: Erich Schmidt, 2008)

Das Märterbuch: Die Klosterneuburger Handschrift 713. Hg. von Erich Gierach, Deutsche Texte des Mittelalters, 32 (Berlin: Weidmann, 1928)

Sekundärliteratur

Bachorski, Hans-Jürgen und Judith Klinger. 1999. 'Religiöse Leitbilder und erzählerisches Spiel: zur mittelalterlichen Legende', in *Literatur als religiöses Handeln?*, hg. von Karl-Erich Grözinger und Jörg Rüpke, Religion, Kultur, Gesellschaft, 2 (Berlin: Berlin-Verlag Spitz), S. 99-133

—. 2002. 'Körper-Fraktur und herrliche Marter. Zu mittelalterlichen Märtyrerlegenden', in *Körperinszenierungen in mittelalterlicher Literatur: Kolloquium am Zentrum für Interdisziplinäre Forschung der Universität Bielefeld (18. bis 20. März 1999)*, hg. von Klaus Ridder und Otto Langer, Körper, Zeichen, Kultur, 11 (Berlin: Weidler), S. 309-33

Bergjan, Silke-Petra und Beaf Näf (Hg.). 2014. *Märtyrerverehrung im frühen Christentum: Zeugnisse und kulturelle Wirkungsweisen*, Wege zur Geschichtswissenschaft (Stuttgart: Kohlhammer)

Christen, Eduard. 1992. 'Martyrium III/2. Systematisch-theologisch', in *Theologische Realenzyklopädie*, hg. von Gerhard Krause und Gerhard Müller, XXII (Berlin: de Gruyter), S. 212-20

Drews, Wolfram und Heike Schlie (Hg.). 2011. *Zeugnis und Zeugenschaft: Perspektiven aus der Vormoderne*, Trajekte (Paderborn: Fink)

Feistner, Edith. 1995. *Historische Typologie der deutschen Heiligenlegende des Mittelalters von der Mitte des 12. Jahrhunderts bis zur Reformation*, Wissensliteratur im Mittelalter, 20 (Wiesbaden: Reichert)

Foucault, Michel. 1977. *Überwachen und Strafen. Die Geburt des Gefängnisses*, übersetzt von Walter Seitter, Suhrkamp-Taschenbücher Wissenschaft, 184 (Frankfurt a.M.: Suhrkamp)

Fuhrmann, Sebastian. 2012. 'Leben verlieren und Leben finden: Nachfolge und Martyrium in den Evangelien', in *Martyriumsvorstellungen in Antike und Mittelalter: leben oder sterben für Gott?*, hg. von Sebastian Fuhrmann und Regina Grundmann, Ancient Judaism and Early Christianity, 80 (Leiden: Brill), S. 167-90

Gerlitz, Peter. 1992. 'Martyrium I: Religionsgeschichte', in *Theologische Realenzyklopädie*, hg. von Gerhard Krause und Gerhard Müller, XXII (Berlin: de Gruyter), S. 197-202

Hartung, Gerald. 1998. 'Strafe II.', in *Historisches Wörterbuch der Philosophie*, hg. von Joachim Ritter unter Mitwirkung von mehr als 700 Fachgelehrten in Verbindung mit Günther Bien et al, X (Basel: Schwabe), S. 218-26

Henze, Barbara. 1997. 'Märtyrer, Martyrium', in *Lexikon für Theologie und Kirche*, begründet von Michael Buchberger, 3. völlig neu bearbeitete Auflage, hg. v. Walter Kasper, VI (Freiburg: Herder), S. 1436-41

Hörner, Petra. 2003. 'Spiritualisierung und Konkretisierung des Martyriumsgedankens in der deutschen Literatur des Mittelalters', *Euphorion*, 97: 327-48

Hühn, Helmut. 1998. 'Strafe I', in *Historisches Wörterbuch der Philosophie*, hg. von Joachim Ritter unter Mitwirkung von mehr als 700 Fachgelehrten in Verbindung mit Günther Bien et al, X (Basel: Schwabe), S. 208-18

Jackson, Timothy R. 1972. 'Konrad von Würzburg's Legends: Their Historical Context and the Poet's Approach to his Material', in *Probleme mittelhochdeutscher Erzählformen: Marburger Colloquium 1969*, hg. von Peter F. Ganz und Werner Schröder (Berlin: E. Schmidt), S. 197-213

—. 1983. *The Legends of Konrad von Würzburg: Form, Content, Function*, Erlanger Studien, 45 (Erlangen: Palm und Enke)

Jolles, André. 1974. *Einfache Form:. Legende, Sage, Mythe Rätsel, Spruch, Kasus, Memorabile, Märchen, Witz*. 5. Auflage, Konzepte der Sprach- und Literaturwissenschaft, 15 (Tübingen: Niemeyer)

Kiening, Christian. 2004. 'Gewalt und Heiligkeit. Mittelalterliche Texte in anthropologischer Perspektive', in *Wahrnehmen und Handeln: Perspektiven einer Literaturanthropologie*, hg. von Wolfgang Braungart , Klaus Ridder und Friedmar Apel, Bielefelder Schriften zu Linguistik und Literaturwissenschaft, 20 (Bielefeld: Aisthesis), S. 19-39

Knape, Joachim. 2003. 'Persuasion', in *Historisches Wörterbuch der Rhetorik*, hg. von Gert Ueding. Redaktion: Gregor Kalivoda und Franz-Hubert Robling, VI (Tübingen: Niemeyer), S. 874–907

Koch, Elke. 2008. 'Formen und Bedingungen von Sprachgewalt in Katharinenlegende und -spiel', in *Blutige Worte: Internationales und interdisziplinäres Kolloquium zum Verhältnis von Sprache und Gewalt in Mittelalter und Früher Neuzeit*, hg. von Jutta Eming und Claudia Jarzebowski, Berliner Mittelalter- und Frühneuzeitforschung, 4 (Göttingen: V & R Unipress), S. 15-30

Köpf, Ulrich 1997. 'Passionsfrömmigkeit', in *Theologische Realenzyklopädie*, hg. von Gerhard Krause und Gerhard Müller, XXVII (Berlin: de Gruyter), S. 722-64

Kraß, Andreas. 2008. 'Der heilige Eros des Märtyrers: eine höfische Georgslegende des deutschen Mittelalters', in *Tinte und Blut. Politik, Erotik und Poetik des Martyriums*, hg. von Andreas Kraß und Thomas Frank (Frankfurt a.M.: Fischer Taschenbuch Verlag), S. 143-68

Lucke, Doris M. 2014. 'Norm und Sanktion', in *Wörterbuch der Soziologie*, hg. von Günter Endruweit, Gisela Trommsdorff und Nicole Burzan, 3. Auflage (Konstanz/München: UVK Verlagsgesellschaft), S. 338-42

Mertens Fleury, Katharina. 2006. *Leiden lesen. Bedeutungen von compassio um 1200 und die Poetik des Mit-Leidens im Parzival Wolframs von Eschenbach*, Scrinium Friburgense, 21 (Berlin/New York: De Gruyter)

Mitchell, Jolyon. 2012. *Martyrdom: A Very Short Introduction* (Oxford: Oxford University Press)

Neukirchen, Thomas. 2008. Siehe oben unter Konrad von Würzburg

Rosenfeld, Hellmut. 1982. *Legende*, 4. verbesserte und vermehrte Auflage, Sammlung Metzler, 9 (Stuttgart: Metzler)

Scheuer, Manfred. 1997. 'Märtyrer, Martyrium', in *Lexikon für Theologie und Kirche*, begründet von Michael Buchberger, 3. völlig neu bearbeitete Auflage, hg. v. Walter Kasper, VI (Freiburg: Herder), S. 1441-44

Slusser, Michael. 1992. 'Martyrium III/1. Christentum (Neues Testament/Alte Kirche)', in *Theologische Realenzyklopädie*, hg. von Gerhard Krause und Gerhard Müller, XXII (Berlin: de Gruyter), S. 207-12

Schirrmeister, Albert. 2000. 'Folter und Heiligung in der Legenda Aurea: Frühchristliche Martern und spätmittelalterliche Körperkonzepte', in *Das Quälen des Körpers: Eine historische Anthropologie der Folter*, hg. von Peter Burschel, Götz Distelrath und Sven Lembke (Köln: Böhlau), S. 133-49

Scholz, Oliver und Heinz-Günther Schöttler. 2009. 'Zeugnis', in *Historisches Wörterbuch der Rhetorik*, hg. von Gert Ueding. Redaktion: Gregor Kalivoda und Franz-Hubert Robling, IX (Tübingen: Niemeyer), S. 1511-29

Schulmeister, Rolf. 1971. *Aedificatio und Imitatio: Studien zur intentionalen Poetik der Legende und Kunstlegende*, Geistes- und sozialwissenschaftliche Dissertationen, 16 (Hamburg: Lüdke)

Stridde, Christine. 2011. 'Pantaleon', in *Deutsches Literatur-Lexikon. Das Mittelalter: Autoren und Werke nach Themenkreisen und Gattungen*, hg. v. Wolfgang Achnitz, II (Berlin: de Gruyter), S. 1175-77

Strohschneider, Peter. 2000. 'Inzest-Heiligkeit: Krise und Aufhebung der Unterschiede in Hartmanns Gregorius', in *Geistliches in weltlicher und Weltliches in geistlicher Literatur des Mittelalters*, hg. von Christoph Huber, Burghart Wachinger und Hans-Joachim Ziegeler (Tübingen: Niemeyer), S. 105-33

—. 2002. 'Georius miles – Georius martyr: Funktionen und Repräsentationen von Heiligkeit bei Reinbot von Durne', in *Literarische Leben: Rollenentwürfe in der Literatur des Hoch- und Spätmittelalters. Festschrift für Volker Mertens zum 65. Geburtstag*, hg. von Matthias Meyer und Hans-Jochen Schiewer (Tübingen: Niemeyer), S. 781-811

—. 2002b. 'Textheiligung: Geltungsstrategien legendarischen Erzählens im Mittelalter am Beispiel von Konrads von Würzburg "Alexius"', in *Geltungsgeschichten: Über die Stabilisierung und Legitimierung institutioneller Ordnungen*, hg. von Gert Melville und Hans Vorländer (Köln: Böhlau), S. 109-48

Till, Dietmar. 2003. 'Poetik', in *Historisches Wörterbuch der Rhetorik*, hg. von Gert Ueding. Redaktion: Gregor Kalivoda und Franz-Hubert Robling, VI (Tübingen: Niemeyer), S. 1304-07

Weigel, Sigrid. 2007. 'Schauplätze, Figuren, Umformungen. Zu Kontinuitäten und Unterscheidungen von Märtyrerkulturen', in *Märtyrer-Porträts: Von Opfertod, Blutzeugen und heiligen Kriegern*, hg. von Sigrid Weigel (München: W. Fink), S. 11-37

Wild, Cornelia. 2007. 'Corona aeternitatis – Der Wettstreit des Märtyrers (Tertullian)', in *Märtyrer-Porträts: Von Opfertod, Blutzeugen und heiligen Kriegern*, hg. von Sigrid Weigel (München: W. Fink), S. 71-73

Williams-Krapp, Werner. 1986. *Die deutschen und niederländischen Legendare des Mittelalters: Studien zu ihrer Überlieferungs-, Text- und Wirkungsgeschichte*, Texte und Textgeschichte, 20 (Tübingen: Niemeyer)

—. 1989. 'Pantaleon', in *Die deutsche Literatur des Mittelalters – Verfasserlexikon*. Begr. von Wolfgang Stammler, fortgeführt von Karl Langosch. 2., völlig neu bearbeitete Auflage unter Mitarbeit zahlreicher Fachgelehrter hg. von Kurt Ruh zusammen mit Gundolf Keil, Werner Schröder, Burghart Wachinger, Franz Josef Worstbrock. Redaktion: Christine Stöllinger-Löser, VII (Berlin/New York: De Gruyter), Sp. 290

German-language Articles
Abstracts

Râche Between 'Retribution for a Wrong Carried Out by the Victim' and 'Punishment': Semantic Game-playing in Rudolf von Ems' *Alexander*
[*râche* zwischen ‚Vergeltung eines Unrechts durch den Geschädigten' und ‚Strafe': Semantische Spielräume im *Alexander* Rudolfs von Ems]

Henrike Manuwald
Georg-August-Universität Göttingen

Responses to acts of violence play a central role in our understanding of the organization of societies. The conventional historiographical model is a progressive one, according to which primitive societies are characterized by individual responses of violent revenge, which can set off a chain reaction of further bloodshed. More developed societies, on the other hand, are attributed a transfer of judicial power to institutions. This progressive model – formulated most famously by René Girard (1972) – has, however, been criticized from the perspectives of ethnology and legal anthropology. The teleological development it expresses has been questioned with regard to both its linearity and the assumption that individual responses to violence are always beyond control. It has been argued that societies which lacked a centralized, institutional means of responding to conflict did not necessarily resort to actions of violent revenge, but often reacted in a more regulated manner.

One example of this is the so-called *Fehdewesen* [principle of feuding] of the Germanic Middle Ages, a regulated process of interaction between victim and culprit that meant the former had the right to enact revenge on the latter. Older scholarship tended to position the *Fehdewesen* in a process of linear development, arguing that the peace movement known as the *Landfriedensbewegung* – which occurred from the eleventh century on – was evidence of the gradual emergence of a state monopoly, which in turn led to the establishment of a public law of punishment. It was further argued that the notion of mediation between victim and culprit (*Täter-Opfer Ausgleich*) was increasingly replaced by a system of punishment focused solely on the perpetrator. In recent years, however, legal scholarship has developed a more differentiated picture: until the late Middle Ages, the German lands are characterized by the juxtaposition of different models of resolving conflict, with systems of revenge and institutional punishment existing concurrently.

This essay considers the existence of concurrent models of resolving conflict in Middle High German (MHG) narrative texts, with a particular focus on the semantic labelling of acts. Vitally, there is no MHG term that corresponds to the New High German (NHG) *Strafe* [punishment]. MHG *strâfe* is first attested in the thirteenth century, referring to verbal reprimand, and other terms (i.e. *zuht*, *pîn*, *buoze*) all have different and nuanced connotations. NHG *Rache* is conventionally translated as 'revenge', but MHG *râche* is used to refer both to acts of retribution carried out by the injured party and to more institutionalized instances of punishment. Due to its wide range of potential usages, *râche* (as well as its cognates) is therefore a particularly pertinent example for an exploration of the ways in which meaning can be fixed contextually. It is investigated here in the context of the thirteenth-century *Alexander* of Rudolf von Ems. Despite the fact that Rudolf's material – the life of Alexander the Great – is taken from classical antiquity, it is also largely 'medievalized' to correspond with contemporary social order and thus offers a window onto the thirteenth-century practice and understanding of responses to violent acts.

Two main aspects are considered through close readings of selected passages, which form the basis for a final discussion about the extent of the legal character of *râche*: 1. legitimate and illegitimate *râche*; 2. *râche* when carried out by God. An exploration of the legitimacy of *râche* suggests that a distinction is drawn between over-hasty acts of revenge guided by subjective emotions and acts of revenge that have the character of punishment, even if they are carried out directly by the injured party. This is illustrated by the example of Dimnus' conspiracy against Alexander. Dimnus plans this conspiracy as *râche*, but it is 'revenge' not for an objective wrong but rather an injury that has been felt subjectively. Alexander's response – the beheading of Dimnus – is also *râche*, but takes on quasi-legal characteristics; although Alexander is the injured party, he also performs the role of judge, demonstrating how *râche* and law can overlap.

The intersection of the roles of judge and injured party is also apparent when God is involved in acts of *râche*. Although the plot is set in an explicitly pre-Christian era, the active presence of God is often felt, not least because Alexander plays a key role in the course of salvation history and can therefore function as a tool of God. The role of God in acts of revenge can be traced back to the Old Testament.

Here, when God is involved directly in responding to an injury perpetrated against him, words with the roots *nqm* are used; in the Vulgate these terms are normally reproduced as *vindicta* or *ultio*, words conventionally translated into NHG as *Rache* (although *Vergeltung* [retribution] might be more appropriate). In these instances God undertakes retribution in the role of a kingly judge, and his actions can be interpreted as jusitifed punishment. In *Alexander*, however, God's 'personal' involvement is sometimes stressed (his 'person', of course, being inseparable from the principles represented by him). Moreover, in instances when God's *râche* is performed by men, discrepancies can occur between subjective and objective motivation; that is, the relationship between God and the person unwittingly carrying out his *râche* is problematized, because the agent has his own motivation. On the whole, the analysis of selected passages shows that an effort is made in the text to differentiate between different kinds of *râche* and thereby create a hierarchy of models of resolving conflict. Whether *râche* is understood positively or negatively seems to depend primarily not on who carries it out, but rather on the character of the original act of violence committed; the most important question of legitimacy is whether retribution occurs for an objective wrong. In this sense, it is unimportant whether the person carrying out the *râche* is personally affected by the crime committed – and this leads to a blurring of the distinction between mediation between victim and culprit (*Täter-Opfer Ausgleich*) and judicial order. In *Alexander*, acts of punishment sometimes seem institutionalized, but at other times are shown to be legitimate even when separate from formal legal processes. The terminological overlap between revenge and legal punishment demonstrated by the word *râche* in this text finds parallels in the medieval Latin terms *ultio* and *vindicta*. In the *Codex Iustinianus*, for instance, the formulation *leges ulciscuntur* [the laws take revenge] is used to signify retribution free of personal emotion.

On this basis a link can be traced back to Girard's argument that a legal trial can be seen as a kind of public revenge, albeit one that restricts revenge to a single act of retribution. Although we need to be careful to contextualize and historicize the distinction between private and public, there is no general way of summing up the relationship between revenge and legal processes. The close textual analysis of Rudolf's *Alexander* shows how for its implied recipients there is no basic contradiction between *râche* and law; rather, *râche* and its cognates are always contextually determined.

Despite the blurred lines between *râche* and law, the diachronic development that eventually separated the two must not be ignored. This is clarified by a concluding examination of the trial of Genelun as told in two German Roland texts: the *Rolandslied* (mid twelfth century) and Stricker's *Karl* (early to mid thirteenth century). In the earlier text, Charlemagne angrily insists on his desire for *râche* for Genelun's betrayal, yet also voices his intention of a legal judgement; this is, then, the justified anger of a ruler, which is even legitimate when he is personally affected. In Stricker's *Karl*, Charlemagne says explicitly that he does not want to act against Genelun 'nâch vîentlîcher râche' [by taking revenge in a hostile way], but demands that he should be judged by princes in the presence of his family. The distinction between the two versions is not so much found in the semantics of *râche*, but rather in the assessment of personal involvement. Much as in Rudolf's *Alexander*, its near contemporary, Stricker's *Karl* shows that *râche* is not automatically connected with personal enmity, but must always be determined contextually.

* * *

Sinner, Preacher, Poet: Role-play in Oswald von Wolkenstein's *Song of Confession*
[Sünder, Prediger, Dichter: Rollenspiele im *Beichtlied* Oswalds von Wolkenstein]

Andreas Kraß
Humboldt-Universität zu Berlin

Foucault uses the image of the panopticon – the prison building designed with a watch-tower at the centre that has a complete view into all cells – in order to illustrate modern disciplinary society. This image can also be an illuminating point of entry to the *Beichtlied* [*Song of Confession*] of the Tirolean poet Oswald von Wolkenstein (c. 1376-1445). In this song, Oswald stages himself as a sinner, providing a full confession of his sins to priests and submitting himself to the disciplinary power of the church. Yet he also takes on the role of the poet, overseeing the catalogue of sins he has committed and 'disciplining' it into the complex strophic form of his song. The song is a play on punishment and poetry: the submissive qualities inherent in the role of the sinner contrast with and overlap the elevation of the self in the role of the poet.

Older scholarship interpreted the *Beichtlied* autobiographically as evidence that Oswald relinquished a worldly life and denied himself earthly pleasures in old age; a more recent study by Regina Toepfer, on the other hand, has suggested that the song is more ironic and self-conscious. According to Toepfer, Oswald plays in a deliberate manner with the contrast between his turbulent autobiography explored in other songs and the moral role of the preacher he assumes here. This essay works outwards from Toepfer's thesis and explores role-play in the song through close reading, adding a new focus on the way in which the speaking voice assumes not only the roles of sinner and preacher, but also that of poet.

The *Beichtlied* can be divided into five sections: 1. a penitent address to the priests to whom the speaker confesses (I, 1-8); 2. a detailed confession of sins (I, 9-V, 4); 3. a self-conscious thematization of the speaker as poet (VI, 5-12); 4. a summary of sins confessed (VI, 1-7); 5. a final address to priests (VI, 8-12). The construction of the song corresponds broadly with the ritual confession prayer or formula, which consists first of a statement of repentance, then a list of sins committed and then a prayer for forgiveness, yet importantly has a section of poetological reflection right at the centre. It is, therefore, constructed in a careful and deliberate manner, a fact further evidenced by the careful subdivision of individual strophes. The song is composed in the *canso* [*Kanzone*] form common to medieval German lyric, with each strophe divided into an *Aufgesang* consisting of two four-line *Stollen* and an *Abgesang* of one four-line *Stollen*. The division of the strophes corresponds here to the internal division of themes and focal points. At the start of the song the voice assumes the role of sinner. This role is characterized through explicit addresses to confessor priests and an emphasis on feelings of repentance, expressed particularly through asyndetic lists of adverbs. Yet the roleplay is already not straightforward, as is evidenced when the sinner states that he has dishonoured the sacrament of priestly investiture. The distinction between the speaker as sinner and the priest (whom he addresses) is broken down, and a certain rivalry becomes apparent, which is taken further when the speaker moves from the role of sinner to that of preacher.

The preaching role assumed by the speaker is made manifest in the confession of sins. The sins confessed are not personal ones; instead, the speaker sets out a complete and systematic catalogue of sins, and this totality suggests that this is an exemplary or a model confession, rather than the confession of an individual sinner. Sixty-four sins are confessed in total, divided into nine categories. Yet it is only after closer reading, aided by the summary of sins confessed at the end of the song, that an underlying systematic catechetical listing of sins becomes apparent. In the main catalogue, categories (such as sins against the Ten Commandments or the Seven Deadly Sins) are maintained but obscured through listing of sins in the wrong order, or combining individual ones in a relatively loose manner. Equally, it is only through close reading that it becomes clear that the sixty sins confessed correspond with the number of lines of the song (excluding the eight-line introduction) and that each category is restricted to one section (*Stollen*) of a strophe. The structural principles of the song are therefore based on a mixture of strict systematic patterning and variation, of clarity and obscurity.

An exploration of formal complexities of this kind points to the empirical role of the author outside the text, but the self-presentation of the voice as poet is also important. In the fifth strophe, the role of poet is differentiated from that of sinner and preacher through a distinction between 'saying' and 'singing', and a connection to God as creator is established through explicit references to the 'creation' of the song. Moreover, a bizarre mention of Bohemian geese, which most likely refers to the Hussites, breaks through the otherwise serious tone of the song, stressing the presence of the poet. It may perhaps even verge on blasphemy, for an implicit parallel is created between the speaker burning in spiritual love for God and the burning of heretics.

Oswald von Wolkenstein is a poet often characterized by the way in which he blurs the boundaries between truth and fiction, blending supposed autobiography with poetic utterance. Fictionality is signalled ironically in this song in the endless catalogue of sins and the statement that his comprehensive sinfulness is the reason that God has chosen the speaker as an effective preacher. In Hartmann's *Gregorius*, it is the greatest sinner who obtains the greatest mercy after performing the most extreme penance. Here, this sort of correlation is turned on its head to create a causal link between sinning, preaching and singing: the ability to sin leads to the ability to sing, and the humility of the sinner becomes the pride of the poet. Oswald – much like his near contemporary the Monk of Salzburg in his Marian song *Das Goldene Abc* – both employs and outdoes traditional forms to prove his own poetic skills, and subordinates himself to God the creator in order to reveal simultaneously his own creative powers as a poet. The way in which Oswald engages in roleplay in this song could perhaps point towards the changing conception of literary authorship in the late Middle Ages. On the one hand he acts as a medieval poet, using known forms and material and reshaping them for his own purpose; on the other, he gestures towards the Early Modern author, who emancipates himself from tradition with his poetic ambition, precarious roleplay and ironic interruption.

* * *

Bodily Use and Corporal (Dis)Order in the Depiction of Asceticism in the *Vita* of Elsbeth von Oye

[so enpfalle ich mir selber also gar, das ich aller meiner geliden ungewaltig wirden: Körpergebrauch, Kontrolle und Kontrollverlust in den Askeseschilderungen der *Vita* Elsbeths von Oye]

Björn Klaus Buschbeck
Stanford University

The *Vita* of Elsbeth of Oye, a Dominican nun of the fourteenth century from the convent Oetenbach near Zurich, provides some extreme examples of physical asceticism: the protagonist whips herself; she ties one nail-studded cross so that it presses into her hip, and another into her back; she wears rotting clothes and voluntarily exposes herself to the vermin and maggots which infest them. In the same way that penance and punishment both have an inherently transformative impetus, Elsbeth's actions aim to bring about a transformation of the self. Nonetheless, given that she is not particularly motivated by an awareness of her own sinfulness, her practices cannot be described as punitive or penitential in any narrow sense: the intended process of transformation is not corrective, but might instead be described as potentially transgressive – not just in the sense of being disturbingly radical, but also in the sense of aiming to go beyond the normal limitations of the human condition so as to share in Christ's divinity.

The notion of *imitatio Christi* forms the immediate context and framework for Elsbeth's practices. Whilst this is not in itself unusual, this *Vita* stands out for suggesting that self-inflicted pain is the only means through which Elsbeth is able to experience the divine presence. God insists that she must torture her own body and he withdraws from her whenever she feels unable to keep up her ascetic practices. The insistence on the satisfaction that God derives from Elsbeth's suffering is one of the more disturbing aspects of the text.

The article focuses on the role of Elsbeth body within the *Vita*. On the one hand, the body is a literary construct within a text that stands in a particular tradition and which has a particular communicative agenda. On the other hand, the text itself presents itself a life writing: as the biography of a real, historical individual, and, for all their severity, the practices described are not fundamentally different from those associated with contemporary figures such as Adelheid Langmann and Heinrich Seuse. However, whereas for other mystics asceticism is typically just one aspect of the spiritual life, for Elsbeth, there is no spiritual life without it. Her body is the medium through which religious experience and knowledge pass. It is the subject that inflicts pain; and it is the object which endures pain.

For Elsbeth, the infliction of pain on her own body becomes a means of self-empowerment and self-sanctification. She uses and transforms her own body to demonstrate an elect status – a stance which, when followed through to its logical conclusion, entails a sense of equality, or even identity, with the crucified saviour whose suffering she has successfully emulated. The transformative nature of her practices is evoked most strongly by the repeated deployment of two clusters of literary images: that of a seal being impressed into wax-like flesh, and that of the exchange of bodily fluids (blood and marrow). The references to the seal are not just literary metaphors – they also draw attention back to the nails that puncture Elsbeth's body. More radically, the flow of blood and marrow between Elsbeth and God serves to underscore the God's hunger for Elsbeth's suffering, whilst also suggesting an obliteration of the boundaries of self: as identity itself becomes fluid and exchangeable, union with the divine seems to be within reach.

Nonetheless, self-empowerment is only one side of the coin. Even as she harnesses the religious and literary authority resulting from her transformed identity, she is constantly on the brink of losing control: neither her mind nor her body is able permanently to bear the amount of physical pain required to perform a constant imitation of Christ. However, any interruption to her practices severs the contact with God and triggers a form of depression. A pattern of addiction unfolds, in which Elsbeth is trapped between the deficient nature of her own body and the need for extreme bodily sensations to keep up the religious experience. Those two aspects of her religious practice, control and loss of control, agency and passivity, are inextricably intertwined. This is shown most clearly when Elsbeth (actively) takes steps to relinquish control over her own body: for example, by tying up her own hands so that she will be forced (passively) to endure the torment of maggots. Furthermore, even the exchanges of bodily fluids can be read as testifying to the passivity of the protagonist who loses herself in the process.

This paradoxical interconnection of agency and passivity underlies the deployment of mirror imagery in the *Vita*. As Elsbeth is transformed into a passively reflected image of the divine archetype, she seems stripped of agency – yet had it not been for her determined pursuit of ascetic control of her own body, there would have been no transformation. Nonetheless, unlike many other medieval mystical texts, Elsbeth's *Vita* does not seek to resolve the paradox within a theoretical model, or to derive any general principles of good spiritual practice. Instead, the focus remains firmly on lived experienced and on the capacity of a particular body to endure suffering. The inner life of the protagonist and her capacity for personal transformation are entirely dependent on her body.

In her radical approach to the body, Elsbeth was unusual even within her own time, and, given the decreasing interest in ascetic practices ever since the fifteenth century, her *Vita* is likely to be perceived as disturbingly different in later periods. Nonetheless, the idea of the body as an instrument for achieving personal transformation continues to resonate in modern art and literature.

* * *

Punishment and Suffering in Martyrdom: Reflections on Konrad von Würzburg's *Pantaleon* [Strafen und Leiden im Martyrium: Überlegungen zu Konrads von Würzburg *Pantaleon*]

Katharina Mertens-Fleury
Universität Zürich

Most definitions of the term 'punishment' focus on the idea of a wrong that must somehow be put right. As such, punishment is tied to a particular legal, political and normative framework; it is within this framework that an appropriate process may be imposed on the culprit. Punishment will alter the status of the culprit insofar as it liberates him from the burden of guilt, but it may also leave tangible marks on his body, or even destroy this physical frame.

Martyrdom provides a challenge to conventional notions of punishment, given that the martyr and those who share his beliefs inevitably operate with a very different system of values to those upheld by the authorities responsible for sentencing him. This difference in perspective is fundamental to medieval accounts of early Christian martyrs who reject the polytheism of the Roman empire: the same stance or action may render an individual guilty in the eyes of the pagan authorities, but innocent and praiseworthy in the eyes of God, of other Christians within the text, and of the medieval narrator and readers. In this context, the term 'sanction' may usefully be invoked, given that its two meanings are almost diametrically opposed ('punishment' versus 'support' or 'approval').

In order to exemplify the complexities of the notion of punishment in relation to martyrdom, this article focuses on the legend of Pantaleon. Most attention is given to the version by Konrad von Würzburg, but with some reference to the shorter versions contained in the *Märterbuch*, in the *Elsässissche Legenda Aurea* and in the *Heiligen Leben*. The analysis covers (1) the divergent norms presented in the legend; (2) the importance of ambiguity and ambivalence; (3) the interplay of speech and action; and (4) the effects of the sanctions.

Religious difference (Christianity versus polytheism) is clearly a source of normative conflict within the legend. However, the fact that Pantaleon is a physician is also highly relevant. The point is not only that he is more successful than the pagan idols associated with medicine (Asclepius and Hippocrates), but also that his approach to the human body is fundamentally different from that of the Emperor: whilst Pantaleon is concerned with the preservation and improvement of health (e.g. by saving a boy who has been strangled by an adder/snake, or by restoring sight to a blind man), the Emperor does everything possible to destroy the physical frame of Pantaleon himself. In Konrad's version, Pantaleon is roasted; immersed in a bath of liquid lead, tied to a heavy stone and dropped in the sea; fed to the wild animals in the circus; and broken on the wheel. Other versions are even more extreme in their accounts of the torments inflicted. Nonetheless, all of these attempts to annihilate Pantaleon are doomed to failure: on every occasion, God spares him suffering and restores his body to its original state of integrity. The martyr's body is thus sanctioned in both senses: it is punished (by the Emperor), but also supported, honoured and affirmed (by God). In fact, martyrdom cannot be imposed on Pantaleon against his own will; in the end, he only dies by the sword because he has asked God to be allowed to join the ranks of the martyrs.

Whilst the sanctions are thus intrinsically ambivalent, the same may be said of other narrative features, including dialogic exchanges. When the Christians pray to God for an earthquake, this phenomenon is understood quite differently by the pagans – namely as a token of the wrath of their gods. When the Emperor kills some of Pantaleon's companions and then claims dishonestly to have sent them on a journey to another country, the central protagonist sees through the literal lie, but affirms its metaphorical truthfulness: the Emperor has indeed sent them on a journey (to heaven), and Pantaleon himself intends to follow them. Other examples provide further evidence for the importance of ambiguity in the construction of the legend.

Whilst the dual 'sanctioning' of Pantaleon's body provides the clearest demonstration of God's power in world, the spoken word is also important for the construction of a normative collision between Christians and Romans. The attempted torments are the direct result of Pantaleon's profession of the faith and of his disputation with the Emperor. The power of prayer is affirmed on numerous occasions, and at the end, the voice of God makes it clear that Pantaleon's prayers have been answered; that he will earn the crown of martyrdom (in contrast to the earthly crown worn by the Emperor) and that he will be able to offer help and healing all those who appeal to him (in contrast to the Emperor who is bent on destruction). However, God's voice also allocates a future punitive role to Pantaleon, who will be the judge and 'durehtere' [persecutor] of the devils. This completes the transformation of Pantaleon from culprit to sanctioning authority.

The Emperor's sanctions are presented as having long-term positive consequences for the Christian community: Pantaleon's virtuous mindset, combined with the miraculous interventions of God, encourage conversion amongst the onlookers, whilst the Emperor himself is diminished, together with the normative framework from which he derives his authority. Indeed, the fact that his repeated onslaughts on Pantaleon look more and more like a personal vendetta also serves to deprive the Roman legal system of legitimacy and credibility. This is consistent with the medieval perspective on pagan polytheism as a dead religion. Pantaleon's significance for the medieval audience is affirmed in a number of ways: he is not only a helper to whom the sick and needy can appeal, but also a model for imitation. In Konrad's prologue and epilogue, the exemplary nature of the martyr is foregrounded, and the narrative itself presented as a 'bischaft' [exemplary tale] for the recipients.

Index

Abelard, Peter 130-31, 134
ascetic practices 9-12, 137-39, 142-43, 155-71, 201-03

Barlaam und Josaphat 29
Bebel, Heinrich 117, 124-25
beheading, *see* capital punishment
Bracciolini, Poggio, *Liber facetiarum* 121-23

capital punishment 1, 3-4, 9-12, 14, 25, 95, 100 115-16, 122-26, 176-77, 184-85, 187, 189
    beheading 24, 95, 180, 182, 196
    hanging
Carolina (criminal code of 1532) 5
Catherine of Siena, *Dialogue* 144
chastity 100, 138-43
Chrétien de Troyes, *Le Conte du Graal* 49, 52, 59-60
Christina von Hane 14, 129-48
Codex Iustinianus 33
compassio 13, 157, 162
confession 3, 8, 13, 65-76, 129-34, 145, 198-200
contrition 6, 9-10, 67-68, 134

Dante, *Divine Comedy* 131, 144, 146
desire 9, 12-13, 80, 91, 103, 138-39, 141, 156, 160-61

Eckhart, Meister 160
Elsässische Legenda Aurea 179-82, 184-85, 189-90, 204
Elsbeth von Oye 14, 155-71, 201-03

ere 96. *See also* honour
execution, *see* capital punishment

fama 13, 96, 107-09
Fehdewesen (principle of feuding) 13, 19, 195
fine (monetary) 4-5, 103-05, 145
flagellation 143, 159, 170, 182
Fortunatus, *Life of St Radegund* 138-39
Foucault, Michel 1-2, 4, 8, 10-11, 65, 83, 85, 92, 175-76, 198
Fourth Lateran Council 6, 129, 145
    omnis utriusque sexus (decree) 6-8
Frey, Jakob, *Gartengesellschaft* 121-25

Girard, René 19, 33-34, 45-46, 195, 197
Gottfried von Strassburg, *Tristan* 140
Gratian, *Decretum* 33, 129, 134
    De penitentia 132-33

hanging, *see* capital punishment
Hartmann von Aue 50
    Gregorius 75, 200
    Iwein 45
Heiligen Leben 179-82, 184-85, 189-90, 204
Heinrich von Hesler, *Evangelium Nicodemi* 30
Hildegard of Bingen 136-37, 139, 145
honour 14, 23-24, 45, 49, 60, 70, 83, 95-109, 119. *See also ere, fama*
Huizinga, Johan 4
humiliation 7, 55, 80, 106, 108
humour 10, 115-26
Hus, Jan 74-76

imitatio Christi 12, 156-60, 162, 164, 168, 187-88, 201-03
incarceration 1, 4, 65, 79-84, 91, 118, 198

Kaiserchronik 28
Kantorowicz, Ernst 11
Katharinenthaler Schwesternbuch 159
Kirchhof, Hans Wilhelm, *Wendunmuth* 116, 124-26
Konrad von Würzburg, *Heinrich von Kempten* 55
  Pantaleon 14, 175-90, 203-05

Landfriedensbewegung (peace movement) 5-6, 19-20, 195
Langmann, Adelheid, *Gnadenvita* 159, 201
Legenda aurea, see *Elsässische Legenda Aurea*
Lindener, Michael, *Rastbüchlein* 116, 124-25

Mären (narrative genre) 95-97, 105-09, 116
Märterbuch 179-82, 184-85, 189-90, 204
martyrdom 8-9, 14-15, 143, 145-46, 175-90, 203-05
Mary, the Virgin 141, 146, 164, 200
Mechthild von Hackeborn 146
Mechthild von Magdeburg, *Flowing Light of the Godhead* 145, 160-61, 168
Monk of Salzburg, *Das Goldene Abc* 75, 200
Montanus, Martin, *Ander theil der Gartengesellschaft* 126
Muling, Adelphus 117
mutilation 11, 95, 121, 142-43, 176

Nibelungenlied 44, 47, 54
Nozick, Robert 43-44
omnis utriusque sexus (decree). see Fourth Lateran Council

Oswald von Wolkenstein 13, 65-94, 198-200
  Beichtlied 65-76, 198-200
  'Durch abenteuer tal und berg' (Kl 26) 79-80
  'Durch Barbarei, Arabia' (Kl 44) 89-92
  Lebenszeugnisse 79-89

pain 20, 79-80, 91-92, 116-17, 125, 129-48, 156-68, 178, 181, 201-03
  'proxy pain' 14, 131, 146
Pauli, Johannes, *Schimpf und Ernst* 115-18, 120-21, 123-25
penance, private 6-7, 129, 137, 142, 145; public 6-7, 145
performance art 170
Peter the Chanter 147
poena 131, 145, 175
prison, *see* incarceration
prostitution 98-100
purgatory 7, 9, 14, 129-31, 142-48

Quintus Curtius Rufus, *Historiae Alexandri Magni* 23, 27

râche (Middle High German term) 5-6, 13, 19-35, 44, 195-98. See also vengeance
revenge, *see* vengeance
Rolandslied 26, 32, 34-35, 197-98
Rosenplüt, Hans, *Spiegel und Igel* 96, 105, 107, 108
Rudolf von Ems, *Alexander* 13, 19-35, 195-98

Schwankbücher 14, 115-26
secret penance, *see* penance, private
self-harm 130-31, 143, 156-57, 161-67
Seuse, Heinrich 170, 201
  Vita 157, 159-60
shame 6, 96, 102, 108, 121, 139
slander 96-103, 142

Spaun, Claus, *Fünfzig Gulden Minnelohn* 96, 105-08
Der Spiegel 96, 107-08
strâfe (Middle High German term) 5, 20, 196
Stricker, Der, Karl 34-35, 197-98

Täter-Opfer Ausgleich (mediation between victim and culprit) 20, 22, 33, 195-97
Thomasin von Zerklaere, *Der welsche Gast* 35, 58
torture 1, 5, 10, 13, 24, 79-94, 117, 161, 170, 176, 181-82, 184-86, 188-89, 201. *See also* self-harm

ultio 30, 33, 197

vengeance 5-6, 13, 19-35, 43-45, 51, 95-96, 103, 131, 175, 188, 195-98. *See also râche, ultio, vindicta*
vindicta 30, 33-34, 197
virginity, *see* chastity

Walter von Châtillon, *Alexandreis* 22
Walther von der Vogelweide 80
wergeld (monetary term), *see* fine (monetary)
Wickram, Georg, *Rollwagenbüchlein* 116, 118-20
Winsbeckin, Die 58
Wolfram von Eschenbach, *Parzival* 13, 43-61

Zaibert, Leo 44-45
Zurich *Ratsgericht* 96-105